Guns *of the* Civil War

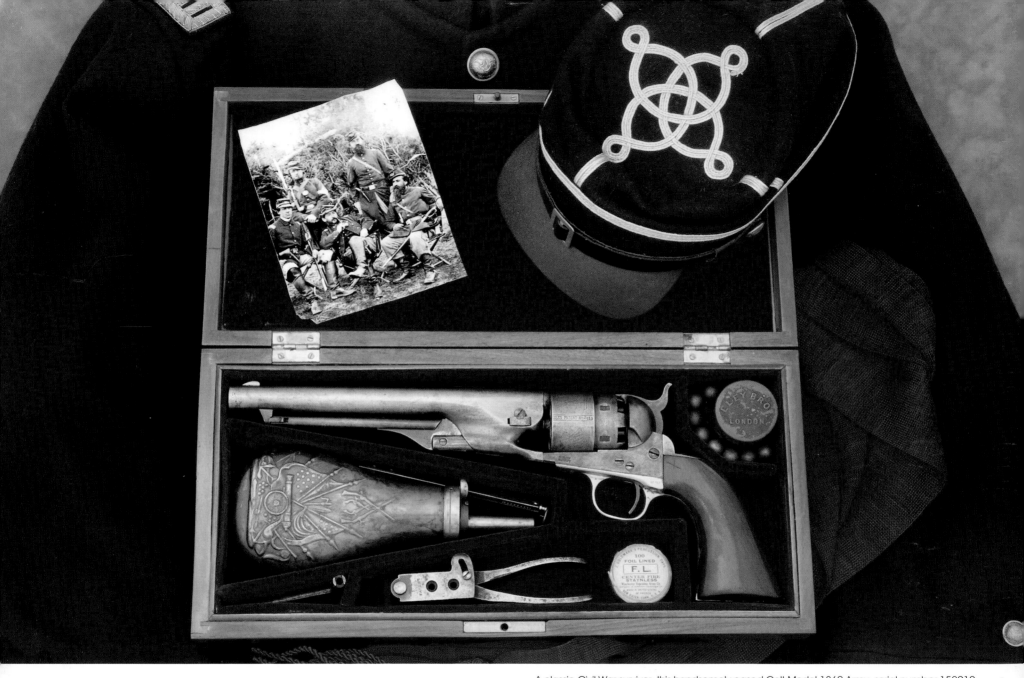

A classic Civil War survivor, this handsomely cased Colt Model 1860 Army, serial number 152919, was produced toward the end of 1864 [1]. The cased gun includes all of the standard accessories that were used in this period. Although the recoil shield and buttstrap are cut for attaching a shoulder stock, this was a civilian model because it does not have the fourth screw in the frame necessary for securing the shoulder stock yoke. Cased sets in this condition are always a wonderful find for Colt and Civil War aficionados. (From the personal collection of John Bianchi. Photography by Dennis Adler [1] Colt's Dates of Manufacture by R. L. Wilson)

Guns *of the* Civil War

WRITTEN & PHOTOGRAPHED BY DENNIS ADLER

ZENITH PRESS

Featuring guns photographed by Dennis Adler from the Mike Clark/Collector's Firearms Collection;
the Dr. Joseph A. Murphy Collection; and the Dennis LeVett Collection, with additional photography provided
by the Rock Island Auction Company Archives

Dennis Adler
Author of *Guns of the American West*

First published in 2011 by Zenith Press
An imprint of MBI Publishing Company,
400 1st Avenue North, Suite 300, Minneapolis, MN 55401 USA.

Zenith Press titles are also available at discounts in bulk quantity for industrial or sales-promotional use. For details write to Special Sales Manager at
MBI Publishing Company, 400 1st Avenue North, Minneapolis, MN 55401 USA.

To find out more about our books, join us online at www.zenithpress.com.

Designed by John Hovenstine

Library of Congress Cataloging-in-Publication Data

Adler, Dennis, 1948-

Guns of the Civil War / Dennis Adler. – 1st ed. p. cm. Includes index.

ISBN 978-0-7603-3971-8 (hb w/ jkt)

1. Firearms--United States--History--19th century. 2. Firearms--Confederate States of America. 3. United States. Army--Firearms--History--19th century. 4. Confederate States of America. Army--Firearms. 5. United States--History--Civil War, 1861-1865--Equipment and supplies. I. Title.

UD383.A35 2011 623.4'42097309034--dc22 2010034524

On the Front Cover: An historic complement of Civil War era firearms. At top, a Springfield Model 1861 rifled musket; below, a handcrafted copy of the Henry rifle presented to President Abraham Lincoln (the original is in the Smithsonian); an S&W 1st Model 3rd Issue .22 caliber revolver; the Remington New Model Army .44 caliber percussion revolver presented to General George Meade; a Starr .44 caliber percussion double action revolver; Colt Model 1849 Pocket Pistol; Colt Model 1860 Army; and two Remington-Elliot "Pepperbox" Deringer models in .22 and .32 caliber rimless, respectively. (All guns are from the collection of Dr. John Wells, with the exception of the Meade Remington New Model Army, S&W No. 1, and Colt Model 1849. Photo by Dennis Adler)

Printed in China

Success and Failure Are History's Co-Conspirators
– Anonymous

To those who laid down their lives 150 years ago in pursuit of a belief, and to those who keep that sacrifice alive through their collections, research, and the understanding that the past must never be forgotten.

At the end of the conflict between North and South,
Between The Union and Confederacy, between brothers,
A massive 1021-page book was written in 1865 to explain
the "Cause, Origin, Progress and Conclusion" of events.
This is the story of how the battle was fought
with the Guns of the Civil War

With the start of any history book there is research, and much of what comprises new books on any subject, is derived from the works of previous authors, historians, and scholars. This is true for *Guns of the Civil War*. While the photography is new, the story has been told time and again over the last 150 years. But each telling is often different; history is a matter of opinions. Sometimes there are different interpretations of events at the time they occurred depending upon which side the authors of various historic documentations may have fought, or where their sentiments laid; new material can be uncovered through comprehensive research of original records, and there are occasional discoveries and revelations through the uncovering of letters and papers from the era. All of this has contributed to the countless volumes written about the Civil War, and it is not the intention of this book to reinterpret history or become a revisionist tale of the events which unfolded prior to or during the War Between the States, but rather to look more closely at the different handguns and longarms which figured so prominently in the bloodiest war in our nation's history.

This story is not just about the guns used by the Union and Confederate militaries, but also by the civilians on both sides of the conflict caught up in the battle between North and South. It wasn't uncommon for a household to gather in fear as troops from either side approached; to anticipate the uncertainty of their future, grasping at whatever weapon was available, an old flintlock musket that had been passed down through the family since the days of the Revolutionary War, a double barreled percussion shotgun, or single shot flintlock or caplock pistol. The Civil War was not only fought by soldiers and politicians; it was fought in our back yards, on our farms, and from town to town across the nation. The guns that were used in the war are the heirlooms of American history.

Many of the revolvers, pistols, and longarms from the conflict, and perhaps more importantly, those that saw little or no use during the war, have become the foundations of great 20th century and even 21st century arms collections. Among the prominent arms collectors who contributed to the content of this book are Dr. Joseph A. Murphy, Dennis Levett, and Mike Clark, who also provided historic guns from Collectors Firearms, his world renowned gun store in Houston, Texas. Mike and his son Donny have a continual stream of historic firearms passing through their hands, and during the spring of 2010 we spent over a week photographing the best of the best both from Mike's personal Civil War arms collection and from among the hundreds of fine quality historic Civil War revolvers, pistols, and longarms in inventory at Collectors Firearms. This book would not have been possible without their valued assistance and friendship.

For generations some of the finest examples of Civil War guns have passed from one private collection to another; great guns with provenance, once owned by legendry soldiers, heroes, and frontiersmen. For nearly a quarter of a century, many of these Civil War arms have changed hands through the Rock Island Auction Company in Moline, Illinois. Company president Patrick Hogan has

Author Dennis Adler
in character for a
Civil War photo shoot in
Guns of the Old West
magazine.

been a great supporter of my books throughout the years and, as in the past, has provided me with historic guns for this work on the Civil War. You will see the credit "Photo courtesy Rock Island Auction Co." in almost every chapter, because Rock Island has been cataloging important, historic guns for almost 20 years, amassing an archive of images that are unrivaled for their diversity and quality. It is my honor to have many of these images in *Guns of the Civil War*. It is also of great benefit to readers to see these photographs of rare Civil War arms that might otherwise never appear in a publication or on display in a museum. I would like to extend my personal thanks to Patrick and the staff at Rock Island Auction Co., for helping make this book possible.

Assistance also comes from smaller collections and individual collectors, as does advice and the voice of experience. One of those voices is Pennsylvania collector and Civil War authority Dr. John Wells, whose name appears frequently throughout this book. John, as always, had just the right piece of missing information, an historical reference, or gun to photograph, to add a little something extra to this book.

Readers will also see a variety of holsters from this period in American history and another great friend, legendary holster maker John Bianchi, was of great assistance in this area. His knowledge of holsters, past and present, never fails to astound, nor does his friendship and generosity.

The author would also like to thank Wes Small and the Small family, owners of The Horse Soldier, in Gettysburg, Pennsylvania, for their assistance in selecting some of firearms for this book. The advice of those who deal in antique arms is invaluable both to arms collectors and those who write about them.

All of this information and photography is like a large tabletop jigsaw puzzle and of little value without a good graphic designer to put the pieces of the puzzle together. Once again I am fortunate to be working with one of the best art directors in the business, John Hovenstine, who also designed *Guns of the American West*. John not only has a feel for designing illustrated books but an appreciation of firearms and American history. And in the end that is what *Guns of the Civil War* is all about.

It has often been said that those who do not learn from the past are condemned to repeat it. The Civil War is a lesson that has touched every American for generations, and we are still learning from the experience 150 years later.

– Dennis Adler

The Colt's Patent Fire-Arms Co. presented this pair of Gustave Young engraved 1861 Navy revolvers to General Robert Anderson, the commander of Ft. Sumter. The guns are pictured with a display of McPherson memorabilia. Representing some of the finest work done by Colt's master engraver, the 1861 Navy Models are regarded as two of the most beautiful engraved Colts in the world.

Contents

Chapter One

A Nation on the Verge of Conflict and the Guns at Hand

Arming the North and South in the middle of a troubled journey

Ours was an unusual circumstance, not only as a nation but as a nation of armsmakers. The United States had no extended history, not politically, having only been resolutely established in 1783 at end of the Revolutionary War, but more so as a nation of armsmakers. Early American pistols and longarms had been built using tools and skills brought from Europe. Many early colonial gunmakers were of German ancestry, and the styles and construction of guns that could be regarded as "American" did not become established until the very end of the 18th century. As for American armsmakers, there were only a handful of well-known names by the early 1800s. Paramount among them was E. Remington & Sons, established in 1816, and Samuel Colt's first enterprise in Paterson, New Jersey, which began manufacturing in 1836. The Springfield Armory had been established in 1794 and the Federal arsenal at Harpers Ferry, Virginia (now West Virginia), which was to figure prominently in igniting the Civil War following abolitionist John Brown's October 1859 raid, first began manufacturing arms for the U.S. in 1801.

In point of fact, at the beginning of the Civil War only 77 years had passed since America's independence from Great Britain. Yes, it had begun in 1776 but it wasn't over until 1783, and was fundamentally fought again from 1812 to 1815. Thus, the United States was still very much a work in progress that had not firmly rooted itself even after its war with Mexico from 1846 to 1848 and the signing of the Treaty of Guadalupe Hidalgo, which increased U.S. territory by over 500,000 square miles, covering what would become the states of California, Nevada, Utah, most of New Mexico and Arizona, as well as parts of Wyoming and Colorado. The Union nevertheless was still quite fragile.

As author and historian Jay Winik wrote in his *New York Times* Bestseller, *April 1865 – A Civil War Saga*, "America was not born out of ancient custom or claim, its people bound

This Civil War era Colt model 1851 Navy, serial number 142,010 was among Colts carried by officers in the 8th and 10th Michigan Volunteer Cavalry in 1863 and was engraved at that time. (Avery Smith collection)

together from the shadows of feudal, marauding bands, emerging as a nation by the time they could primitively write their own history. Where in most countries a sense of nationhood spontaneously arose over tens of centuries, the product of generations of common kinship, common language, common myths and a shared history, and the collective ties of tradition, America was born as an artificial series of states, woven together by negotiated compacts and agreements, charters and covenants. It did not arise naturally, as in Europe, or China, or Persia, but was made, almost abstractly, out of ink and paper, crafted by lawyers and statesmen."

There were broad distinctions between the states, their individual heritages and old allegiances to England and France. The Southern states held more to Old World traditions, and the discord that existed since the late 18th century had festered and multiplied for almost 50 years. The states that comprised our nation – the North and South still being an arbitrary distinction before the war – had each established their own self rule and independence, their own militias and governing bodies to oversee each state's individual interests, even their own currency. Coastal states established their own navies, some with impressive fleets of warships and merchant vessels. Like pieces of a puzzle, America was composed of citizens from 33 separate states [1]. Our nation spanned from the Atlantic to the Pacific, from its borders with Canada in the North, to the then established boundaries with Mexico in the South. The United States was nothing less

The United States as it appeared in a map from 1860. The nation was comprised of 33 states at the time. Kansas became the 34th state in January 1861. The map was created to illustrate the separation of Union and Confederate states in December 1860, four months before the Civil War began! (Courtesy Frank Oppel)

MAJOR ROBT ANDERSON.
De Brow et full beauff

While many regard John Brown's raid on the arsenal at Harpers Ferry, Virginia, in 1859 as the catalyst for igniting The War Between the States, it was the attack on Fort Sumter in April 1861 that finally forced Lincoln's hand. Located in South Carolina's Charleston Harbor, Ft. Sumter was under the command of then Maj. Robert Anderson (top). After a gallent three-day standoff against Confederate artillary, in which the Fort had been heavily damaged by 34 hours of bombardment, Brig. Gen. Pierre Beauregard (above and right), Anderson's former student at West Point, initiated a series of cordial letters couriered back and forth asking for Anderson's surrender. With food running out and what all parties agreed was a hopeless situaiton, Anderson finally ordered the evacuation (surrender) of Ft. Sumter on the April 14, 1861. (Photos courtesy Library of Congress)

Confederate Brig. Gen. Pierre G. T. Beauregard was at the vanguard of the intial attack that is attributed to starting the Civil War in April 1861. Beauregard is pictured here among the top generals in the Confederacy (top of left row), along with Robert .E. Lee (center), and Generals Thomas "Stonewall" Jackson, James Longstreet, John C. Breckenridge, A.P. Hill, Fitz Hugh Lee, Richard S. Ewell, and the legendary "Gray Ghost" of the Confederate Cavalry, Col. John Singleton Mosby. (Illustration from *The History of the Civil War*, by Samuel M. Schmucker, L.L.D., 1865, Bradley & Co.)

enterprising than half the land mass of South America, and Latin America was comprised of only 22 separate states (individual nations) at the time, all with varying allegiances and cultures. Why then should a country as vast as the United States have a unified heritage or even one governing body? States Rights were so great an issue that the nation was already on the verge of coming apart at its seams by the late 1850s. There had been threats of Southern states seceding from the Union for more than a decade, as early as June of 1850. In the North, New Jersey threatened secession in the 1850s, California and Oregon flirted with the idea of forming a Pacific Coast nation, and Utah had fought against federal control for years. Thus the seeds of secession had long been sewn.

With eleven Southern states having filed articles of secession from the Union between December 1860 and May 23, 1861, along with the seizure by state's militias of as many U.S. Forts as possible, the military was divided along political lines. Between the 12th and 13th of April, when the first shots were fired upon Ft. Sumter in Charleston Harbor, South Carolina, by Brigadier General Pierre Gustave Toutant-Beauregard and his Confederate forces, the United States of America officially began to dissolve as a unified nation.

The Arms at Hand

The majority of soldiers, who remained loyal to the North, were armed with smoothbore and rifled muskets, Colt revolvers, and various single shot pistols

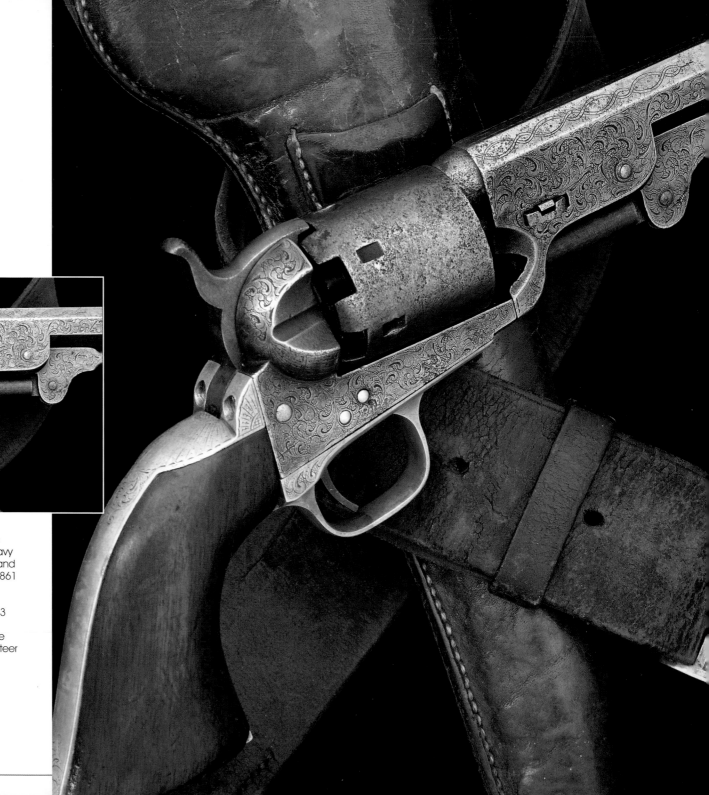

At the beginning of the Civil War the predominant military sidearm for both Union and Confederate troops was the .36 caliber Colt's Model 1851 Navy revolver. By 1855 the Colt Navy had been fully integrated among U.S. branches of service, and of course, at the time this included troops who would after 1861 give their allegiance to the Confederacy. The fine example shown, serial number 142010 was among Colts carried by officers in the 8th and 10th Michigan Volunteer Cavalry in 1863 and was engraved at that time. Officers were required to purchase their own sidearms. The 8th and 10th were under the command of George Armstrong Custer's all Michigan Volunteer Cavalry Units. (Avery Smith collection)

that had been developed and in use by the military since the 1840s and early 1850s. The predominant military sidearm was the .36 caliber Colt's Model 1851 Navy revolver. Larger caliber arms were older .44 caliber Colt Dragoons: 1st, 2nd, and 3rd Models, (the latter with detachable shoulder stocks to make them into carbines for the cavalry), and the .58 caliber, single shot, U.S. Springfield Model 1855 Pistol-Carbine.

The Pistol-Carbine, derived from the 1855 U.S. Springfield Rifled Musket, had been designed by the Ordnance Department specifically for use by the cavalry as it provided both a saddle pistol and, with the detachable stock, a carbine that was reasonably effective, both on horseback, or for dismounted cavalry. The 12-inch barrel was also short enough to be easily reloaded from the saddle. The guns tested in 1855 proved accurate up to 500 yards.[2]

By 1856 the US Cavalry and Dragoons were variously armed with muzzle-loading Model 1841 rifles, Musketoons, rifle carbines, breech-loading Hall and Sharps carbines, and the new U.S. Springfield Pistol-Carbine.[3] All of these weapons were in use by the U.S. military when the Civil War erupted, thus troops loyal to the South had the same complement of weapons as those on the Union side. It would take well into 1861 before the U.S. military was rearming with the new .44 caliber Colt 1860 Army and improved U.S. Springfield Model 1861 Rifled Muskets, thus many soldiers in the field were still wielding .44 caliber Dragoons, single shot pistols, and muskets.

As the war carried on into the 1860s the demand for arms of any type made the use of older style weapons

In 1861 the majority of Union officers were armed with the Colt's Model 1851 Navy. Though 10 years old, it remained the most common U.S. military sidearm until issue of the new .44 caliber Model 1860 Army began in 1861. The .36 caliber, six-shot Navy models were one of the most popular guns manufactured by Colt's and second only in total sales to the 1849 Pocket Model. (Author's collection)

The lineage of Dragoons spanned the period from 1847 to 1861. Changes in grip, cylinder stop slot (oval to rectangular), and triggerguard designs (square back to oval) are the most obvious indicators of specific models. From top to bottom: Whitneyville-Hartford Dragoon, First, Second, and Third Model Dragoons. Until the 1860 Army was issued, they were the primary .44 caliber arms used by the U.S. military. For the most part, the Confederacy was unable to acquire the Colt 1860 Army unless they were captured in battle, thus they relied more heavily on older .44 caliber Colt Dragoons: 1st, 2nd, and 3rd Models from the late 1840s and early 1850s. (Dr. Joseph A. Murphy collection)

Among the legendary guns of the Texas Rangers and Texans fighting for the Confederacy, were Samuel Colts Dragoons. Pictured atop a painting of the Texas Rangers by Jack Terry, are an engraved Third Model, top, a First Model, center, and a Second Model, bottom. (Dr. Joseph A. Murphy collection)

The U.S. Springfield Pistol-Carbine had been designed by the Ordnance Department specifically for use by the cavalry as it provided both a saddle pistol and, with the detachable stock, a carbine that was reasonably effective, both on horseback, or for dismounted cavalry. The 12-inch barrel was also short enough to be easily reloaded from the saddle. This somewhat outmoded single shot pistol was still in use by the Union Cavalry at the beginning of the Civil War. The guns utilized the Maynard tape-type priming device intended to replace percussion caps. Instead of caps, a paper tape roll, which contained the mercury fulminate, was automatically fed every time the gun was cocked, and ignited the powder charge in the barrel breech when struck by the hammer. Basically the first cap pistol! (Gun photos courtesy Rock Island Auction Co. Background photo by Dennis Adler. Special thanks to Charlie Doutt, Dr. John Wells, and Eric Dilling.)

Pictured is a Sharps Model 1851 Navy Carbine. A former apprentice under John Hall (of Hall Rifle fame) at the Harpers Ferry Arsenal, Christian Sharps wanted to make loading and charging a rifle even faster, and his idea was to do it all from the breech end. Sharps received his first patent in 1848 and introduced his first model a year later. The original Sharps breech-loading design, of which less than 100 were made, also incorporated an automatic capping device, but he abandoned this design in 1850, and by 1851 had advanced through two further improvements, neither of which had the automatic capping device. The example shown is fitted with the capping device. U.S.N. is stamped on the buttplate and a five pointed brass star inlaid on the right of the stock matching the stars used for periods in the U.S. Navy. (Photos courtesy Rock Island Auction Co.)

By 1852 the familiar Sharps rifle (first with slanting breech as shown) and side hammer had come into being. Within three years Sharps had sold more than 5,000. In the interim he had also come up with several variations; the 1853 carbine, breech-loading shotgun, and long barrel military rifle. More than 10,000 of the 1853 models (mostly carbines) had been produced by 1857 and Sharps had set up his own manufacturing facilities in Hartford, Connecticut. Previously he had his rifles made by Robbins & Lawrence in Windsor, Vermont. (Photos courtesy Rock Island Auction Co.)

C.SHARPS' PATENT. 1852.

Confederate volunteers often brought their own rifles and muskets with them. Longrifles dating back to the early 1830s, like this example of a Bedford, Pennsylvania-style by maker Wm. Border, were not uncommon, as were numerous flintlocks dating from the 1780s. The South made do with what was at hand, especially in the very last years of the conflict. (Photographed by the author at the historic Dobbin House Tavern in Gettysburg, Pennsylvania)

Civilians were often drawn into the war simply defending their homes, property, and families. This famous photo from the Library of Congress shows John L. Burns of Gettysburg, Pennsylvania. Wounded in the leg Burns defended his home and fought against Confederate troops at the Battle of Gettysburg, armed only with an old flintlock musket.

necessary, including as many single shot pistols as could be rounded-up by both Union and Confederate forces. The South had to virtually start from scratch with a volunteer Army comprised of estranged U.S. soldiers who had forsaken the Union and sworn their oath to defend the Confederacy, and others who, only months before, had been farmers, laborers, plantation owners, and businessmen. Most were armed with what was at hand, old percussion rifles, rebuilt muskets, even flintlock muskets and pistols dating back to the post Revolutionary War period. Thus, in the beginning, handguns like the Springfield Model 1855 and similarly-styled single shot percussion lock models from the 1840s; large caliber horse pistols carried by mounted troops, or stuffed into a sash or makeshift belt holster, were being used on both sides of the Mason/Dixon Line.

Arming the States' Militias

In the late 1850s, after the Colt's Model 1851 Navy had been successfully integrated into the U.S. military, the Ordnance Department turned over to the states for use in their militias over ten thousand single shot pistols. [4] This, of course, at the time included militias in the Southern States. As early as 1860 the state of Mississippi issued 462 single shot pistols to volunteer militia. Virginia withdrew 116 pistols from the arsenal along with another 1,231 pistols issued to that state's militia. On the Union side, as the Civil War carried on into the summer of 1861, the Ordnance Department procured over 650 holster pistols in August and an additional 772 in October, which were issued to cavalry units in 1862-63.[5] There were still more than 4,000 single shot pistols in U.S. arsenals by the end of 1862, many of which would be issued to Union troops before the end of the war.

Samuel Colt in his youth cut quite a striking figure and this rather imperious portrait was also indicative of his showmanlike personality, which not only helped establish his first enterprise but generated sales. Despite the failure of the Patent Fire-Arms Manufacturing Company, Colt had secured his place in the industry, and when he came back in 1847, he was there for the duration. (Mary Evans Picture Library/Alamy)

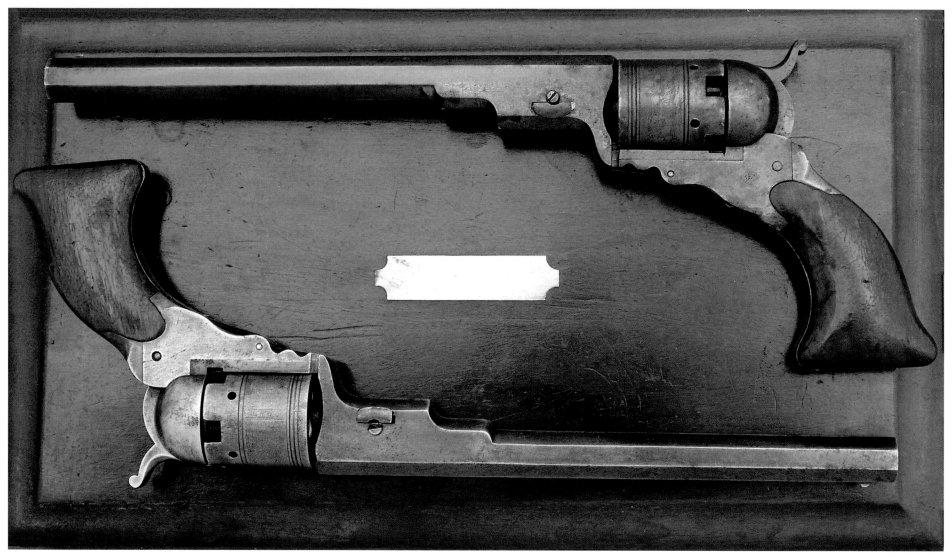

This very rare cased pair of No. 5 Holster Models with 9-inch barrels is one of only two cased sets known to exist. One set is in the Hartford Museum, and the other in the Dennis LeVett collection. LeVett's (pictured) is a very early set with square backed cylinders. The No. 5 Models were the guns used by Capt. Jack Hays, Samuel Walker and the Texas Rangers in the famous Comanche Indian battle of 1844. While Patersons were well out of date by 1861, chambered in .36 caliber, or smaller calibers, depending upon the model, the memories of Hayes' success in 1844 were not lost on those in the South who had little else at hand.

technically part of Mexico, under American military occupation as the result of the Mexican-American War. With the signing of the treaty between Mexico and the U.S. on February 2, 1848, California became a part of the United States, but a unique part – it was neither a formal territory nor a state. California was in political limbo, a region under U.S. military control but without the benefit of a civil legislature, executive or judicial body. Local citizens operated under a confusing and changing mixture of Mexican rules, American principles, and personal dictates. And more than a few disputes were settled at the end of a Colt barrel.

Gold turned California into a melting pot. Within a year $30,000 to $50,000 worth of gold in the form of dust and nuggets was coming out of California every day. Boom towns rose and folded, men, women, families from

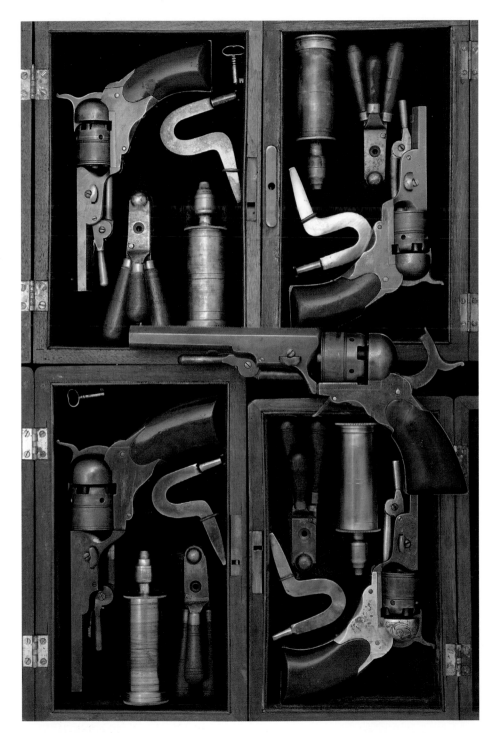

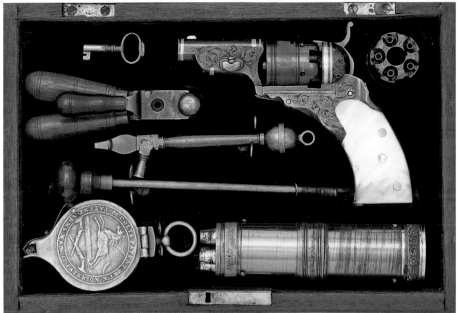

all over the country, and from as far as China, Peru, Chile, and Europe came in search of fortune. Some found it; others found the end of their lives, often on the wrong end of a claim jumper's gun. Some never struck it rich and found themselves working in the towns that sprang up near mining camps. Men who had dreamed of pockets filled with gold became storekeepers, laborers, farmers, or gamblers, those who could ride and knew their way around cattle became cowboys, while others joined the Army. Many were immigrants, settlers or drifters of one kind or another. Like breaths of air the nation inhaled and exhaled people and their dreams in the 1850s like wind filling the sails of ships. By the end of the decade the nation was about to be tested as never before. The winds that blew now were the winds of war.

At the start of the American Civil War in 1861 Colt's Patent Fire-Arms Manufacturing Company was one of the largest and most successful business concerns in the country. By the time of the attack on Fort Sumter, there was an entire range of Colt revolvers from small-caliber pocket-sized pistols to the mighty .44 caliber Dragoons, the highly regarded .36 caliber 1851 Navy, and brand new .44 caliber 1860 Army, the latter two

Colt's first revolvers were 5-shooters. The smallest cased examples are often called "Baby Ehlers" but are actually the New Improved First Model Baby with ramrod (loading lever). "Everyone thinks that John Ehlers, who took over Samuel Colt's first arms manufacturing concern in 1842 did these but they had been designed before the Patent Firearms Manufacturing Company went bankrupt and Ehlers acquired the guns in inventory," says noted collector Dennis LeVett. The larger example is a .31 caliber Ehlers Model. The Baby Ehlers are all .28 caliber. The single gun resting atop the cases is a very rare .34 caliber Ehlers Model with loading lever.

The men who made Colts famous in the 1840s: Texas Ranger Captain Samuel H. Walker and Captain (later Major) John Coffee "Jack" Hays. The newly appointed Captain of the United States Mounted Rifles, Walker sought to make improvements in the Colt's revolver, making it more powerful and better suited to mounted troops engaging hostiles. Walker was not only instrumental in designing the new revolver but in securing Colt's initial order for 1,000 new .44 caliber Holster Model revolvers (later renamed the Walker Colt following the Captain's death in battle during the Mexican-American War in 1847). Pictured are Walker revolvers number 1009 and 1010 which were sent to Captain Walker by Col. Colt in July 1847. Walker used the .44 caliber revolvers at the time of his death at the Battle of Humantala, Mexico in October 1847. The two revolvers were returned to the Walker family in 1848. Pictured with the *Weekly Herald* carrying Walker's obituary is the Mexican-American War Medal won by Capt. Walker. (Guns, Dr. Joseph A. Murphy collection; Jack Hays photo courtesy Former Texas Rangers Association)

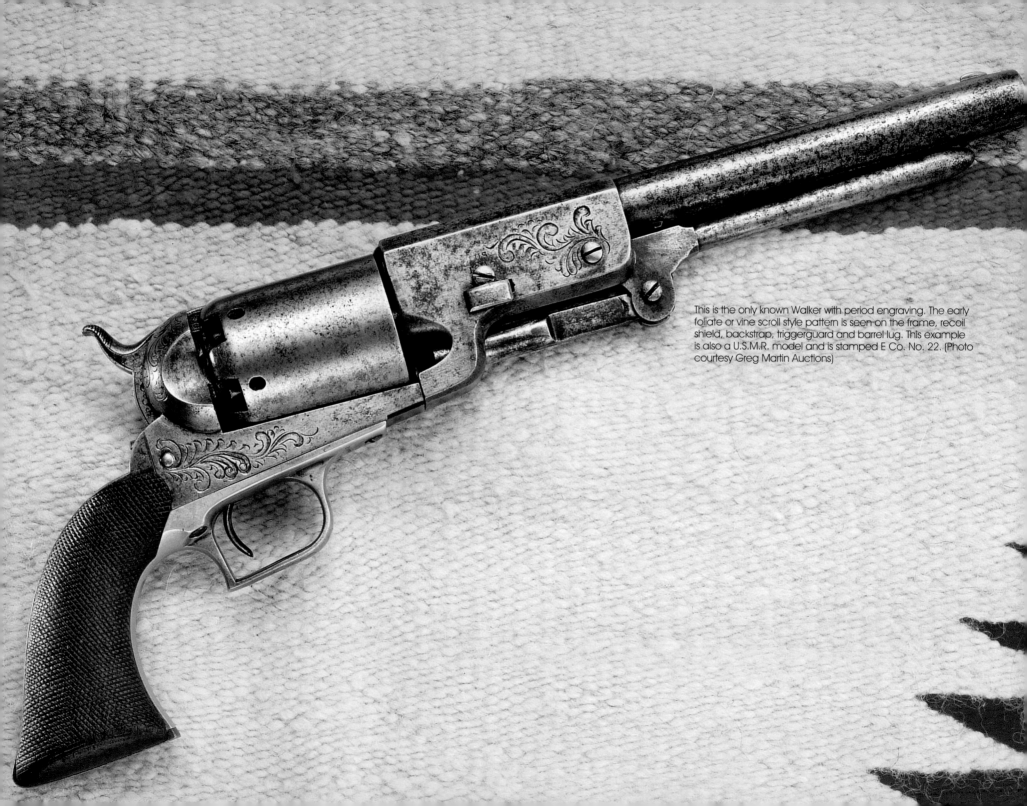

This is the only known Walker with period engraving. The early foliate or vine scroll style pattern is seen on the frame, recoil shield, backstrap, triggerguard and barrel lug. This example is also a U.S.M.R. model and is stamped E Co. No. 22. (Photo courtesy Greg Martin Auctions)

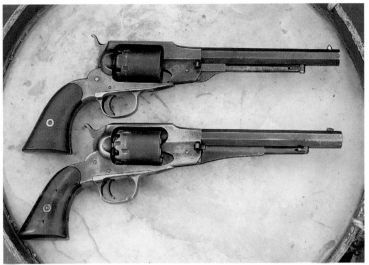

As soon as the Colt's patent extension expired E. Remington & Sons began manufacturing single action revolvers of their own design. The earliest .44 and .36 caliber models were the Remington-Beals Army and Navy. Designed by Fordyce Beals, the new Remington models featured a solid top strap and a fixed (threaded) barrel, providing greater strength and ease of operation compared to Colt's wedge-pinned barrel and open top design. Note the two different styles of front sight, early bee-hive shape and later pinched style, which was used throughout the remainder of production on both Army and Navy revolvers. (Guns courtesy Mike Clark Collection/Collector's Firearms)

being the principal sidearms of the U.S. military throughout the War Between the States.

Sam Colt may have perfected and patented the design for the mechanically-operated revolving cylinder pistol, but he wasn't alone in the American firearms business; he was instead the catalyst for an emerging industry that flourished throughout the early half of the 19th century. Among Colt's most successful contemporaries was E. Remington & Sons in Ilion, New York. After the Colt's patent extension expired, Remington introduced the revolutionary 1858 Remington-Beals Army Model revolver chambered in .44 caliber, and the lighter .36 caliber Navy version. The Remington revolvers featured a solid top strap and a fixed (threaded) barrel, providing greater strength and ease of operation compared to Colt's wedge-pinned barrel and open top design, which by 1858 was now almost 20 years old. One could change out a Remington cylinder in seconds, without having to remove the barrel. The top strap added strength to the frame, and above all, the threaded Remington barrels assured greater accuracy. In the heat of

The large .44 caliber Colt Dragoons succeeded the Walker in 1848. Pictured is a civilian First Model Dragoon cased with accessories; 500 count Eley cap tin, "Walker" style powder flask, large nipple wrench, and brass and iron bullet mold. Serial number 6116, this is one of the finest examples known of the First Model Dragoon. One of the defining characteristics of the First Model is the oval (also referred to as round) cylinder bolt stops. This design was changed to rectangular in 1850 when the Second Model Dragoon was introduced. (Dr. Joseph A. Murphy collection)

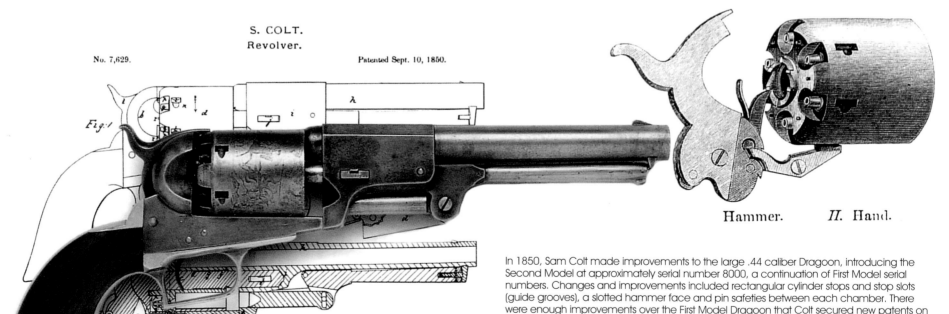

S. COLT.
Revolver.

No. 7,629.

Patented Sept. 10, 1850.

Fig. 1

Hammer.   H. Hand.

Fig. 4

Fig. 3 Aa

In 1850, Sam Colt made improvements to the large .44 caliber Dragoon, introducing the Second Model at approximately serial number 8000, a continuation of First Model serial numbers. Changes and improvements included rectangular cylinder stops and stop slots (guide grooves), a slotted hammer face and pin safeties between each chamber. There were enough improvements over the First Model Dragoon that Colt secured new patents on September 10, 1850, to protect the rectangular cylinder stops and guide grooves, slotted hammer face, and pin safeties. The latter, (small projections between the chambers on the cylinder breech in the illustration) were intended to secure the hammer at rest between chambers. Cocking the hammer from this position completed the rotation of the cylinder into battery. This was a significant improvement but hardly a safety by today's standards. Only around 2,700 Second Models were built, with a portion of those examples used to fill a government order for 1,000 Army pistols received in February 1850. (Photos courtesy R.L. Wilson (patent drawing), Herbert G. Houze/Wadsworth Atheneum (hammer-hand), and Greg Martin Auctions, Second Model Dragoon)

Sam Colt made presentations of cased engraved models to military and government officials as a common practice. He also made presentations to foreign leaders in hopes of gaining foreign contracts for guns. Often this ploy was quite successful. Pictured is an exquisite pair of engraved Third Model Dragoons, serial numbers 11790 and 11850, presented by Col. Colt to King Victor Emmanuele II, of Italy in 1851 (or 1852). Both guns are profusely engraved and have blued frames (rather than case colored), silver plated backstraps and triggerguards, and ivory grips. The undersides of the triggerguards are engraved with the Coat of Arms of The House of Savoy and the United States, respectively. Third Model Dragoons are easily distinguished by the use of a round triggerguard. (Dr. Joseph A. Murphy collection)

battle, a Colt barrel wedged too tightly could easily bind the cylinder. Colt nevertheless remained the dominant American revolver of the Civil War era, and well into the postwar expansion west in the late 1860s and early 1870s. For more than 35 years the percussion revolver, either manufactured by Colt's, Remington, or others, both here and abroad, remained the prevailing design despite the obvious advantage of cartridge firing revolvers. For the Union, the primary revolvers issued to its soldiers were the Colt's 1851 Navy and 1860 Army, followed by the Remington Army and Navy, and the Starr double and single action models, the latter built at the request of the Ordnance Department.

Colt had rebuilt his arms company with the success of the 1847 U.S.M.R. (United States Mounted Rifles) Holster Model revolver, later renamed the Walker after co-designer Capt. Samuel Walker was killed in the Mexican War at the Battle of Humantala on October 9, 1847. At the time of his death, Walker's fame was nationwide and was reported in every major newspaper across America.

The Walker revolver had nearly been, as Walker wrote, "...the most perfect weapon in the World for light mounted troops..." except for a few minor refinements, which Sam Colt began to make by the summer of 1847. In battle, the Walkers had "occasionally" been prone to malfunctioning if vibration caused the loading lever to drop from its V-shaped locking pin that pressed into a recess in the top of the loading lever. The fallen lever then forced the plunger into the first open chamber jamming the action. Colt rectified this on the Whitneyville-Hartford Dragoon by adding a spring loaded retention pin to the end of the lever and a latch under the barrel. Colt also shortened the barrel from 9-inches to 7-1/2

Sitting atop a framed advertisement for Colt's Second Model Dragoon c. 1850, are a Second Model and the first pocket pistol built in Hartford, the 1848 Pocket Model, or more popularly, "Baby Dragoon." The little 5-shot, .31 caliber pistols were carried as backup guns in the 1850s, particularly during the California Gold Rush, and found similar use throughout the Civil War tucked into soldier's waist belts or hidden in a pocket. (Dr. Joseph A. Murphy collection)

This historically significant First Model Dragoon, serial number 3969, was originally a gift from Connecticut Governor Thomas H. Seymour to Franklin Pierce (later to become 14th President of the United States 1853-1857). At the outbreak of the Mexican War in 1846, the former New Hampshire Senator and U.S District Attorney enlisted in the Army as a private. Serving under General Winfield Scott in the campaign against Mexico City, he was commissioned a Brigadier General. Pierce later presented the cased Colt Dragoon to Colonel Thomas J. Whipple (a fellow veteran of the Mexican campaigns, and later commander of the 4th New Hampshire during the Civil War). All of this is handsomely documented by the revolver's inscription on the silver-plated brass backstrap. (Dr. Joseph A. Murphy collection)

Following the First Model Dragoon, Sam Colt reverted to his penchant for small pocket pistols introducing the Model of 1848. Chambered in .31 caliber, the 5-shot revolvers were offered with a standard octagonal barrel measuring 4-inches in length. The square back frame was a scaled version of the Dragoon which led to the gun's being nicknamed the Baby Dragoon. The cased example has a 3-inch barrel, the shortest offered. The other examples are fitted with a 5-inch and a 6-inch barrel, which was the longest offered. (Dr. Joseph A. Murphy collection)

Colt followed the 1848 Baby Dragoon with the most successful percussion revolver ever built, the Model 1849. This extraordinary cased example with a 6-inch barrel shows the finest engraving of the period on a pocket model Colt. The 1849 was also a 5-shot pocket pistol like the 1848, but with the addition of a loading lever. Later models (after 1850) could also be purchased with a 6-shot cylinder. The Union soldier in the photo case is holding a Pocket Model. Note the new Colt's Patent powder flask with crossed Dragoons beneath the American eagle, which is grasping arrows, an olive branch and a shield. The legend E. Pluribus Unum appears below within a banner. (Dr. Joseph A. Murphy collection)

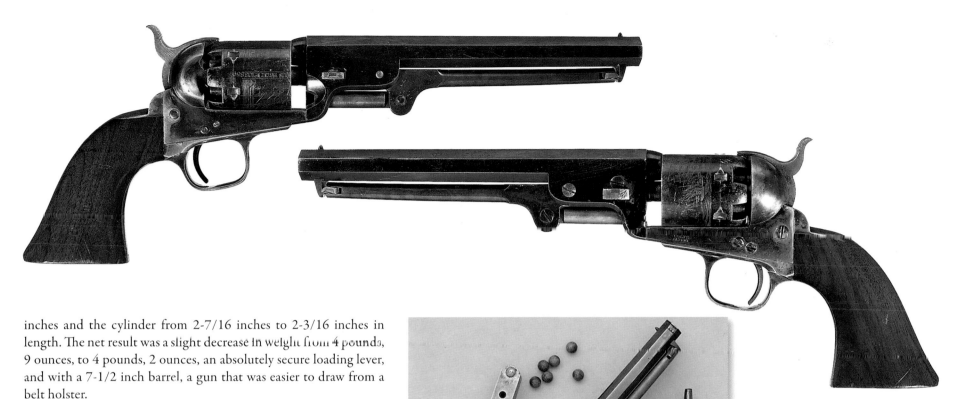

inches and the cylinder from 2-7/16 inches to 2-3/16 inches in length. The net result was a slight decrease in weight from 4 pounds, 9 ounces, to 4 pounds, 2 ounces, an absolutely secure loading lever, and with a 7-1/2 inch barrel, a gun that was easier to draw from a belt holster.

Production of the Whitneyville-Hartford Dragoon was short-lived, from the fall of 1847 through the end of the year with the total amounting to no more than 240 examples, with the serial number range continuing from the civilian Walkers through No. 1340. The majority of the guns used the old Walker frames, accounting for the added distance between the shortened cylinder (still left in the white as on the Walker) and the barrel. The grips were also Walker style, although a few later examples transitioned to the square shoulder grip and grip strap design seen on the 1st Model Dragoon in 1848.

As the first models built by Samuel Colt the barrel lug top flat was stamped – ADDRESS SAML COLT NEW-YORK CITY –. Why New York instead of Hartford, Connecticut? New York was recognized as a center of world commerce even in the

The second most successful percussion model in Colt's history was the 1851 Navy. By 1855 the .36 caliber, 6-shot revolvers had become the standard issue sidearm of the U.S. military. After the Civil War began, soldiers on both sides were carrying the Colt Navy. This example features the round triggerguard. The silver plating over brass used on the triggerguard and backstrap has long worn away on this historic Colt. (Gun courtesy Mike Clark Collection/Collectors Firearms)

The 1851 Navy was carried by officers on both sides during the Civil War. This is an exceptional example of a Colt Navy with documented history. This revolver belonged to Confederate Colonel James Gregory Hodges who was killed in Pickett's Charge at the Battle of Gettysburg on July 3, 1863. Hodges was one of eight Confederate Colonels who died during Pickett's Charge. (Photos and documentation courtesy Rock Island Auction Co.)

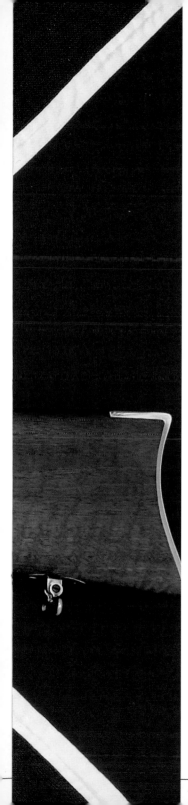

There are many ironies to the Civil War; one was that Jefferson Davis, U.S. Senator from the State of Mississippi and later Secretary of War under Franklin Pierce, would become the President of the Confederate States of America in 1861. This is a commemorative reproduction of the engraved and shoulder stocked 1851 Navy presented to Jefferson Davis while he was Secretary of War. The limited edition cased guns were produced for the U.S. Historical Society in 1990. The edition was limited to 1,000 examples. An additional 250 cased guns were sold through The American Historical Foundation (later to become America Remembers).

Jefferson Davis (center) and his cabinet, Vice President Alexander Stephens, Secretary of State Judah P. Benjamin (bottom), and Confederate Diplomatic Envoys James Mason and John Slidell, as illustrated in *The History of the Civil War*, written in 1865. (Illustration from *The History of the Civil War*, by Samuel M. Schmucker, L.L.D., 1865, Bradley & Co.)

distinguished by its square shoulder grip and grip strap (where the grip strap meets the frame), and oval cylinder stop slots.

Weighing 4 pounds, 2 ounces, and fitted with a 7 1/2 inch barrel (same as the Whitneyville-Hartford Dragoon), the 1st Model Dragoon was an unprecedented success for Colt, not only with the military, but with a growing civilian market hungry for a big, six shot revolver suitable to frontier use. A year later when gold was found in California, the Colt Dragoons would be among the front line weapons in use for one's self preservation. The most popular, however, would be Sam Colt's next two revolvers, the 1848 and 1849 Pocket Models.

Colt had always favored small concealable handguns, and he returned to his Paterson roots with the 1848 Pocket Revolver, or more popularly, the "Baby Dragoon." A scaled down version of the First Model Dragoon, the 1848 featured a full octagonal barrel in 3-inch, 4-inch, 5-inch, and 6-inch lengths and, like the first Paterson Pocket Models, without loading lever. Chambered in .31 caliber, the new pocket model harkened back to its New Jersey heritage by being a 5-shot revolver.

Occasionally, cased sets were comprised of two different Colt models. One of the most famous was this 1851 Navy and 1849 Pocket Model (serial Nos. 2847 and 84624) set engraved and gold inlaid by Colt's master engraver Gustave Young. The guns were presented to Captain James West on January 4, 1854, by the 30 passengers who had crossed the Atlantic aboard the U.S.M. Steamer Atlantic. The set was in appreciation for Capt. West's heroics in saving the ship during its 1853 trans-Atlantic voyage. Note that there are both round ball and conical lead bullets in the partition at lower right. (Dr. Joseph A. Murphy collection)

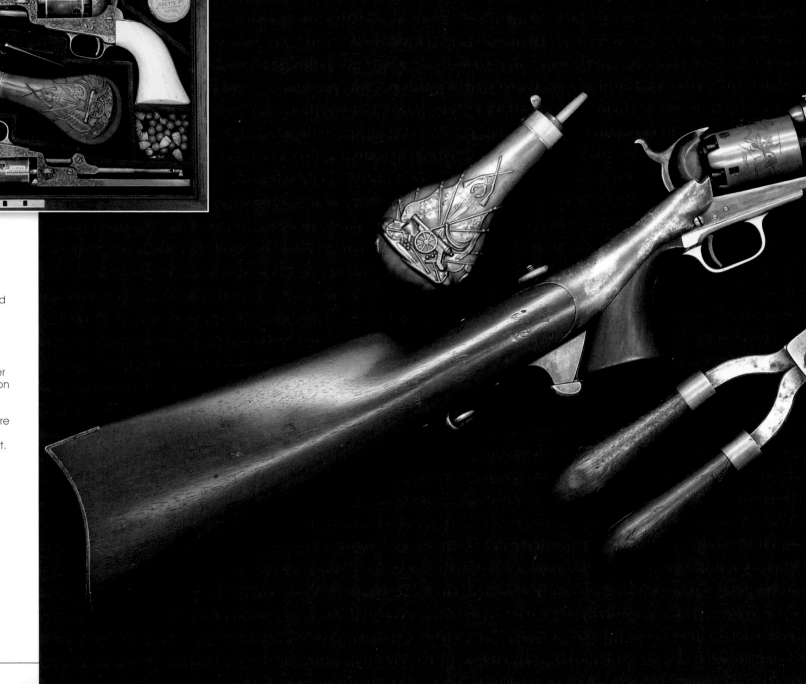

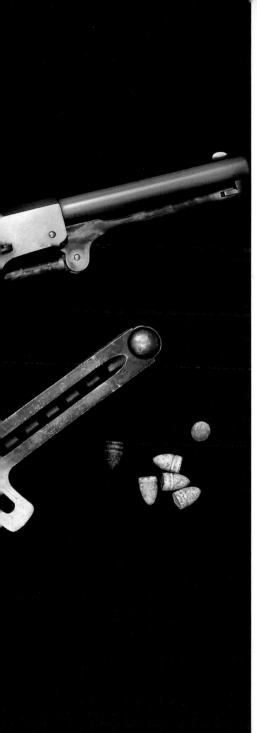

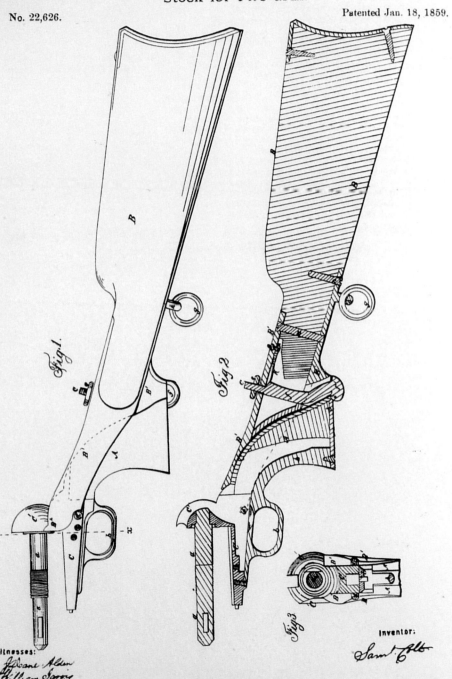

N PETERS, PHOTO-LITHOGRAPHER, WASHINGTON D C.

wilds of California in search of gold in 1849, the Colt 1848 and 1849 Pocket Models were favorites for their small, concealable size, reliability and light weight, just 24 ounces. The 5-shot (and 6-shot beginning in 1851) pistol became the concealed carry gun of choice in the 1850s, and during the Civil War many a soldier carried an old Colt as an extra measure of safety. Throughout its production life, and even afterward, there were more variations of the 1849 Pocket Model than any other Colt revolver. We say "afterward" because the 1849 continued on as a .38 caliber cartridge conversion revolver manufactured by Colt's until 1880, giving this gun a total production history spanning three decades.

In 1850 Colt introduced the gun that would become the most famous six-shooter of the early American West and Civil War, the .36 caliber Belt Pistol, more popularly known today as the 1851 Navy. Colt had finally produced the perfect gun, small enough to be carried in comfort, yet powerful enough to get the job done. Both the U.S. military

Colt's Third Model Dragoon was also manufactured with a removable shoulder stock. Intended for the U.S. Cavalry, the "Carbine Pistol" was specially designed with cutouts in the base of the recoil shield and large "4ᵗʰ" screws at the back of the frame to engage the yoke of the shoulder stock. A channel cut into the base of buttstrap, corresponding to a latch at the bottom of the yoke, was used to lock the stock to the frame. The example shown, serial number 17462 is one of the finest examples extant. Colt's patent for the third variation shoulder stock and modifications to the Colt frame is dated January 18, 1859. The various components, bottom latch and knurled screw for tightening, yoke contour and recoil shield cutouts are illustrated. (Dr. Joseph A. Murphy Collection)

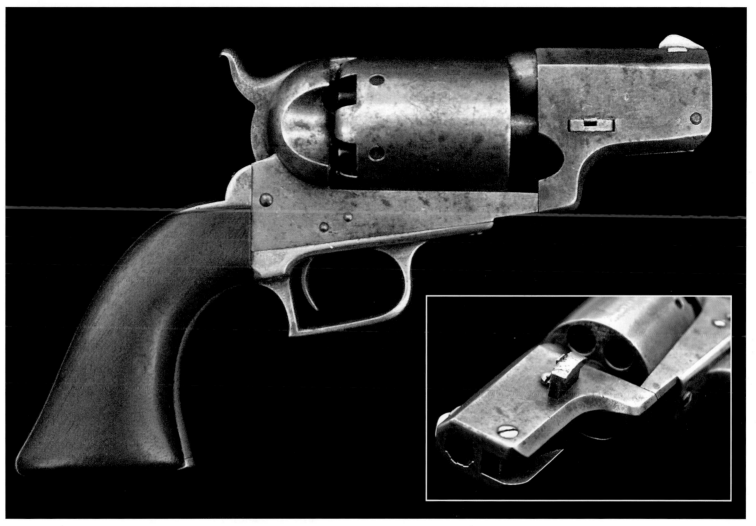

Dragoons with shoulder stocks were generally fitted with a folding rear sight on top of the barrel lug. Accuracy with the stock attached was greatly enhanced and point of aim was more accurate than with the pistol's hammer notch rear and bead front sight.

and civilian market was once again standing at Samuel Colt's doorstep saying "more please."

There were two basic versions of the elegant octagonal barreled repeater, one with a square back triggerguard and another with a round triggerguard. The gun's name was not derived from its use by the Navy (although it was used by both the U.S. Navy and Army), but rather from its Ormsby engraved cylinder scene depicting the famous May 16, 1843, battle at sea between Texas and Mexico. Patented in September 1850, the first examples of

The biggest of small guns, this unusual 1st Model Dragoon was shortened to a barrel length of only 2-3/4 inches, literally cut off at the end of the barrel lug. This particular .44 caliber model, from the collection of Lt. Col. Gerald E. Dickerson, Jr., has a very colorful and documented history having been carried by Deputy U.S. Marshal William Stokes who pursued and captured John D. Lee, the leader of a Mormon raiding party that murdered 123 immigrants passing through Utah on their way to California in September 1857. Because of the Civil War the investigation had been curtailed until the early 1870s. Lee managed to evade arrest until Stokes caught up with him in 1874. In his memoirs Stokes remarked that Lee admitted he had never seen a gun like that before in his life, and he got a pretty good look at it. Stokes had the gaping .44 caliber barrel less than a foot from Lee's head at the time of the arrest.

the Belt Model were being produced by early fall. As Wilson notes in *The Book of Colt Firearms*, "the Navy was the '.38' caliber of its day, and quickly outshone the Dragoon arms in commercial sales." By 1855 the Navy Model had also been adopted by the U.S. government, which ultimately purchased a total of 35,000 guns. Total production, which continued through 1873, amounted to more than 255,000 guns, plus another 40,000 manufactured in London during the brief period from 1853 to 1857 when Colt maintained a factory in England.

Not forgetting the need for large caliber firepower, Colt's Third Model Dragoon (put into production the same year as the 1851 Navy) was the best selling large caliber revolver in America by 1855. The Third Model was a continuation of its predecessor but easily distinguished by having an oval triggerguard. All of the improvements from the Second Model were carried over, including the flat mainspring, notched roller bearing hammer, and cylinder locking pins intended to provide a hammer rest between chambers, so that the gun could be safely carried with a fully loaded cylinder.

There were seven variations of the 1855 Root Sidehammer pistol incorporating numerous design changes and improvements. Pictured are three variations (left to right) a No.4 with 3-inch octagon barrel, fluted cylinder and ivory grips, a rare No.6A with round barrel and round cylinder, and two No. 5A Models with 4-inch round barrels and fluted cylinders. (Dennis LeVett collection)

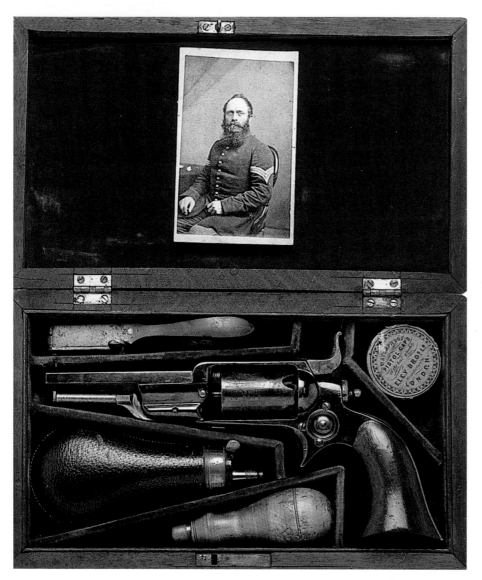

Though a small caliber pistol, the Roots sidehammer revolver, in either .28 or .31 caliber, made a good hideaway gun during the Civil War and many were carried by soldiers in the field. No more than 40,000 examples in all seven variations, Colt and Root were continually changing the design, and to such extent that there were distinctive physical and mechanical differences from one version to another.

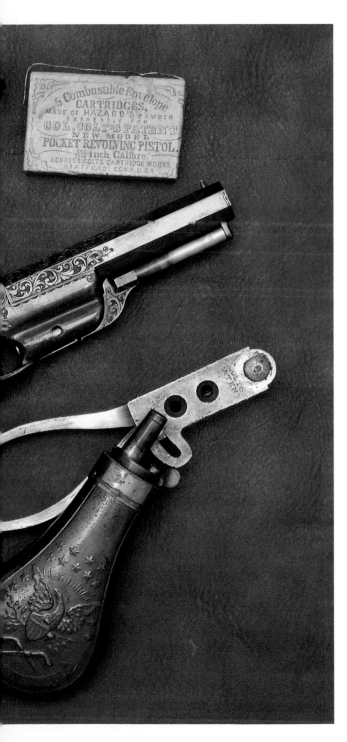

One of the rarest of all Root Sidehammer models, this No. 2 (or Model 2) bears elegant scrollwork by Gustave Young, and is silver plated with a matching silver plated powder flask.

Production of the Third Model continued through 1861 with total production over a 10 year period reaching 10,500 of which approximately 4,330 were Ordnance issue. Of that number 946 were supplied with detachable shoulder stocks. As noted by Wilson, "Government issued Pistol Carbines were in pairs, with only an issue of a single matching detachable shoulder stock." These have become the rarest and most desirable sets of Third Model

This pair of beautifully engraved Sidehammer Pistols exhibits some of the finest engraving on this model Colt revolver. The ivory gripped No. 7 Model, serial No. 12076 I.E., was factory engraved and presented by Colt to James McClatchie, a longtime employee of the company, and Samuel Colt's timekeeper. He worked for Colt's from 1853 through 1864, two years after Sam Colt's death. One of the finest Root Sidehammer pistols known, the cost of this beautifully engraved gun was $28.88. The second example is a No. 2 Root Pistol known as the "Charter Oak Model 1855 Sidehammer". No. 5886, it is from a series of guns presented to Colt's wholesalers or "jobbers" in 1856. The name comes from the wood used to make the grips, the famed Charter Oak, which had been toppled by a storm. (Dr. Joseph A. Murphy collection)

Dragoons. Still weighing 4 pounds, 2 ounces, the Third Model Dragoon marked the end of Colt's large frame, 1847 Walker-derived revolvers. The .44 caliber mantle would be passed to a new generation of smaller, lighter Colts in 1860.

Elisha King Root

In Hartford, Samuel Colt had begun purchasing parcels of property back in 1853, in what was then called the South Meadows, an area that fronted on the banks of the Connecticut River. As lowland, it was swampy, prone to spring flooding, and considered of little value, thus Colt was able to acquire the land, 250 acres total, at a remarkably low price of $60,000. He then spent another $125,000 to build a dike nearly two miles long between the river and the ground upon which his new factory was to be built. By August 1855 the Colt assembly plant fronting the Connecticut River shoreline was open for business. The new facilities were equipped with the most up-to-

The Root design was not limited to pistols. Root rifles, muskets, and carbines (shown) were also produced by Colt's in a wide variety of calibers. (Photo courtesy Herbert G. Houze/Wadsworth Atheneum)

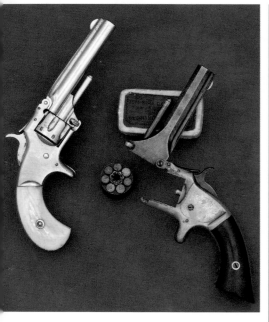

Pictured are two early Smith & Wesson Tip-Up .22 caliber rimfire revolvers, a 1st Model 3rd Issue (left), and 1st Model 2nd Issue. The inimitable Samuel Clemens once described the Smith & Wesson seven-shooters as carrying "a ball like a homeopathic pill." Indeed the .22 rimfire wasn't much of a cartridge but it was enough in a tight scrape to maybe get away with your life. (Guns from the Mike Clark Collection/Collectors Firearms)

date metalworking machinery available, the installation of which had been overseen by Colt's childhood friend, Elisha King Root, one of the most talented mechanical engineers of the era.

The two had met when Sam was 15 years old. While attending private school at Amherst he became interested in chemistry and electricity, and it was here that Colt first conceived of the idea for underwater explosives. He fashioned a rudimentary mine filled with gunpowder that could be detonated from shore by an electric current passing through a wire wrapped inside a tarred rope. On July 4, 1829, he distributed a handbill boasting that, "Sam'l Colt will blow a raft skyhigh on Ware Pond." His proclamation brought out a crowd of curious locals dressed in their holiday best to witness this improbable feat. Young Sam's experiment worked as declared, in fact, better. The raft exploded with such force that everyone along the shoreline was doused with water. Soaked to the skin the crowd ran after Colt, probably with the intension off tossing him headfirst into Ware Pond. Their pursuit ended when a tough looking young man who had watched the events unfold placed himself between Colt and the mob. His name was Elisha King Root. A quarter of a century later he was setting up the tooling in Hartford.

Along with the new assembly plant, the Colt's Patent Fire-Arms Manufacturing Company was officially incorporated in Connecticut in 1855, with an initial

Smith & Wesson took a back seat to Colt and Remington during the Civil War, but was the only American arms maker allowed to manufacture a cartridge firing revolver. In 1855 S&W had acquired the White patent for the bored through, breech-loading cylinder. As such, throughout the war no American gunmaker could build a breech-loading revolver that fired a self-contained metallic cartridge. This didn't stop both the Union and Confederacy from importing European-made cartridge guns and ammunition. S&W had patented the .22 caliber short cartridge before the war and countless soldiers on both sides of the conflict purchased the small, easily-concealed, 7-shot .22 revolvers as a backup gun. Pictured are a 1st Model Second Issue .22, a 1st Model 3rd Issue (with fluted cylinder) and a New York (possibly Nimschke shop) engraved 1st Model 3rd Issue with round cylinder. (Ricky Biagi collection and author collection, engraved gun)

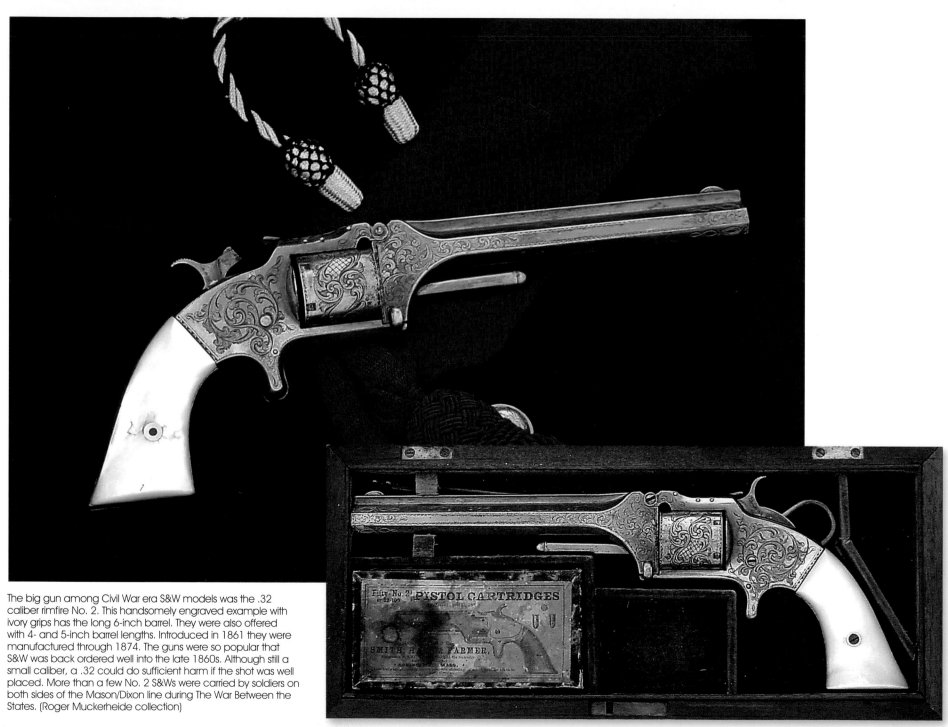

The big gun among Civil War era S&W models was the .32 caliber rimfire No. 2. This handsomely engraved example with ivory grips has the long 6-inch barrel. They were also offered with 4- and 5-inch barrel lengths. Introduced in 1861 they were manufactured through 1874. The guns were so popular that S&W was back ordered well into the late 1860s. Although still a small caliber, a .32 could do sufficient harm if the shot was well placed. More than a few No. 2 S&Ws were carried by soldiers on both sides of the Mason/Dixon line during The War Between the States. (Roger Muckerheide collection)

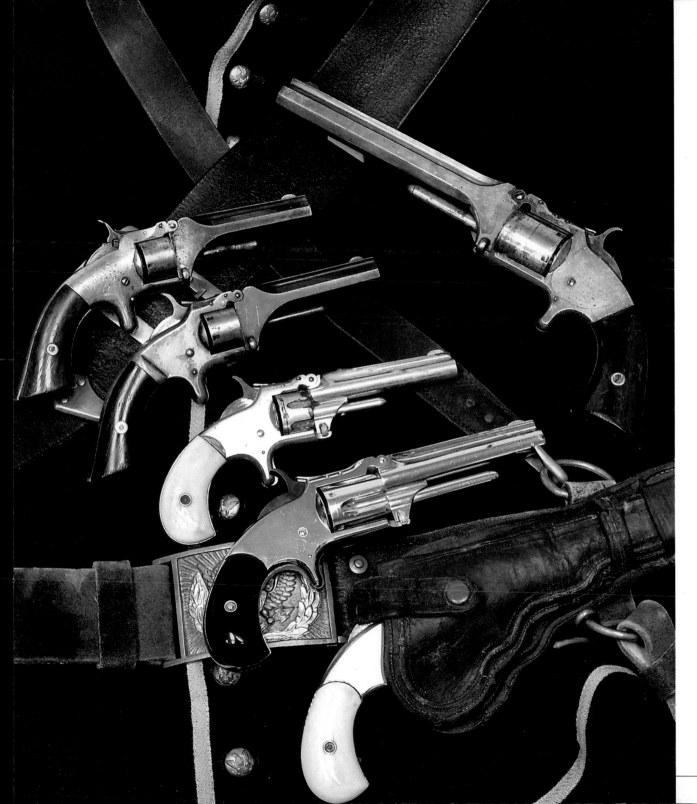

issuance of 10,000 shares of stock, of which Sam Colt retained ownership of 9,996 shares, giving one share to each of his business associates, including Root, now his factory superintendent. Within a year Colt's was manufacturing 150 weapons a day and "Colonel" Samuel Colt had become one of the ten wealthiest businessmen in America. As a loyal Democrat he had finally won his long-sought military commission, becoming a colonel and aide-de-camp to his good friend, Connecticut Governor Thomas Seymour. Even though it was an honorary commission, like everything else, Colt used it to his best advantage for sales and marketing. Decades later Sam Colt would be recognized by industry as one of the earliest Americans to take full advantage of marketing and sales promotion programs through publicity, product sampling, advertising, and public relations.

In many ways Sam Colt was to the handgun what Henry Ford and Henry Martyn Leland would be to the automobile in the 20th century. In 1902 Leland established the Cadillac Automobile Company. Six years later his cars won the coveted Dewar Trophy in England, successfully completing a standardization test involving parts interchangeability. Three Cadillacs were disassembled, their 2,163 components completely intermixed and then another 89 random parts removed and replaced with spares. The three cars were then reassembled from the commingled parts, started up and driven for 500 miles! Cadillac became the first American automaker ever to win the Dewar Trophy. What does this have to do with Colt? Henry Leland began his engineering career in Hartford, Connecticut, working for Samuel Colt. Other

A family of small arms, the S&W No. 1, No. 1-1/2, and No. 2 revolvers were in such high demand during the war that Smith & Wesson was never able to produce enough guns to fill all of its orders. Pictured among Civil War era models is a No. 1-1/2, introduced in 1865 and a 2nd Issue with fluted cylinder and bird's head grips, which replaced the 1st Issue model in 1868 and remained in production through 1875. Pictured top to bottom, S&W No. 2 with factory silver plated finish; No. 1 1st Model, 1st issue; No. 1 1st Model 2nd issue; No. 1 Model 3rd issue, No. 1-1/2 with rosewood grips; and a No. 1-1/2 with ivory grips in a Mexican slim Jim holster. (Mike Clark/Collectors Firearms collection)

Simply pressing up on the barrel latch at the bottom of the lug released the barrel and lug allowing it to "tip up" on its hinged top and expose the cylinder and short arbor. The cylinder was simply slipped out and reloaded, replaced, and the barrel dropped down into the locked position. An extra loaded cylinder could be changed out in a matter of seconds. Pictured are a No. 2 (top) and a No. 1-1/2 .32 rimfire. (Mike Clark/Collectors Firearms collection)

A pair of handsome New York-style engraved S&W Tip-Ups. In addition to the .22 caliber rimfire models (top left), S&W also produced two .32 caliber rimfire model. The second gun is a No. 1-1/2 (2nd Issue model c.1868). (Author's collection)

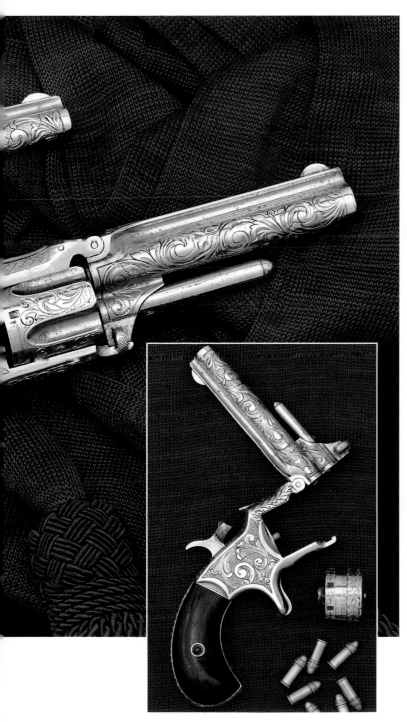

A rare and exceptional S&W No. 1, First Issue Number One, Sixth Type with an extremely rare Gutta Percha case. The S&W lineage is one of the most complicated because of the continual variety of models and changes in individual nomenclature with each alteration in design. (Photos courtesy Rock Island Auction Co.)

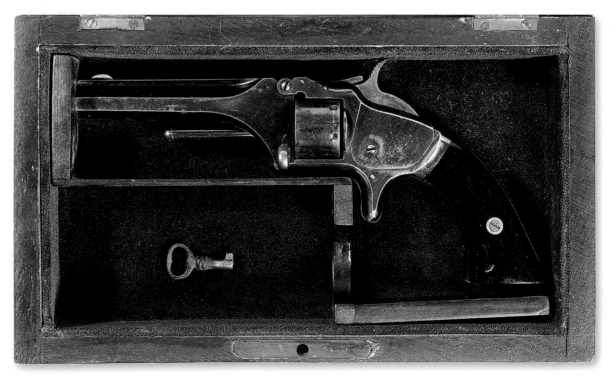

Pictured is a cased S&W Model No. 1 Second Issue with a U.S. Navy inscription. (Photos courtesy Rock Island Auction Co.)

Little S&W .22 rimfire seven-shooters were sometimes given to soldiers by their families in hope that, in time of need, the gun might bring a loved one home safe from the war. This photo shows a Union soldier posing with his S&W Model No. 1 Second Issue. The company sold out its entire production between 1860 and 1865 and was still filling backorders after the war ended. (Photos courtesy Rock Island Auction Co.)

famous Colt alumnus included Christopher M. Spencer (inventor of the Spencer rifle used in the Civil War; the first hammerless slide action shotgun; and the first screw-making machine), Francis A. Pratt, and Amos Whitney.

Although two other Connecticut gunmakers, Simeon North, and Whitney, had been the first to standardize parts, by the late 1850s Colt had perfected the technique to the point where eighty percent of his gun making was done by machine alone. Hartford was where the standards for mass production and parts interchangeability were established in the 1850s; the very underpinning of American auto making in the early 20th century. Leland had learned the value of precision engineering at Colt's and put it to use making automobiles. Henry Ford was similarly inspired by Colt's in his establishment of the moving assembly line.

The man who had been behind much of this, and behind Sam Colt from 1849 on, was Elisha King Root. As noted by historian Herbert G. Houze in *Samuel Colt, Arms, Art and Invention,* "...had it not been for Root's inventive genius, Colt's dream of mass production would never have been realized."

In addition to setting up the assembly lines in Hartford, Root the machinist, was also Root the teacher, instructing his personnel (including Leland and Spencer) in manufacturing techniques. And as Colt's factory superintendent, he was also Root the inventor.

Colt has often been accused of "staying too long at the fair," building open top revolvers for decades when it had long been established that a revolver with a solid frame and topstrap was a stronger design. E. Remington & Sons knew this is 1858 when they introduced their first revolvers. Horace Smith and Daniel B. Wesson knew this too when they began selling their first cartridge revolvers in 1857, the same year Sam Colt's patent extension expired. Why then did Colt's continue to manufacture open top revolvers until 1873? There are two answers. First, they didn't, and secondly, sales of established models, such as the 1849 Pocket Revolver, Third Model

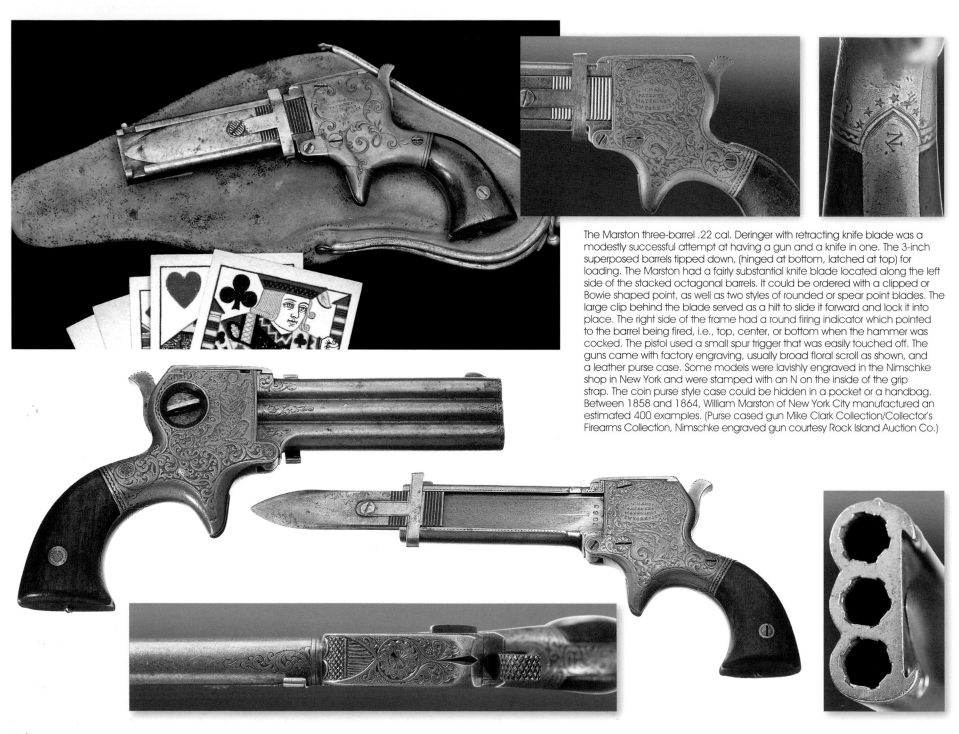

The Marston three-barrel .22 cal. Deringer with retracting knife blade was a modestly successful attempt at having a gun and a knife in one. The 3-inch superposed barrels tipped down, (hinged at bottom, latched at top) for loading. The Marston had a fairly substantial knife blade located along the left side of the stacked octagonal barrels. It could be ordered with a clipped or Bowie shaped point, as well as two styles of rounded or spear point blades. The large clip behind the blade served as a hilt to slide it forward and lock it into place. The right side of the frame had a round firing indicator which pointed to the barrel being fired, i.e., top, center, or bottom when the hammer was cocked. The pistol used a small spur trigger that was easily touched off. The guns came with factory engraving, usually broad floral scroll as shown, and a leather purse case. Some models were lavishly engraved in the Nimschke shop in New York and were stamped with an N on the inside of the grip strap. The coin purse style case could be hidden in a pocket or a handbag. Between 1858 and 1864, William Marston of New York City manufactured an estimated 400 examples. (Purse cased gun Mike Clark Collection/Collector's Firearms Collection, Nimschke engraved gun courtesy Rock Island Auction Co.)

Getting to the point....some gun knives were more the latter such as the French made double barrel .32 caliber from the Civil War era. The double triggers folded up when not needed and the weapon appeared more like a large pocket knife. The hammers were individually cocked. (Mike Clark Collection/Collector's Firearms)

Dragoon, and 1851 Navy were so lucrative only a fool would dare tamper with such success.

There were a handful of experimental revolvers built by Sam Colt and E. K. Root that employed a topstrap (these experimental models are on display at the Wadsworth Atheneum), as well as various means of fixed barrels and break open designs. None were as good as the original save for E. K. Root's 1855 patent model revolver, the fountainhead for a separate line of Colt's pistols and rifles featuring a solid frame and unique side mounted hammer. The prototype design had been finalized by Root and Colt in 1854 and a patent issued in E. K. Root's name on Christmas day 1855. Subsequent patents for the Root pistols (May 4, 1858) bore Samuel Colt's name with Root signing as witness. The first patent issued (December 25, 1855) had been for the prototype, which was never put into production. It employed a unique self cocking method activated by sliding the trigger ring forward and pulling it back, the rearward motion also discharging the weapon. A zig-zag channel in the cylinder acted upon by sliding the trigger rotated the cylinder.[6]

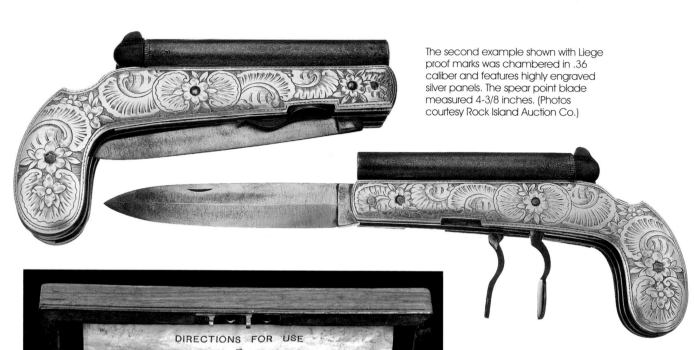

The second example shown with Liege proof marks was chambered in .36 caliber and features highly engraved silver panels. The spear point blade measured 4-3/8 inches. (Photos courtesy Rock Island Auction Co.)

DIRECTIONS FOR USE
of
SHARPS' PATENT REPEATER.

First—Half-cock the arm. **Second**—Hold the Pistol in the right hand and press the thumb on the screw-head under the barrel; at the same time, with the left hand, draw the barrel forward to its stop; then insert the cartridges, return the barrel to its place, and it is ready for use.

The Sharps Patent four-barrel, .32 caliber Pepperbox Derringer was one of the most successful small, multi-barrel pistols of the 1860s and 1870s. It was also one of the earliest, designed by Christian Sharps in 1859 and manufactured through 1874. The fluted Sharps barrels were 2-1/2 inches in length. This is a C. Sharps Tipping & Lawden version with silver plated factory engraved frame and grips. The standard model had an engraved brass frame and gutta-percha grips. The gun was loaded by depressing the release on the underside of the frame, which allowed the four barrel group to slide forward on the frame. Also sold as the Sharps & Hankins Breech-Loading 4-Shot Pepperbox, the Philadelphia armsmaker produced more 168,000 Pepperbox pistols in 23 different model variations over 15 years and in four calibers, .22, .30, and .32 short and long rimfire. (Mike Clark Collection/Collector's Firearms)

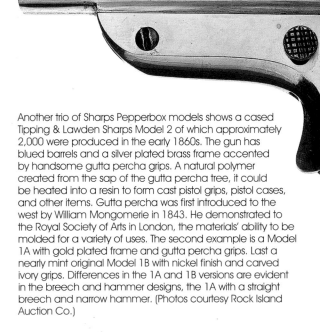

Another trio of Sharps Pepperbox models shows a cased Tipping & Lawden Sharps Model 2 of which approximately 2,000 were produced in the early 1860s. The gun has blued barrels and a silver plated brass frame accented by handsome gutta percha grips. A natural polymer created from the sap of the gutta percha tree, it could be heated into a resin to form cast pistol grips, pistol cases, and other items. Gutta percha was first introduced to the west by William Mongomerie in 1843. He demonstrated to the Royal Society of Arts in London, the materials' ability to be molded for a variety of uses. The second example is a Model 1A with gold plated frame and gutta percha grips. Last a nearly mint original Model 1B with nickel finish and carved ivory grips. Differences in the 1A and 1B versions are evident in the breech and hammer designs, the 1A with a straight breech and narrow hammer. (Photos courtesy Rock Island Auction Co.)

The Root pistols and rifles became eminently popular during the War Between the States, particularly the latter which allowed a soldier to have a large caliber rifle, carbine, or shotgun with up to six shots.[7]

The Root pistols were built from 1855 through 1873 in seven different series variations chambered in either .28 or .31 caliber. Seven versions for a gun that saw no more than 40,000 examples built might sound strange but Colt and Root were continually changing the design, and to such extent that there are distinctive physical and mechanical differences from one version to another.

The most obvious visual changes are from the octagon barrels used in the First through Fourth series to the round barrels used on Fifth through Seventh. Cylinders changed from round in the First and Second Models, to fluted cylinders on the Third and Fourth Models, and then back to round cylinders. Cylinder scenes changed from the first round cylinder series to the second. The original engraving by W. L. Ormsby was a settler armed with a pair of pistols fighting Indians in front of his cabin. The second cylinder scene used was Ormsby's Stagecoach Holdup adopted from 1849 Pocket Pistol. Changes too were made in loading lever designs and shapes, and factory patent stampings.

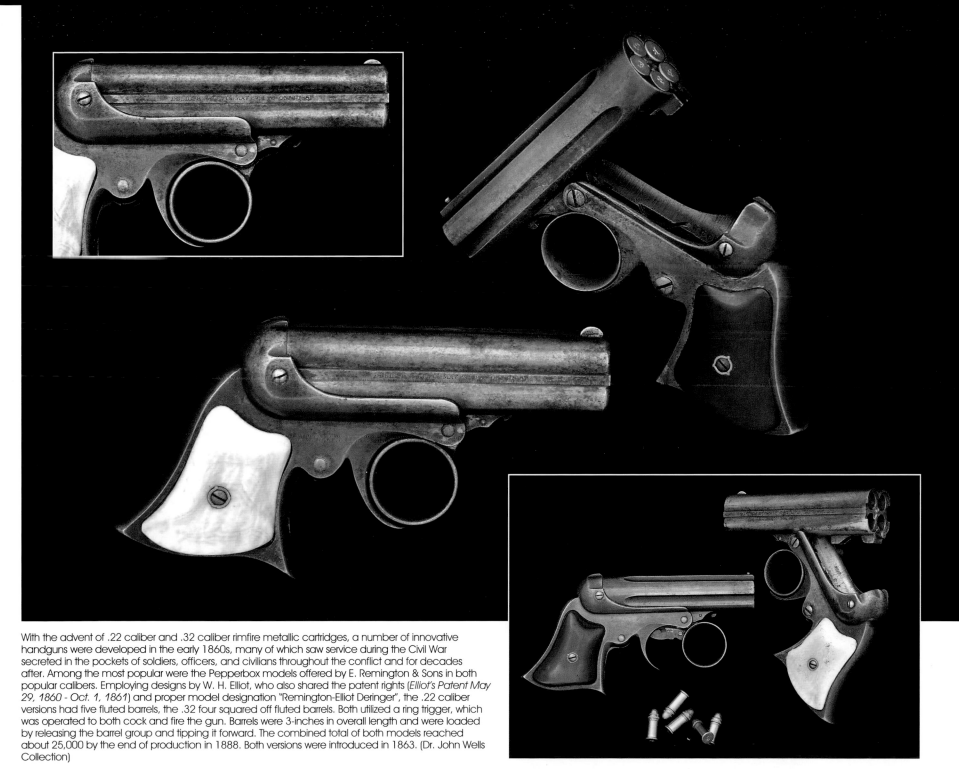

With the advent of .22 caliber and .32 caliber rimfire metallic cartridges, a number of innovative handguns were developed in the early 1860s, many of which saw service during the Civil War secreted in the pockets of soldiers, officers, and civilians throughout the conflict and for decades after. Among the most popular were the Pepperbox models offered by E. Remington & Sons in both popular calibers. Employing designs by W. H. Elliot, who also shared the patent rights (*Elliot's Patent May 29, 1860 - Oct. 1, 1861*) and proper model designation "Remington-Elliot Deringer", the .22 caliber versions had five fluted barrels, the .32 four squared off fluted barrels. Both utilized a ring trigger, which was operated to both cock and fire the gun. Barrels were 3-inches in overall length and were loaded by releasing the barrel group and tipping it forward. The combined total of both models reached about 25,000 by the end of production in 1888. Both versions were introduced in 1863. (Dr. John Wells Collection)

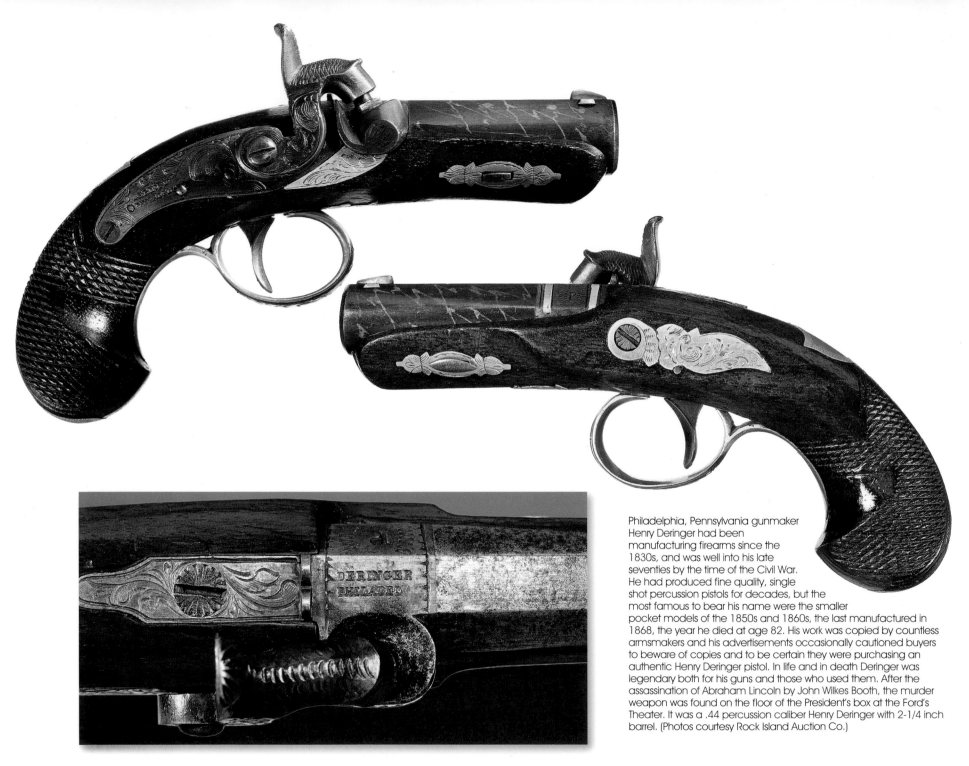

Philadelphia, Pennsylvania gunmaker Henry Deringer had been manufacturing firearms since the 1830s, and was well into his late seventies by the time of the Civil War. He had produced fine quality, single shot percussion pistols for decades, but the most famous to bear his name were the smaller pocket models of the 1850s and 1860s, the last manufactured in 1868, the year he died at age 82. His work was copied by countless armsmakers and his advertisements occasionally cautioned buyers to beware of copies and to be certain they were purchasing an authentic Henry Deringer pistol. In life and in death Deringer was legendary both for his guns and those who used them. After the assassination of Abraham Lincoln by John Wilkes Booth, the murder weapon was found on the floor of the President's box at the Ford's Theater. It was a .44 percussion caliber Henry Deringer with 2-1/4 inch barrel. (Photos courtesy Rock Island Auction Co.)

As a small caliber pocket pistol, both the .28 and .31 caliber Root Models were only modestly successful despite being the highly touted solid frame design. The traditional small caliber open top Colt revolvers of the late 1840s continued to outsell and outlast the Root Pistols.

One Shot...Maybe two, or three?

There are many arguments for and against small caliber pistols. Smith & Wesson's popular .22 caliber "Tip-Up" revolvers were often regarded as a "Ladies gun" but during the Civil War many a soldier and civilian could be found with an S&W or other small caliber single or multiple-shot pistol on their person. As for the "potency" of Daniel Wesson's patented .22 short, and even some slightly larger calibers of the 1860s, celebrated author Samuel Clemens wrote in his book *Roughing It*, "I was armed to the teeth with a pitiful little Smith & Wesson's seven-shooter, which carried a ball like a homeopathic pill, and it took the whole seven to make a dose for an adult. But I thought it was grand. It appeared to me to be a dangerous weapon. It only had one fault – you could not hit anything with it."

Indeed, the .22 was an anemic cartridge, but so many .22 caliber pocket pistols and single shot Derringers were produced prior to and throughout the Civil War that one has to admit to there having been some accepted standard, that no one wanted to be shot by any caliber pistol, especially at very close range where several of Mr. Clemens' "homeopathic pills" could have been a fatal enough dose.

More potent, and eminently more popular as time went on, was the .32 caliber cartridge and the eclectic variety of devices built to discharge it, everything from the practical to the improbable such as the combination Belgian brass knuckle and stiletto pinfire revolver, Marston three barrel .22 caliber Derringer with retracting knife blade, and French made double barrel .32 folding blade knife

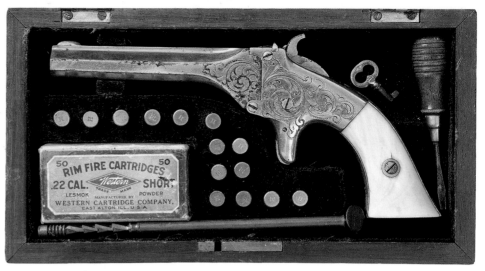

With the availability of the .22 rimfire cartridge in the 1860s a considerable number of single and multiple shot pistols were manufactured to fire them. This is one of the more elegant examples of the early 1860s manufactured in New Haven, Connecticut by the T.J. Stafford Co. The barrel is nickel plated and the frame is silver plated over brass. Barrel length measured 3-1/2 inches. The guns came in a wooden case with a box of cartridge and an additional 14 rounds in the cartridge block. This example is handsomely engraved in the period vine scroll style and fitted with ivory grips. The grip design is reminiscent of the early S&W No. 1 First and Second Issue .22 revolvers c.1857-1868. (Photos courtesy Rock Island Auction Co.)

Another deluxe presentation model of the Moore's No. 1 with vine scroll engraving on a punch dot background. This rare silver plated example also shows the carrying case and examples of the early .41 caliber rimfire cartridge. (Photos courtesy Rock Island Auction Co.)

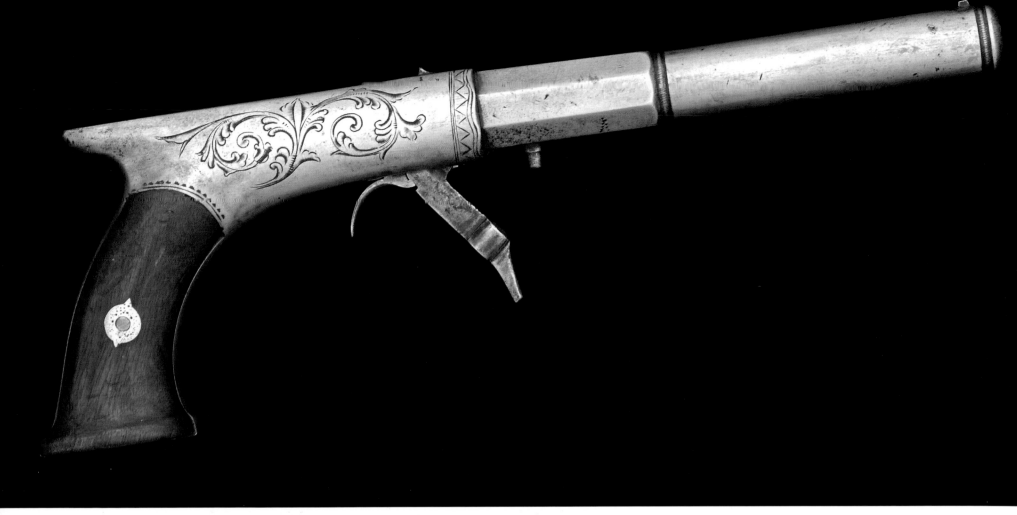

A great place to hide a back-up gun was in your boot, same place a lot of men hid a dagger or small Bowie knife. The Anderson Underhammer was a large caliber caplock pistol with a part octagonal, part round barrel measuring 4 to 5 inches. The action was cocked by pulling down on the under barrel lever. Nearly 50 different makers produced simple, affordable Underhammer "boot pistols" before, during and after the Civil War, all pretty much the same style, though a few also had triggerguards. (Mike Clark Collection/ Collectors Firearms)

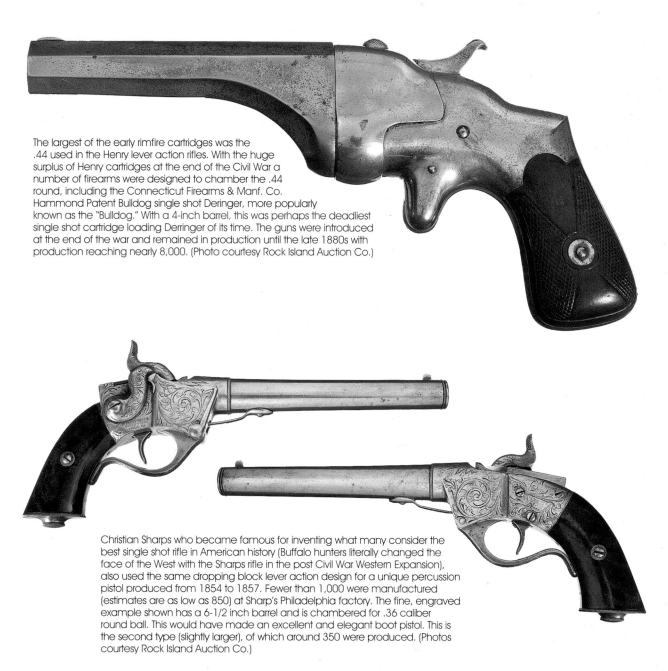

The largest of the early rimfire cartridges was the .44 used in the Henry lever action rifles. With the huge surplus of Henry cartridges at the end of the Civil War a number of firearms were designed to chamber the .44 round, including the Connecticut Firearms & Manf. Co. Hammond Patent Bulldog single shot Deringer, more popularly known as the "Bulldog." With a 4-inch barrel, this was perhaps the deadliest single shot cartridge loading Derringer of its time. The guns were introduced at the end of the war and remained in production until the late 1880s with production reaching nearly 8,000. (Photo courtesy Rock Island Auction Co.)

Christian Sharps who became famous for inventing what many consider the best single shot rifle in American history (Buffalo hunters literally changed the face of the West with the Sharps rifle in the post Civil War Western Expansion), also used the same dropping block lever action design for a unique percussion pistol produced from 1854 to 1857. Fewer than 1,000 were manufactured (estimates are as low as 850) at Sharp's Philadelphia factory. The fine, engraved example shown has a 6-1/2 inch barrel and is chambered for .36 caliber round ball. This would have made an excellent and elegant boot pistol. This is the second type (slightly larger), of which around 350 were produced. (Photos courtesy Rock Island Auction Co.)

The most handsomely styled and perhaps most successful of all four-barrel models was created by one of the war's most famous rifle makers, Christian Sharps. Renowned for making what many consider the single most important series of rifles in American history, he also created the Sharps Patent .32 caliber four-barrel Pepperbox Pistol (Derringer). It is estimated that more 168,000 Sharps Pepperbox pistols (in 23 different model variations over 15 years and in four calibers, .22, .30, and .32 short and long rimfire) were produced. Models were also produced under the Sharps & Hankins, Philadelphia, and Sharps Patent Tipping & Lawden names. The best looking of all the Sharps models is considered to be the Model 1A with a straight standing breech (the gun is loaded by sliding the barrel block forward), engraved frame and barrel, and gutta-percha grips.

Another series of guns developed in the 1850s and 1860s was designed by Frank Wesson, the younger brother of Daniel and Edwin Wesson. While Daniel's success with his associate and partner Horace Smith has completely eclipsed the works of either of the other Wesson brothers, Frank's contribution to American arms making is fairly significant both for his unique 19th century gun designs and his later association with another famous manufacturer, Harrington & Richardson.

Most of Frank Wesson's designs were, in a word, "different" from other guns of the period. His rifles were innovative for the 1850s and 1860s, but it is his small arms – pistols and "pocket rifles" – that have become the younger Wesson's trademark guns. His single shot pistols first began appearing in the late 1850s chambered in the new .22 short rimfire cartridge invented by his brother Daniel. There is, however, one Frank Wesson pistol that stands head-and-shoulders above the rest, the medium Frame Tip-Up Pocket Rifle c.1862-1870, with either a 10 or 12-inch barrel and a detachable skeleton shoulder stock.

While none of these various firearms were ever approved by the Ordnance Department for military use,

that didn't preclude the private purchase of small backup guns by soldiers. Many were given to them by family members in hopes that the little gun might in some way help return a son, brother, or father safely from the war.

Here Comes Everybody

With the expiration of the Colt's patent the floodgates of industry were flung wide open. Armsmakers sprang up throughout the New England states, many in Connecticut, some right in Colt's own back yard in New Haven, others in Pittsburgh and Philadelphia, Pennsylvania; in New York; at the Springfield Armory (Springfield Arms Co. and Warner Patent revolvers) in Massachusetts, and at the historic Whitney Arms Co. Whitneyville, Connecticut, founded in the late 18th century by Eli Whitney, inventor of the Cotton Gin. After his death in 1825, his nephews Eli Whitney Blake and Philos Blake operated the company until Whitney's son took control in 1842. A Princeton graduate in 1841, Whitney, Jr. had inherited his father's business sense and talent as a designer. His first venture, at age 22, was to negotiate a U.S. government contract to manufacture the U.S. Model 1841 rifle. Between 1842 and 1855 Whitneyville produced 22,500 rifles. It was Whitney, Jr. who also helped Sam Colt produce the 1847 Walker for the United States Mounted Rifles, and the transitional Whitneyville-Hartford Dragoons, before Colt established his own works in Hartford.

The Pepperbox was one of the first successful revolving pistols, only instead of a cylinder with multiple chambers; one had a gun with multiple barrels. The guns were always somewhat controversial as their greatest advantage was also their greatest weakness. Because of the design aiming and accuracy were always difficult, consigning the Pepperbox to close in work. The action was cumbersome and the weight of as many as six barrels made the guns muzzle heavy. Nonetheless until the late 1850s they were very popular sidearms and offered in a variety of sizes and calibers. The most successful were the Allen Pepperboxes first manufactured in Massachusetts in the 1830s by Ethan Allen. These were the inspiration for countless variations including versions of the Allen designed double action Pepperbox. The guns are their own category of arms and too numerous to discuss in detail. The examples shown are Allen & Thurber Dragoon sized models chambered for .36 caliber percussion. The barrels are 5-1/4 inches in length. (Photos courtesy Rock Island Auction Co.)

Just as Colt had many imitators, so too, did Smith & Wesson. Fire Manhattan Arms Co. was adept at making facsimiles of both Colt's and S&W models in the 1860s. This is the Manhattan First Model Pocket Revolver chambered in .22 rimfire. Its similarity to the S&W No. 1 Tip-Up revolver is unmistakable. Approximately 1,600 of the 7-shot revolvers were manufactured between 1860 and 1861. It is rare to find an example in such fine condition and with its original pasteboard picture box. (Photos courtesy Rock Island Auction Co.)

formerly limited to the heavier Dragoons, and do so in a revolver that weighed 2 pounds, 8-1/2 ounces, almost half that of a Third Model Dragoon, which tipped the scales at 4 pounds, 2 ounces. Not only was the 1860 Army lighter, but smaller, measuring 13-5/8 inches overall with an 8-inch barrel, compared to the Third Model Dragoon at just under 14-inches with a 7-1/2 inch barrel. The extra 1/2 inch in barrel length gave the 1860 Army a bit more weight up front and a longer sight radius. When fitted with a detachable shoulder stock, the military version of the 1860 Army also made a reasonably decent six shot carbine. More than a new handgun, it was a work of design art, as different in appearance from the 1851 Navy and Dragoons as the Walker had been from a Paterson. Here was a slim firearm with a tapered round barrel, compound curves, a trim, shallow frame, and a long, contoured grip.

Not surprisingly, with the start of the Civil War, the United States government became the single largest purchaser of 1860 Army models.

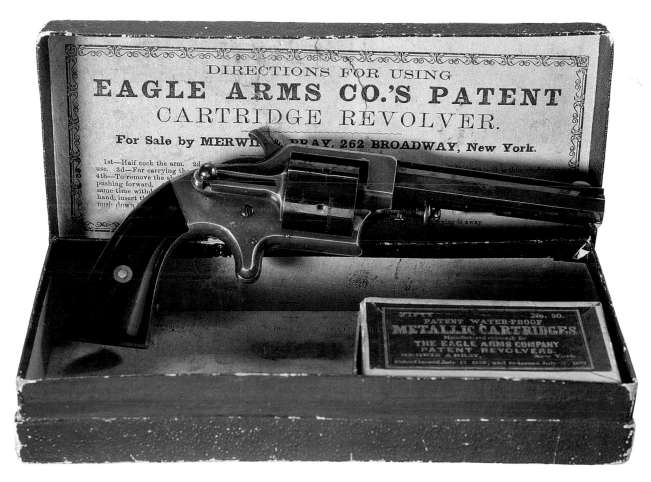

Alexander Thuer wasn't the only inventor to come up with a way around the S&W Rollin White Patent in the late 1850s. Eagle Arms Co. patented a front loading 6-shot revolver in July 1859 (marked *Patented July 12, 1859 & July 21, 1863*), which used a specially made .30 caliber cup primed cartridge loaded from the front of the cylinder. The ejector, along the right side of the frame, protruded through a small hole in the back of each cylinder chamber and was pushed forward to dislodge spent casings. Designed by W.C. Ellis and J.H. White, there were several versions but the pocket model pictured was the most successful with production reaching approximately 20,000 by the end of the Civil War. Once again this would have been a sidearm purchased by individual soldiers. The single action, spur trigger pistols used a solid frame like the Remington, and could also be refitted with a percussion cylinder, making this a versatile little gun. (Photos courtesy Rock Island Auction Co.)

Military versions often had notched recoil shields and a fourth screw in the frame to mount a detachable shoulder stock, whereas Civilian models had full recoil shields. There were also two cylinder types, rebated and fluted, the latter being the earliest and rarest. It is estimated that Colt's produced only around 4,000 fluted models (some noted in factory records as the "cavalry" model, though this pertained to their stronger construction to meet Ordnance Department specifications), out of a total production run exceeding 200,000 built between 1860 and 1873. It was an elegant looking gun that would endure long after production ceased; both in its original form and as one of the most popular metallic cartridge conversions of the early 1870s.

E. Remington & Sons

Remington was one of America's oldest armsmakers, founded in 1816 by Eliphalet Remington II. Originally, the company did not manufacture guns, only barrels, and quite successfully. In 1828 Remington moved to larger facilities in Ilion, New York, along the Erie Canal, a major trade route in the 19th century. It wasn't until 1848, following the purchase of the Ames Company of Chicopee, Massachusetts, that Remington produced an entire gun, a breech loading percussion carbine built under contract to the U.S. Navy. It was followed by a contract for 5,000 U.S. Model 1841 percussion "Mississippi" rifles. As for pistols, nearly a decade would pass before E. Remington & Sons introduced their first handgun, the Remington-Beals pocket revolver, patented June 24, 1856, and May 26, 1857, and introduced just as the extension on the Colt's patent expired. Designed by Fordyce Beals, who shared not only the name but the patent rights, he would go on to design many of Remington's most successful models throughout the 1860s and 1870s.

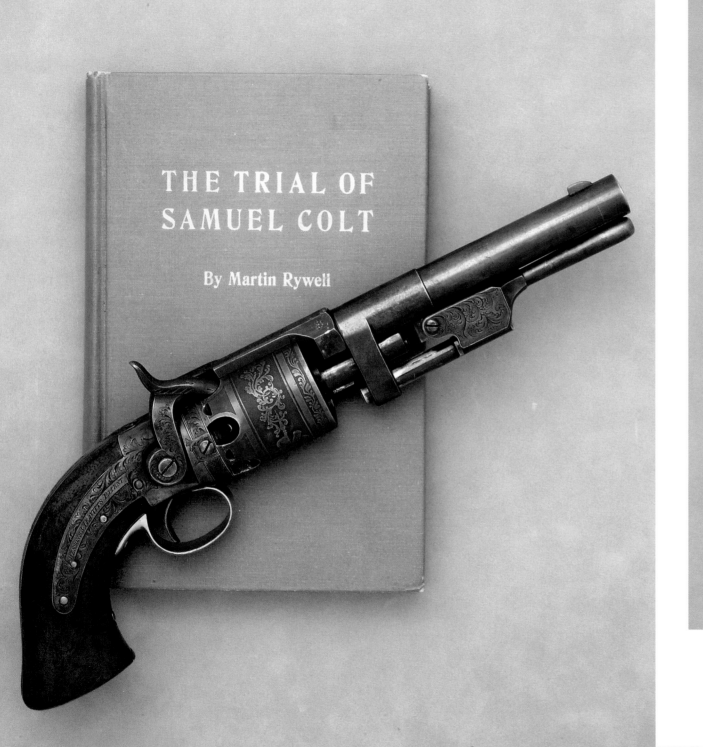

In his landmark case against the Massachusetts Arms Company (1851) Samuel Colt filed patent infringement charges against the Mass. Arms Co.'s use of mechanisms covered in his 1836 U.S. patent. The gun was originally designed by Daniel B. Wesson and Daniel Leavitt and manufactured by Wesson, Stevens & Miller of Hartford. Production was then taken over by the Massachusetts Arms Co., at which point Colt filed suit. What is so striking about this gun, other than its sheer size, is that it is a sidehammer design! As a result of losing the suit, Massachusetts Arms Co. continued to build versions of this revolver without a mechanically rotated cylinder (rotated by cocking the hammer, which had been Colt's grounds for patent infringement). Pictured is one of the finest engraved examples of the legendary lawsuit revolver. (Dr. Joseph A. Murphy collection)

In 1858 Remington raised the bar for .44 caliber handgun designs with the introduction of the Remington-Beals Army model, an immediate and successful rival to the Colt revolvers and their comparatively out-dated construction. Followed by the .36 caliber Navy Model, Remington did not rest on its laurels during the Civil War but continued to make design improvements to its original Army and Navy revolvers, introducing the improved Army in 1861 and New Model Army in 1863, which was to become the most revered of all Civil War revolvers from the Ilion, New York armsmaker. Remington produced the second largest quantity of handguns used by the U.S. Army and Navy, a total of nearly 130,000, over 115,000 of which were chambered in .44 caliber.

While Colt could claim considerable celebrity for its 1851 Navy being the favored sidearm of James Butler "Wild Bill" Hickok, E. Remington & Sons would also have equal notoriety bestowed upon its 1863 New Model Army as the gun carried during the Civil War and for years after by William F. "Buffalo Bill" Cody. A true cowboy in the tradition of the American Frontier, at age 11 he was herding cattle and driving wagon across the Great Plains. In 1860, after a brief try at trapping and mining, at age 14 he joined the Pony Express. Most of his time was spent crossing Kansas, although occasionally he traveled into northeast Colorado and cut north into Nebraska and Wyoming, but Cody's career as a rider was short-lived, the Pony Express suspended operations on October 28, 1861. It was during the Civil War that Cody first met Bill Hickok, who had just signed on as a Union scout. Cody was still too young for regular military duty in 1861 but three years later, after joining the Seventh Kansas, he was involved in the Battle of Tupelo, in which Confederate General Nathan Bedford Forrest was forced to retreat.

With his background as a Pony Express rider, hunter and tracker, Cody was hired as an Army scout, more of a spy really, wearing a Confederate uniform and riding well ahead of his regiment. In point of fact a very dangerous job in which he could have accidentally been shot by Union soldiers or hung as a spy by the Confederates!

The Wesson and Leavitts sidehammer revolver design for Massachusetts Arms Co. was relatively short lived. Introduced in 1850, Samuel Colt forced the company to suspend production in 1851. Roughly 800 guns were built chambered in .40 caliber percussion with 7-1/8 in barrels. This is a very early example without loading lever. Another 1,000 belt models were produced with shorter barrels and slightly smaller frame. (Mike Clark Collection/Collectors Firearms)

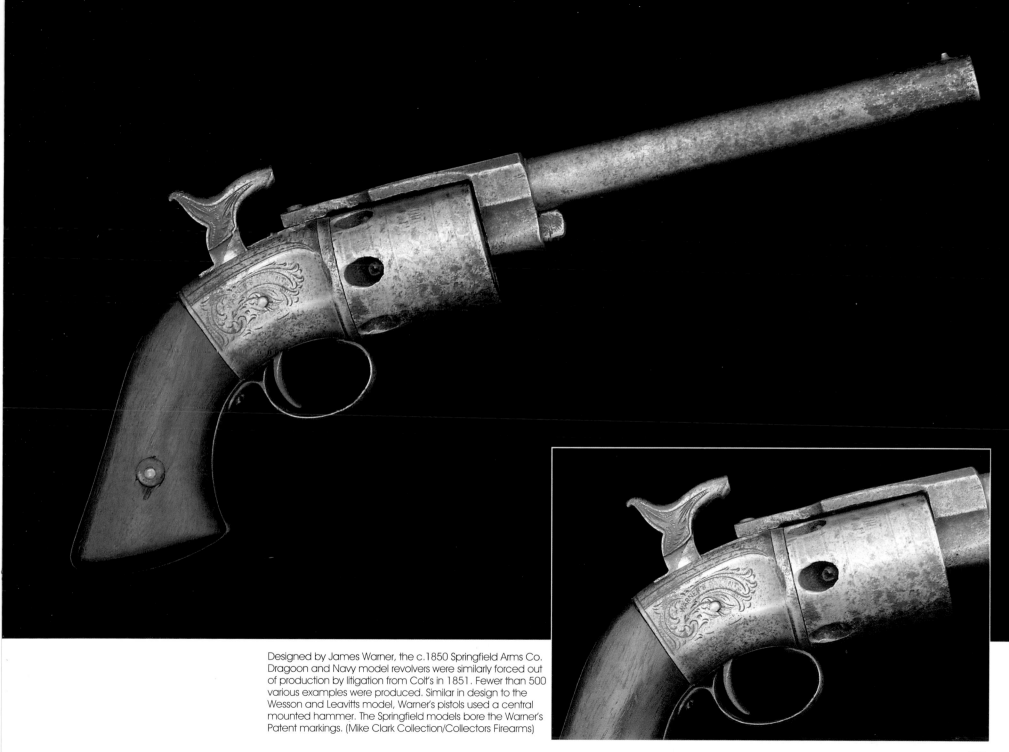

Designed by James Warner, the c.1850 Springfield Arms Co. Dragoon and Navy model revolvers were similarly forced out of production by litigation from Colt's in 1851. Fewer than 500 various examples were produced. Similar in design to the Wesson and Leavitts model, Warner's pistols used a central mounted hammer. The Springfield models bore the Warner's Patent markings. (Mike Clark Collection/Collectors Firearms)

The big Pettengill Army Model six-shot, .44 caliber double action only hammerless revolvers were issued to U.S. Cavalry regiments during the Civil War. (Photo courtesy Rock Island Auction Co.)

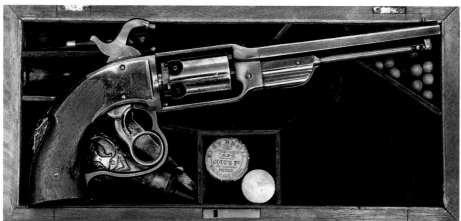

A fine cased example of the Savage Army model revolver. The gun was fired by first pulling the lower ring trigger which when drawn to the rear cocked the hammer and rotated the cylinder. Pulling the upper trigger released the hammer. A somewhat cumbersome design, production ended in 1865. (Mike Clark/Collectors Firearms collection)

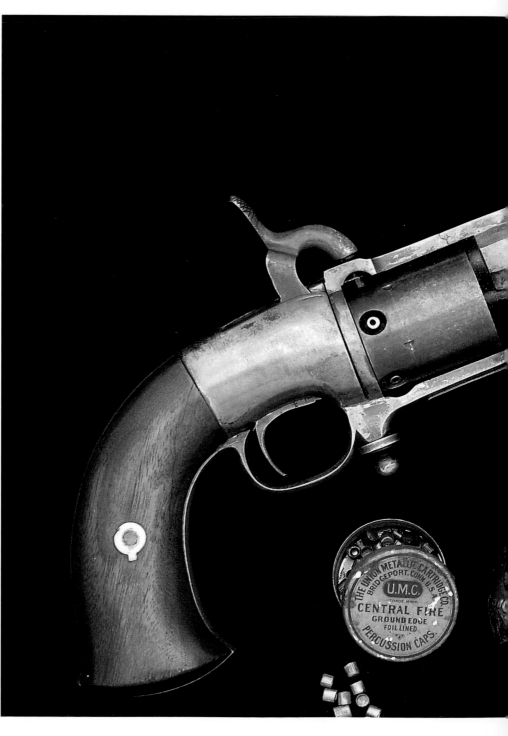

Another unique design from the late 1850s was the Butterfield which offered a better way to fire a revolver by pre capping each chamber as the gun was cocked and thereby eliminating one of the early failings of percussion revolvers, a hammer resting on a loaded and capped chamber, or worse, the percussion cap on an un-detonated chamber falling off. The Butterfield was patented by Josiah B. Butterfield (J.B. Butterfield & Co.) in 1861 and manufactured in Philadelphia until 1862. When an expected government contract to purchase the arms fell through, the company was forced to cease production. Only around 2000 were made. The unique, 5-shot, .41 caliber revolvers carried a stack of special percussion caps (flat detonating discs) in a spring loaded tube screwed into the bottom of the frame. Each time the revolver was cocked a fresh detonator was stripped from the tube, and held ready over the cylinder nipple as the hammer dropped. (Mike Clark Collection/ Collectors Firearms)

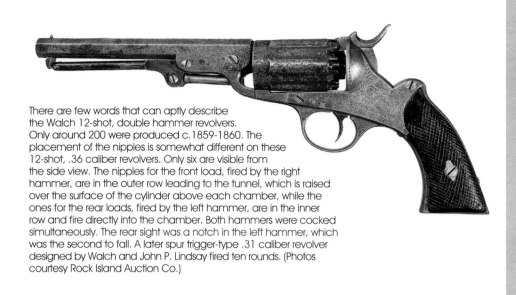

There are few words that can aptly describe the Walch 12-shot, double hammer revolvers. Only around 200 were produced c.1859-1860. The placement of the nipples is somewhat different on these 12-shot, .36 caliber revolvers. Only six are visible from the side view. The nipples for the front load, fired by the right hammer, are in the outer row leading to the tunnel, which is raised over the surface of the cylinder above each chamber, while the ones for the rear loads, fired by the left hammer, are in the inner row and fire directly into the chamber. Both hammers were cocked simultaneously. The rear sight was a notch in the left hammer, which was the second to fall. A later spur trigger-type .31 caliber revolver designed by Walch and John P. Lindsay fired ten rounds. (Photos courtesy Rock Island Auction Co.)

Navy. The U.S. military only took delivery of 11,984 with the balance of guns being sold to the civilian market. The unique design was based on the earlier Savage & North Figure 8 Model revolvers, built in the late 1850s by Simeon North and Josiah Savage. S&N became the Savage Revolving Fire-Arms Co. in 1859. The hefty .36 caliber guns were discharged by first pulling the lower ring trigger, which when drawn to the rear cocked the hammer and rotated the cylinder. Pulling the upper trigger released the hammer. A somewhat cumbersome design, production ended in 1865.

In 1851, in defiance of the Colt's patent extension, Springfield Arms Company (founded in 1850) in Springfield, Massachusetts, introduced a Dragoon Model revolver

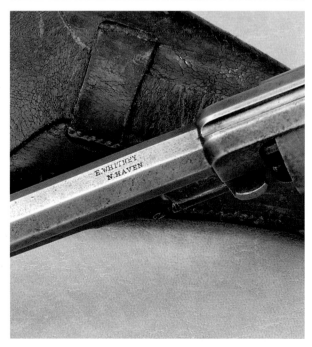

The historic Whitney Arms Co. of New Haven, Connecticut, "Whitneyville" was originally founded in the late 18th century by Eli Whitney, the inventor of the Cotton Gin. His nephews, Eli Whitney Blake and Philos Blake, took over management of the company after their Uncle's death in 1825. Upon graduating from Princeton in 1841, Eli Whitney, Jr. (born in 1820) stepped into the management role. His first involvement with revolvers was helping Samuel Colt produce the Walker revolver for the United States Mounted Rifles in 1847. His factory also assisted in manufacturing the transitional Whitneyville-Hartford Dragoons built while Colt was establishing his own factory in Hartford. Immediately after the expiration of the Colt's patent, however, Whitney felt no obligation to stay out of the revolver market and built a copy of the Colt 1851 Navy. That was quickly followed with Whitney's own design for a percussion revolver in 1858. Much like the guns of E. Remington & Sons, the Whitney revolvers were a solid frame design with a screwed in barrel. Examples like this 2nd Model Navy in .36 caliber percussion, shown with a period military flap holster, were carried by both Union and Confederate troops. The Union purchased over 7,000 Whitneyville revolvers during the war. (Mike Clark Collection/Collectors Firearms)

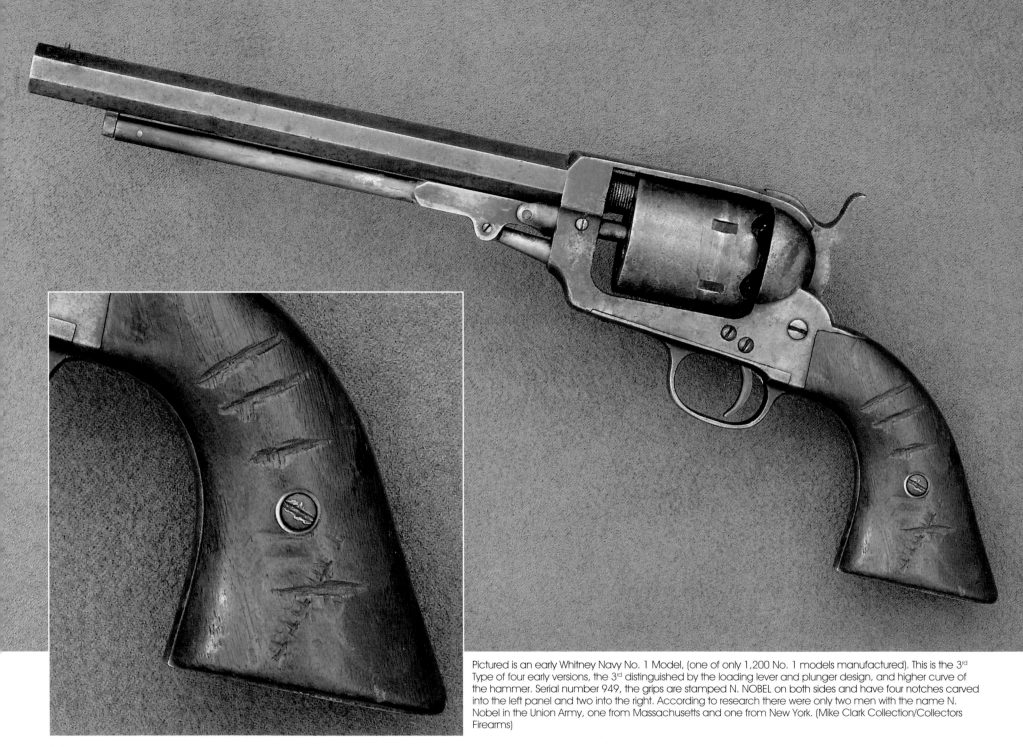

Pictured is an early Whitney Navy No. 1 Model, (one of only 1,200 No. 1 models manufactured). This is the 3rd Type of four early versions, the 3rd distinguished by the loading lever and plunger design, and higher curve of the hammer. Serial number 949, the grips are stamped N. NOBEL on both sides and have four notches carved into the left panel and two into the right. According to research there were only two men with the name N. Nobel in the Union Army, one from Massachusetts and one from New York. (Mike Clark Collection/Collectors Firearms)

Whitney Pocket Model revolvers were carried by Union and Confederate soldiers, probably as an extra gun. Chambered in .31 caliber percussion they were produced in 1st Model and 2nd Model versions, the pair shown being of the 2nd Model, 2nd Type with eagle, shield, lion, and navy battle scenes on the cylinder. The shield is just barley visible on the example at right. Barrel length was 3-inches, cylinder capacity, 5-shots. (Mike Clark Collection/Collectors Firearms.)

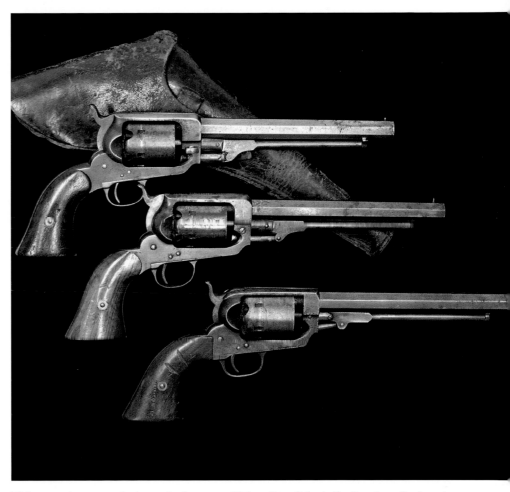

Whitney revolvers were also known by the name Whitney Navy & Eagle Co. Revolvers. Produced through the early 1860s, the design was similar to other solid frame revolvers of the period, like the Remington, Rogers & Spencer, Marston, and Freeman, but the Whitney was among the first to use this design. Most of the 1860's production was purchased by the Army and Navy during the Civil War. Pictured at top is a .36 caliber 2nd Model with holster; middle, another 2nd Model; and bottom a 1st Model. There were a total of 10 variations in the 1st and 2nd Models. Whitney revolvers of all types and calibers amounted to over 30,000 guns during the Civil War, most of which were purchased by civilians or individual soldiers. (Mike Clark/Collectors Firearms collection)

chambered in .40 caliber, a Navy Model in .36 caliber, and a .28 caliber Pocket Model. The guns were all designed by the armory's James Warner, who would also produce his own Warner Patent Models of similar design in 1851. (Late in 1857, after the Colt's Patent had expired, James Warner began manufacturing a .28 caliber revolver marked *James Warner Springfield, Mass. U.S.A.* He built more 10,000 before production ended). Colt's fierce litigation had forced Springfield to cease production in 1852, as it did James Warner and

The earliest versions of the new Colt Model 1860 Army had fluted cylinders. A cased pair with shoulder stock is an exceptionally rare find. This consecutively numbered pair, 2259 and 2260, were a presentation from Samuel Colt to Colonel Charles Augustus May, a longtime friend and supporter. May was a distinguished Dragoon officer in the Mexican wars and Colt had also presented him with a pair of shoulder stocked Third Model Dragoons. Col. May was among the pall bearers at Colt's funeral in January 1862. The fluted pair of 1860s Army revolvers remain in exceptional condition. (Photo Courtesy Greg Martin Auctions)

Early on, Colt had problems with the early fluted cylinders on 1860 Army models which, in random occasions failed Ordnance Department testing, almost always as a result of a burst or swelled cylinder. Colt's solution was to make the bore conical leaving more material under the bolt stops. This began in the latter part of 1861. Between July and September the now familiar rebated cylinder replaced the fluted cylinder as standard production on the 1860 Army. The fluted cylinder example pictured was shipped April 1861 at the start of the Civil War. (Mike Clark Collection/Collectors Firearms)

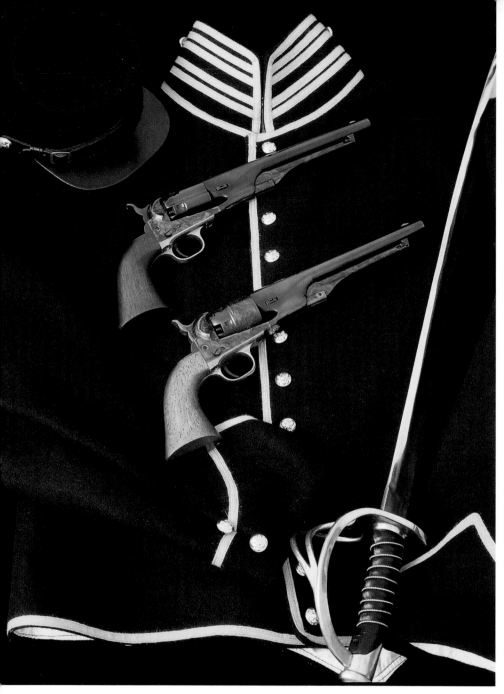

Pictured are a fluted cylinder 1860 Army (top) and a rebated cylinder model, illustrating the change in the design. The U.S. government was the largest purchaser of Colt's Model 1860 Army. Both examples shown have frames cut for mounting a shoulder stock and the large 4th screw necessary to anchor the yoke of the stock.

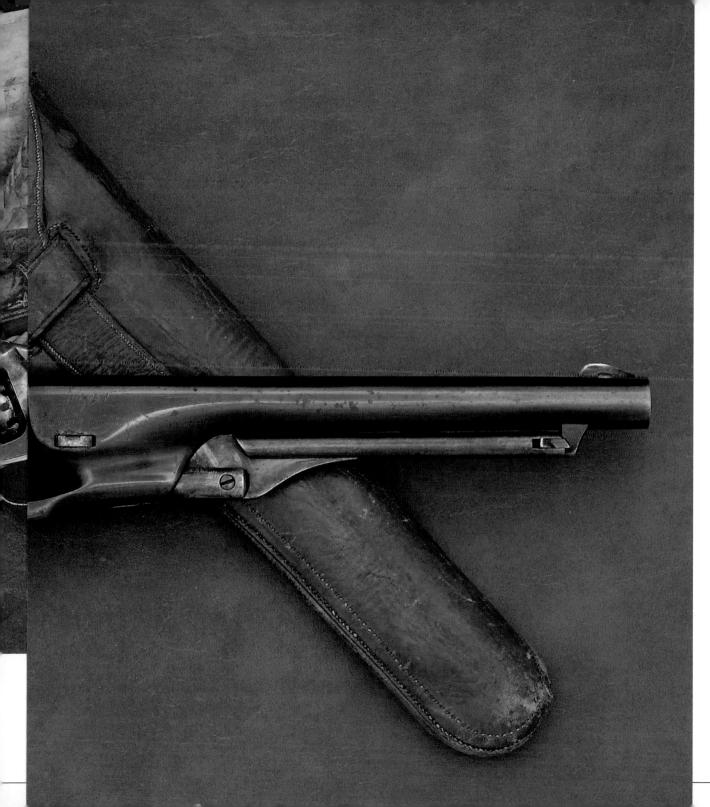

others producing revolvers utilizing its patented operating mechanism. The most famous litigation was against the Massachusetts Arms Co., which lost its landmark patent infringement case to Colt's in 1851. Massachusetts continued to manufacture its Wesson & Leavitt designed revolvers without a mechanism to automatically rotate the cylinder when the hammer was cocked, the principal feature for which Colt's had brought suit. This downgraded the Massachusetts revolvers to something more akin to early Collier revolvers built from 1819 to 1827. Like the Collier, the Massachusetts revolvers manufactured through 1857 operated by manually rotating the cylinder after hitting a release button located above the trigger. To make the guns more appealing they were also equipped with the Maynard self-priming device first seen on the U.S. Springfield Model 1855 Rifled Muskets and Pistol Carbines.

Some of Massachusetts Arms early associates were none other than Horace Smith, two of the Wesson brothers, Daniel B. and Edwin; Joshua Stevens (later the successful J. Stevens Arms Co.); and J. T. Ames of the Ames Mfg. Co. Even with all of this talent, no one could stand up to a legal skirmish with Colt's attorneys. The Massachusetts Arms Co. did find one way to circumvent the Colt's patent in 1857, by building licensed copies of the British Adams Patent double action revolver, which helped introduce the double action concept to America. The use of British double actions during The War Between the States was not uncommon on either side, and a considerable number of Adams and British Kerr revolvers were imported between 1861 and 1865, in addition to the more than 5,500 Adams and Kerr's Patent .36 caliber double action revolvers manufactured in Massachusetts by 1861.

This is an 1860 Army with rebated cylinder and recoil shield notched for attaching a shoulder stock. However, this gun is a civilian model with ivory grips and a modified, dovetailed front sight. It does not have the 4th screw necessary for mounting a shoulder stock to the gun's frame. It is shown with a civilian flap holster. (Mike Clark Collection/Collectors Firearms)

Colt's most ardent competitor and imitator during the 1860s was the Manhattan Arms Co. which was formed in 1856, a year prior to the expiration of the Colt's Patent. The company manufactured a variety of pistols and revolvers in Newark, New Jersey, (despite its New York address, another idea borrowed from Samuel Colt), and began producing revolvers remarkably similar to Colt's Model 1851 Navy and 1849 Pocket Model in 1858. Manhattans did have one very distinctive feature, cylinders on 5-shot, .31 caliber percussion models used 10 cylinder stops, 6-shot .31 caliber models had 12 cylinder stop slots. The .36 caliber Navy Models had 12 stop cylinders. The majority of Manhattan revolvers had very stylish roll-engraved cylinders and many with hand engraving at a price far less than a Colt. The company remained very successful throughout the 1860s though there were no significant military orders other than from individual regiments, officers or soldiers. The majority of Manhattan revolvers were sold to the civilian market. The example shown is a .36 caliber Navy Model. (Mike Clark Collection/Collectors Firearms)

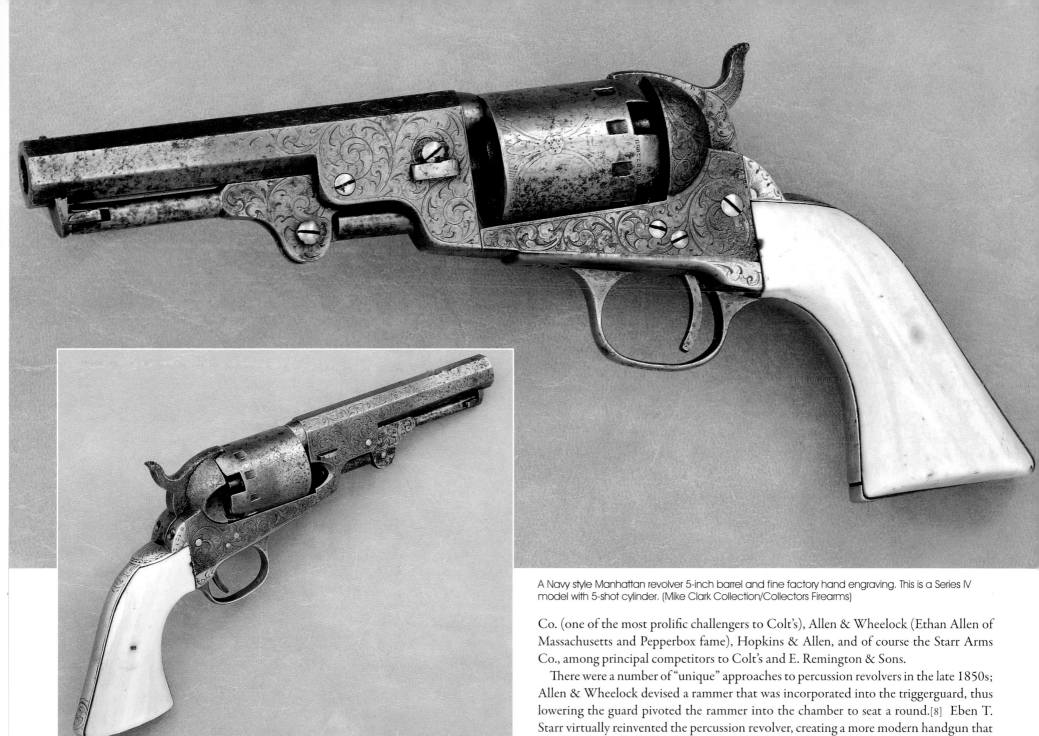

A Navy style Manhattan revolver 5-inch barrel and fine factory hand engraving. This is a Series IV model with 5-shot cylinder. (Mike Clark Collection/Collectors Firearms)

Co. (one of the most prolific challengers to Colt's), Allen & Wheelock (Ethan Allen of Massachusetts and Pepperbox fame), Hopkins & Allen, and of course the Starr Arms Co., among principal competitors to Colt's and E. Remington & Sons.

There were a number of "unique" approaches to percussion revolvers in the late 1850s; Allen & Wheelock devised a rammer that was incorporated into the triggerguard, thus lowering the guard pivoted the rammer into the chamber to seat a round.[8] Eben T. Starr virtually reinvented the percussion revolver, creating a more modern handgun that many years later would influence the design of S&W's first .44 caliber cartridge revolvers.

Chapter Two

Handguns of the Union:
Arming a Nation at War with Itself

A pair of Colt revolvers had the firepower at close range of eight single shot muskets

War is an ugly thing. In the harsh light of reality it has neither the glamour nor romance it has gained through literature and films. Glorious visions fade in combat; training either sustains one or fails when the moment of truth arrives. Certainly, most certainly, there was a national pride, a desire to enlist and take up arms in defense of the nation; after all, it was our heritage, we were born as a country from such valor.

In April 1861, the newly elected President and his advisors believed the War Between the States would only last a few months; such thoughts had no doubt filled the minds of American patriots in 1776, but no victory of such consequence comes quickly, the Revolutionary War lasted seven years. However, unlike 1776, this war was not being fought to free a nation from a foreign antagonist; this was a nation at war with itself. By the mid 1860s, Abraham Lincoln and Jefferson Davis, who had been inaugurated as President of the Confederate States of America on February 18, 1861 (two weeks before Lincoln's inauguration!), had learned the cost of such unbridled passions, having paid with the blood of Americans at Bull Run, Shiloh, Antietam, and Gettysburg. Lincoln's stirring Gettysburg Address in November 1863 was a eulogy for fallen men that might well have been for the nation. Every facet of the war was greater than had been imagined, as was the need for guns to facilitate what was now a long and hardened battle between North and South to either preserve the Union, or break its back.

The Colt 1861 Navy presentation to General James B. McPherson (pictured to the left in a copy of *Harpers Weekly*), was inscribed on the backstraps: FROM HIS FRIENDS/O.N. CUTLER; W.C. WAGLEY. The sequentially serial numbered guns, 11756/I and 11757/I were done en suite with a pair of matching 1862 Police models. McPherson was an 1853 West Point graduate, the same class as Sheridan, Schofield, and Hood, all of whom were destined for glory in the War Between the States. McPherson, however, graduated head of the class. Promoted to Lt. Col. in 1861, by the autumn of 1862 he was in command of an infantry brigade at the battle of Corinth. His outstanding service led to a field promotion to Major General of volunteers and command of an entire division. After his success in the battle of Vicksburg in 1863, McPherson was promoted to the regular rank of Brigadier General on the recommendation of General Grant. Tragically, engaged in battle against one of his old West Point classmates, John Bell Hood, McPherson was mortally wounded on July 22, 1864. Ulysses S. Grant wept at the news, saying "The country has lost one of its best soldiers, and I have lost my best friend." (Dr. Joseph A Murphy collection)

The Colt's Patent Fire-Arms Co.

The guns of Samuel Colt and the Colt's Patent Fire-Arms Manufacturing Company were the principal sidearms of the Union after 1861, but the Hartford works could only produce so many guns, and Colt's was still catering to its civilian market as well, though many of its clientele were individual soldiers or their families purchasing Colt's magnificent .36 caliber pocket models, to which Sam Colt had added the Police Model in 1862 and the soon to be introduced Pocket Model of Navy Caliber, often erroneously called the Pocket Navy. This was to be the last revolver designed under the guiding eye of the company's founder. On January 10, 1862, at the age of 47, Samuel Colt died after suffering a brief illness, never to know the outcome of the war that had divided a nation he'd worked so diligently to arm.

At the beginning of the Civil War, Sam Colt had not been ambivalent about the issues. He regarded slavery not as much a moral issue but one of poor economics. After the October 16, 1859, attack on the Harpers Ferry arsenal, Colt had denounced John Brown as a traitor, and he later had opposed the election of Abraham Lincoln for fear it would divide the Union. In this Colt had been correct.

Prone to indulgences, his work was all consuming and his health was not good for a man of his age. Bothered by frequent attacks of inflammatory rheumatism and distressed by the death of an infant daughter, he began driving himself as if he knew his days were numbered. Smoking Cuban cigars, Colt ruled his domain from a roll-top desk at the Hartford Armory. Though one of the wealthiest men in the country, he found himself short on heirs; two of his brothers, John and William had died, and the third, James, had proven to be a hot-tempered ne'er-do-well who could neither be trusted with money nor responsibility. At the time of his death Colt's estate was reportedly worth $15 million, a vast sum for the 1860s. He was survived by his wife Elizabeth and their young son Caldwell. Elizabeth, whom he had married in June of 1856, was the daughter of the Reverend William Jarvis, and it would be Elizabeth's brother Richard in whom Colt would find the assurance of talent and dedication necessary to carry on the family business. Shortly before he died, he handed the company reins to his brother-in-law, writing to Richard in 1862: "You and your family must do for me now as I have no one else to call upon. You are the pendulum that must keep the works in motion." Richard Jarvis saw the company through the end of the Civil War and into the postwar era. Control of Colt's remained in the hands of Elizabeth and her family until 1901, when the company was sold to a group of investors.

A classic Civil War survivor, this handsomely cased Colt Model 1860 Army, serial number 152919, was produced toward the end of 1864 [1]. The cased gun includes all of the standard accessories that were used in this period. Although the recoil shield and buttstrap are cut for attaching a shoulder stock, this was a civilian model as it does not have the fourth screw in the frame necessary for securing the shoulder stock yoke. Cased sets in this condition are always a wonderful find for Colt and Civil War aficionados. (From the personal collection of John Bianchi. Photography by Dennis Adler. [1] Colt's Dates of Manufacture by R.L. Wilson)

Deluxe engraved and cased pair of 1862 Police models, consecutively serial numbered, 15859/I and 15860/I, were engraved by the Gustave Young shop and presented to Major General James B. McPherson. Pictured with the cased guns is an August issue of *Harper's Weekly* telling of the death of General McPherson. Also shown is a portrait of McPherson alongside his Medal of Honor for the Vicksburg Campaign, and Col. Elmer E. Ellsworth's own Zouave Medal from the 17th Corps at far right. Col. Ellsworth was one of Lincoln's closest friends, having helped him get elected in 1860. The Col. was also one of the first casualties of the War, murdered in Alexandria, Virginia, on May 24th, 1861 after removing a Confederate Flag flying above the Marshall House Inn, which was in plain view of the White House. Ellsworth volunteered to go over and retrieve the flag for Lincoln. As he was descending the staircase after cutting down the flag, the Inn's owner killed him with a shotgun blast to the chest. (Dr. Joseph A. Murphy collection)

Often called a Pocket Navy, the Pocket Model of Navy Caliber was introduced in 1865, a year after the fire that razed part of the Colt factory in 1864. A throwback to the extremely popular 1849 Pocket Model, the new model used the same frame as the 1849, and the same roll engraved cylinder scene. Chambered in .36 caliber, the 5-shot revolver became nearly as popular as the 1849, remaining in production through 1873. This particular example was a presentation gun from Colt's to L. T. Pearson, Esq. Serial number 16619/E it exhibits the late vine scroll style of engraving. The grips are hand checkered walnut in a volute (decorative spiral) motif. This same type of grip design was used on an 1860 Army and was also likely done by Charles J. Helfricht. (Dr. Joseph A. Murphy collection)

A little more than a year before his death, Samuel Colt had revisited one of his greatest successes, the Model 1851 Navy which had sustained the company for years and was still in production even though the 1860 Army was a far more powerful sidearm. The 1860 was, for lack of a better word, elegant in its design with a gracefully contoured round barrel and newly engineered loading lever that made the Army model appear streamlined in comparison to the angular, octagonal barreled 1851 Navy. In 1861 Colt introduced

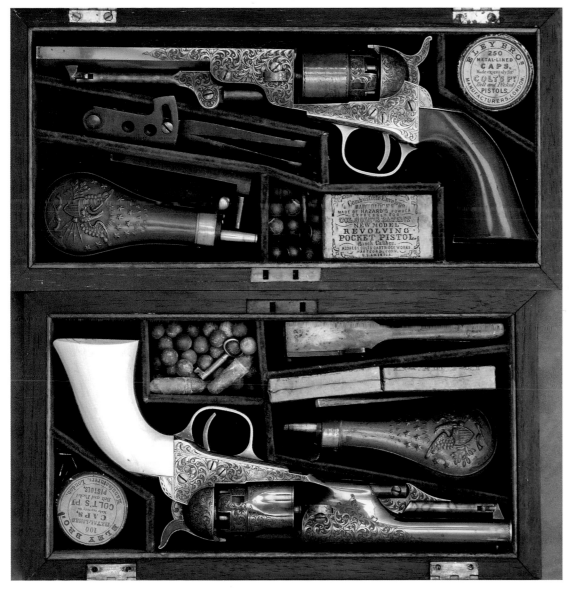

Sharing the same frames, the 1862 Police Model (bottom) and 1865 Pocket Model of Navy Caliber were equally popular throughout the late Civil War era and well into the 1870s. Both examples pictured were engraved by Gustave Young in a graceful exhibition-grade vine scroll style on the barrels, frames, and loading levers. Both guns have a hand engraved London barrel address, and hand checkered trigger spurs. Neither gun was ever shipped to England and remained at Colt's, with the 1862 being purchased by James Bryant, a longtime Colt employee. The pair, serial numbers 39220/IE (I for ivory, E for engraved) and 17986/IE (which nevertheless has deluxe walnut grips) are together again as part of the Dr. Joseph A. Murphy collection. Note the two Colt's paper cartridges amongst the round balls in the Police presentation case.

Samuel Colt was a gifted engineer who, with the assistance of Elisha King Root, developed efficient means to mass produce high-quality revolvers with interchangeable parts. The Hartford works was one of the first uses of assembly line manufacturing. Before his untimely death at age 47, Colt designed three of the greatest revolvers of the Civil War era, the 1861 Navy, 1862 Police Model, and 1865 Pocket Model of Navy Caliber. (photo courtesy R.L. Wilson)

The Colt's Patent Fire-Arms Co. presented this pair of Gustave Young engraved 1861 Navy revolver to one of the Civil War's most renowned Union officers, General Robert Anderson, the commander of Ft. Sumter. The guns are pictured with a display of McPherson memorabilia including family portraits, his military belt, medals, and engraved ivory handled saber. Representing some of the finest work done for Colt's by the company's master engraver, the presentation 1861 Navy Models of General Anderson are regarded as two of the most beautiful engraved Colts in the world. The fine engraved Colt 1861 Navy models presented to General Anderson are inscribed on the backstrap: TO GEN. ROBERT ANDERSON U.S.A. WITH COMPLEMENTS OF COLT'S PT. F.A. MFG. CO. (Dr. Joseph A. Murphy Collection)

of Ft. Sumter, which was accomplished without a single shot fired on either side as Union forces withdrew. This marked the "official" beginning of The War Between the States.

A month later President Lincoln promoted Major Anderson to the rank of Brigadier General. Anderson received a hero's welcome in New York City, where he proudly carried Fort Sumter's 33-star American flag to a Union Square patriotic rally regarded today by historians to have been the largest public gathering in North America up to that time. Gen. Anderson then went on a highly successful recruiting tour of the Northern States before taking a leave of absence due to ill health. He retired from the Army on October 27, 1863.

His gallantry at Ft. Sumter was never forgotten by President Lincoln. Just days after Robert E. Lee's surrender at Appomattox, on April 9, 1865, Anderson was invited to return to Charleston in the uniform of a Brevet Major General, and four years to the day after lowering the Fort's flag in surrender, he raised it in triumph over the recaptured, but badly battered fortress.

The pair of Gustave Young engraved 1861 Navy models presented to General Anderson bore the standard factory markings which included the barrel address:

– ADDRESS COL. SAM^L COLT NEW-YORK U.S. AMERICA. – ff and the COLTS/PATENT stamping on the left side of the frame. The cylinders used the roll engraved naval engagement scene from the 1851 Navy and 1860 Army.

The .36 caliber revolvers were fitted with 7-1/2 inch barrels and weighed 2 pounds, 10 ounces empty. The military demand for this model was modest and between April 1861 and the end of the Civil War only 2,363 were purchased. The civilian market, on the other hand, gladly embraced the new model with sales reaching over 25,000 by 1866. When Colt's finally discontinued the 1861 Navy in 1873, more than 38,000 had been sold.

The 1860 Army, upon which the 1861 Navy had been based, was the primary .44 caliber percussion sidearm carried by Union forces throughout the war. The initial 1860 models had fluted cylinders but production began to decline after the rebated cylinder was introduced. A fair portion of early fluted models issued to the Cavalry came with their frames cut for a shoulder stock, and were generally cased as a pair with a single stock. It is estimated that around 4,000 fluted cylinder Army revolvers were manufactured. Of those, the first 1,000 had shorter 7-1/2 inch barrels like the

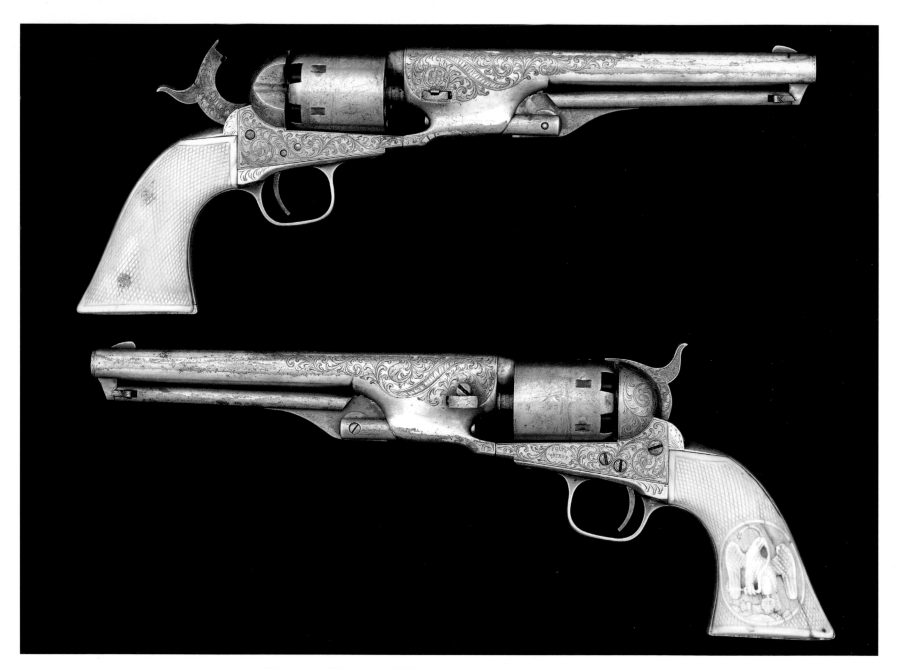

This is a beautifully engraved 1861 Navy done by Gustave Young in a running vine scroll pattern. Note the scrollwork over the top of the barrel (gun is shown from both sides) which is similar to the scrollwork banner used for the U.S. Grant 1860 Army presentation gun. This example was silver plated with a gold washed rammer and cylinder, and fitted with carved and checkered eagle and snake ivory grips. The "E" suffix in the serial, No. 18185E, indicates that it was an original factory engraved gun. (Mike Clark Collection/Collectors Firearms)

AT HUNTSVILLE, ALABAMA—DANCING THE "VIRGINIA REEL."—[SEE PAGE 235.]

Another example of superior engraving of the period, this 1860 Army, serial number 65137/2 bears the late vine scroll design but in a very tight and heavily embellished pattern. This example also has the barrel address hand engraved. In addition, this gun has rarely seen hand carved and checkered select walnut grips, with piano finish varnish, possibly the work of Charles Helfricht, father of Colt engraver Cuno A. Helfricht. The illustration of the Colt's factory shows the original three-story complex facing the Connecticut River. It was in this building that the 1860 Army models were manufactured. The entire structure was lost in the great factory fire of February 4, 1864.

109

The detachable shoulder stock made the 1860 Army a suitable revolving carbine for cavalry use. Guns were issued in pairs with a single shoulder stock. The cased example shown is a deluxe presentation model given by Colt's to Colonel Charles Augustus May. The rare cased set was auctioned off by Greg Martin Auctions in June 2002 with an estimated value between $150,000 and $200,000.

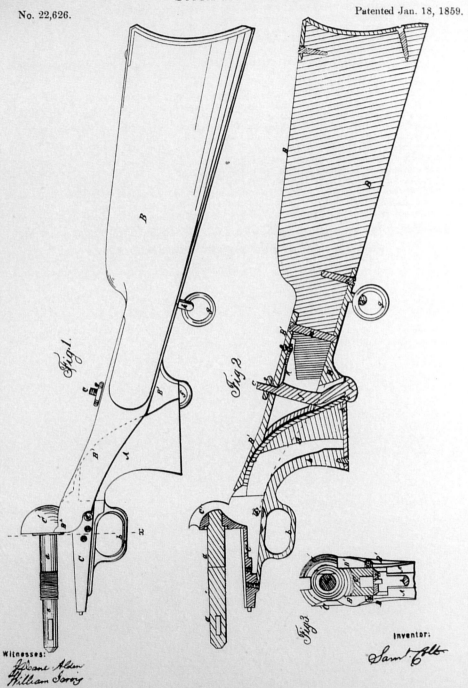

S. COLT.
Stock for Fire-arm.

No. 22,626.

Patented Jan. 18, 1859.

Fig. 1

Fig. 2

Fig. 3

Witnesses:

Inventor:
Sam¹ Colt

N. PETERS, PHOTO-LITHOGRAPHER, WASHINGTON. D. C.

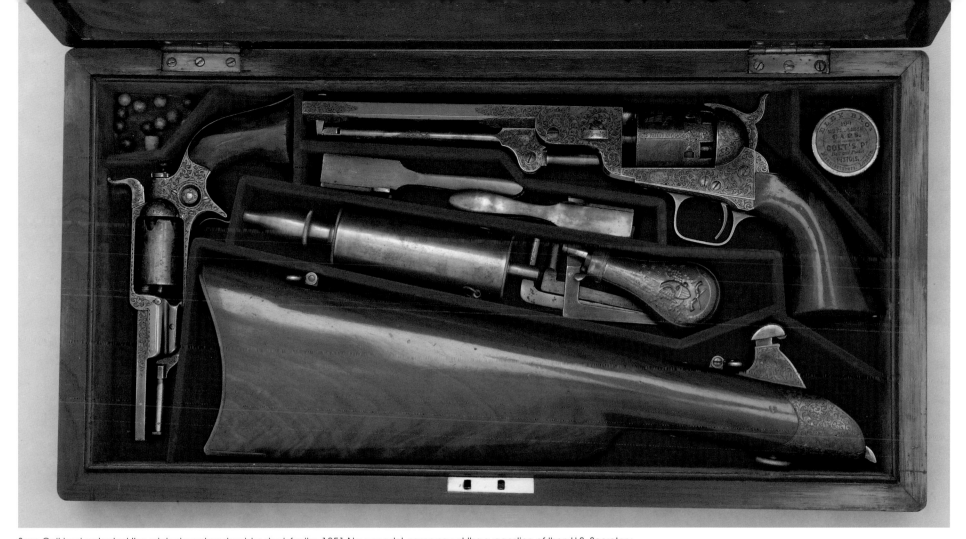

Sam Colt had patented the original revolver shoulder stock for the 1851 Navy model, some say at the suggestion of then U.S. Secretary of War Jefferson Davis, who may even have had a hand in the design. Pictured is an exceptional presentation pairing of 1851 Navy with shoulder stock and a No. 2 style 1855 Root Sidehammer revolver both profusely engraved by Gustave Young with his most intricate scrollwork. This striking rosewood cased set was a gift from Col. Colt to H.A.G. Pomeroy. Note the exceptional select walnut used for the shoulder stock in this presentation set. Pomeroy incidentally was neither a government official nor head of state. He was the architect who designed the new Hartford armory. He was also Sam Colt's nephew. (Dr. Joseph A. Murphy collection)

This is the patent drawing for a detachable shoulder stock to fit the 1860 Army model revolver. Not surprisingly, with the start of the Civil War, the United States government became the single largest purchaser of the 1860 Army. Military models often had notched recoil shields and a fourth screw in the frame to mount a detachable shoulder stock, and this applied to both rebated and fluted cylinder variations. Colt patented this design for the 1860 Army, January 18, 1859.

The Police Model was stamped with two different barrel addresses, as well as the London address on guns sold in Great Britain. The principal style seen is:

– ADDRESS COL. SAM^L COLT NEW-YORK U.S. AMERICA –

Alternately the address was also stamped in two lines:

ADDRESS SAM^L COLT
HARTFORD CT.

The COLTS/PATENT stamping was also used on the left side of the frame. The half fluted half rebated cylinders were stamped PAT. SEPT. 10th 1850 on one of the flutes. The left shoulder of the triggerguard was marked 36 CAL.

Not as concealable as Colt's earlier Pocket Models, there was one very limited exception, which has become the most intriguing pocket pistol of the percussion era, the snub nose Police revolver, what one might regard as the first Colt Detective Special. Based on the Police frame it is a most curious and controversial gun. Most were

A rarely seen combination: a gun with its original holster and belt. This example, originally owned by Corporal John Gilbert Ray, Jr., Company E, 43rd Regiment of Infantry, 1st Brigade, 1st Division of the Volunteer Militia of Massachusetts, remains intact with a Bowie Knife and scabbard and cartridge pouch. Ray, who later became a Union Pacific Railroad construction engineer, is pictured in the tintype photo c. 1867, wearing the belt, holster and his 1860 Army, serial number 155981. Traveling through the American West it was claimed that he smoked the pipe of peace with the chief of the Sioux tribe, and was present when they drove the golden spike that connected the east and the west by rail on May 10, 1869. Born in 1843, Ray lived long enough to see the turn of the century and even own a Stanley Steamer before he died on October 28, 1907. (Photo courtesy Greg Martin Auctions)

Pictured are variations of the 1860 Army. At top, an ivory griped 3-screw civilian frame not cut for shoulder stock; center left, a 4-screw with silvered triggerguard and backstrap and cut for stock; center right, a New York engraved model with carved Mexican eagle and snake ivory grips, inscribed inside of grip to General Mariano Escobedo 1864; bottom right, 3-screw civilian model not cut for shoulder stock; bottom left, a 4-screw cut for stock in an unusual 149,000 serial range, which is unusually high and the letter "s" appears by each number indicating made for shoulder stock. Military holster at top, carved flap holster at bottom. (Mike Clark Collection/Collectors Firearms)

AGENTS FOR COLT'S FIRE ARMS.
Bought of H. D. NORTON & BRO.,
Hardware, Iron, Nails, Castings, Stoves, Tin Plate, Lead and
AGRICULTURAL IMPLEMENTS AND GARDEN SEEDS,
WINDOW GLASS AND WOODEN WARE, LEATHER AND SAD
United States
50
United States
25
UNITED STATES
TWENTY FIVE
25
CARTRIDGES,
REVOLVING BELT PISTOL

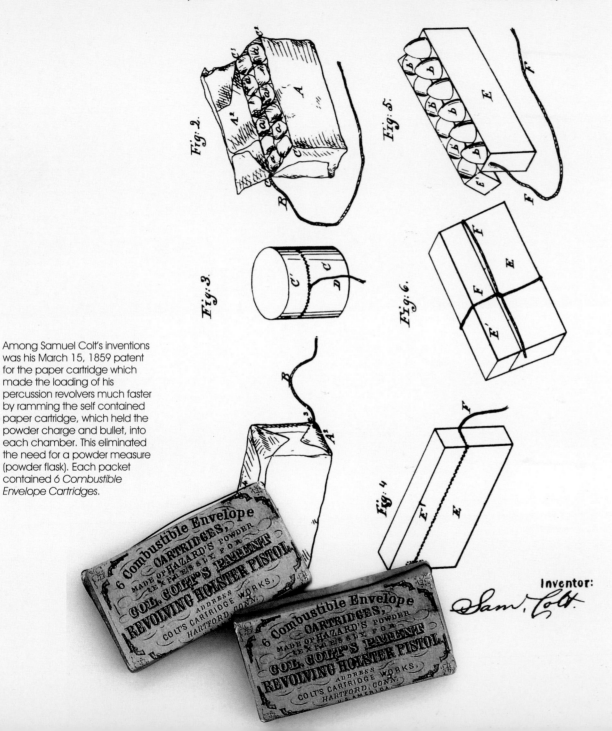

S. COLT.
Cartridge Box.

No. 23,230.

Patented March 15, 1859.

Fig. 2.

Fig. 3.

Fig. 5.

Fig. 6.

Fig. 4.

Inventor:

Sam. Colt.

Among Samuel Colt's inventions was his March 15, 1859 patent for the paper cartridge which made the loading of his percussion revolvers much faster by ramming the self contained paper cartridge, which held the powder charge and bullet, into each chamber. This eliminated the need for a powder measure (powder flask). Each packet contained 6 *Combustible Envelope Cartridges*.

fitted with a with 2-inch barrel which Colt's produced on special order only, and as noted by R.L Wilson in *The Book Of Colt Firearms*, the production total was estimated at only 25 to 50 guns. There is very little factual data on these unique Colt pocket pistols other than that they had plugged barrel lugs, crowned muzzles (indicating that they were not just longer barrels cut down) and many had dovetailed front sights (as shown). The serial number of one such example, #10578 places its date of manufacture late in 1862, thus they were in production during the Civil War. Surviving examples have also been seen with 2-1/2 inch barrels and a simple brass pin front sight.

There is one other rarely seen variation of the Police Model bearing a 3-1/2 inch barrel without loading lever. The guns, known as the "Trapper" model, had a rammer channel beneath the barrel lug and came cased with a brass ramrod. Examples are known to have been within the 4165 to 4265 serial number range, with perhaps fewer than 50 built.

The last percussion revolvers manufactured in Hartford were the Pocket Models of Navy Caliber, produced c.1865 to 1873. The frames from the last Pocket Models were also used to build the first Colt Pocket Pistol cartridge conversion in the 1870s. Essentially a bigger version of the 1849 Pocket Model, or if you choose, a smaller version of the 1851 Navy, this was the last vestige of Colt's octagonal barreled revolvers. Also chambered in .36 caliber percussion, the 5-shot Navy was offered with barrel lengths of 4-1/2, 5-1/2, and 6-1/2 inches. A bit heavier than the Police model, which weighed 26 ounces with the 6-1/2 inch barrel; the Navy tipped the scales at

The 1860 Army, in both the early fluted cylinder design (top) and improved rebated cylinder design were primarily carried by the Union Army. The Ordnance Department purchased nearly the entire inventory of Colt 1860 Army and 1851 Navy models during the Civil War. Sam Colt did, however, ship guns to the South in 1860 and 1861. His last shipment of 500 revolvers left for Richmond three days after the attack on Fort Sumter, packed in boxes marked "hardware." The pair of 2nd Generation Colts shown (serial Nos. 209154 and 205932) is one half of a consecutively numbered set, fluted and rebated, produced c.1980, and 1978, respectively.

Union private Frank A. Remington (left) and two other Union soldiers are shown in this ambrotype (an early method of photography made by placing a glass negative against a dark background), holding Colt 1860 Army revolvers. (Library of Congress)

28 ounces in the same barrel length. Since the frames were identical, the additional two ounces were accounted for by the old style octagonal barrel and barrel lug. The Navy cylinders were roll engraved with the old W. L. Ormsby stagecoach holdup scene that had been used on the 1849 Pocket Model.

Historians speculate that the Colt factory fire in 1864, claimed the tooling for the 1862 Police model, and the reason for the Pocket Model of Navy Caliber in 1865, is that tooling for the 1849 Model survived the fire, providing Colt's with a means to get pocket models quickly into production. As it turned out, people liked the Navy Model. Demand was such that the .36 caliber pocket pistol remained in production until the early 1870s.

By April of 1862 Custer had risen to the rank of Captain. He is pictured here at Falmouth, Virginia with General Alfred Pleasonton. Note that Custer (left) is wearing a holstered 1860 Army. (Library of Congress)

Pictured are Lieutenant George A. Custer (seated), and Union officers Nicolas Bowen, and William G. Jones. Note that Custer is cradling an 1860 Army in his lap. The photograph was taken between May and August 1862 during the Peninsular Campaign. (Library of Congress)

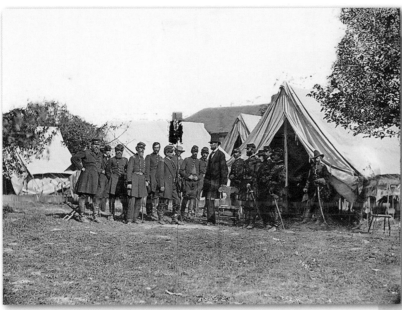

This photograph was taken after the Battle of Antietam, September–October 1862. Pictured are (L to R) Col. Delos B. Sackett, I.G.; Capt. George Monteith; Lt. Col. Nelson B. Sweitzer; Gen. George W. Morell; Col. Alexander S. Webb, Chief of Staff, 5th Corps; Gen. George B. McClellan; an Army scout named Adams; Dr. Jonathan Letterman, Army Medical Director; a Union officer; President Abraham Lincoln; Gen. Henry J. Hunt; Gen. Fitz-John Porter; an unknown individual behind Gen. Porter; Col. Frederick T. Locke, A.A.G.; Gen. Andrew A. Humphreys; and at far right against the tent, then Capt. George Armstrong Custer. (Library of Congress)

George Armstrong Custer was one of the most charismatic and controversial characters of the Civil War. He advanced through the ranks ahead of many of his classmates and even superiors, from Lieutenant, after graduating from West Point in 1861, to Captain by 1862, and after first being passed over for the rank of Colonel early in 1863, at age 23, he was given a field promotion to Brigadier General in June. By the end of the war he had become the youngest Major General in the nation. Many believe his bravery at Gettysburg, leading a cavalry charge against Confederate General J.E.B. Stuart's position, and thereby stalling Stuart's crucial offensive during Pickett's Charge, contributed to the Confederate's defeat. (George A. Custer Museum of the Monroe County, Michigan, Historical Museum)

E. Remington & Sons

In need of as many firearms as could be acquired, and more importantly, firearms that could pass Ordnance Department and military inspections, manufacturers in the North were lining up to provide muskets, rifles, and revolvers. The second most significant source of the latter was E. Remington & Sons, America's oldest armsmaker. The company had already established itself as a staunch competitor to Colt's less than a year after Samuel Colt's patent extension expired. The Model 1858, designed by Fordyce Beals, was a more modern handgun, built with greater efficiency, and fewer parts, thus Remington could build them for less than a comparable Colt's model revolver.

Early in 1861 the U.S. Ordnance Department purchased 3,950 Remington-Beals Navy revolvers, and between August 1861 and March 1862, another 7,250 Navy models plus 850 Remington-Beals Army revolvers on the open market, all through retailers like Schuyler, Hartley and Graham in New York and Tyler Davidson & Co. In June 1862 the U.S. military contracted directly with E. Remington & Sons to supply another 5,000 Navy models and 15,000 Army revolvers (.36 caliber and .44 caliber percussion, respectively).

As the war escalated, an additional order came in July 1863 simply stating, *"All the army .44 revolvers they can deliver within the present year..."* resulting in another 18,902 revolvers which the Army purchased for $11.82 each. Shortly before Thanksgiving in November 1863,

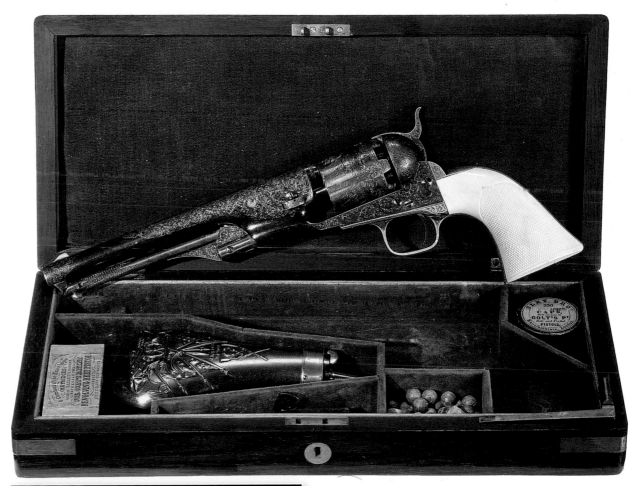

It is estimated that Colt's produced around 200,000 examples of the 1860 Army, approximately 4,000 with fluted cylinders, between 1860 and 1873. Army frames, barrels, and cylinders were also used c.1873 to the early 1880s for Richards Type I, Type II, and Richards-Mason .44 caliber cartridge conversions. The example pictured with ivory grips would be considered a civilian model as the recoil shield is not notched for a shoulder stock. That, however, would not have precluded it from being used by the military during the Civil War. (Mike Clark Collection/Collectors Firearms)

The Battle of Gettysburg and Abraham Lincoln's Gettysburg Address were two turning points in The War Between the States. So touched by the unprecedented loss of life at Gettysburg, Colt's master engraver, Gustave Young, created what could be regarded as the first commemorative revolver in the company's history. Known as "Tears of Gettysburg", Young expressed his grief and patriotism through his artistic mastery. He engraved this 1861 Navy in his finest traditional scrollwork pattern, incorporating animal heads (dogs, wolves, and American eagles) within the scrolls and on the hammer flats, much as he had done on other master engraved Colts, only on this one revolver, every figure is crying.

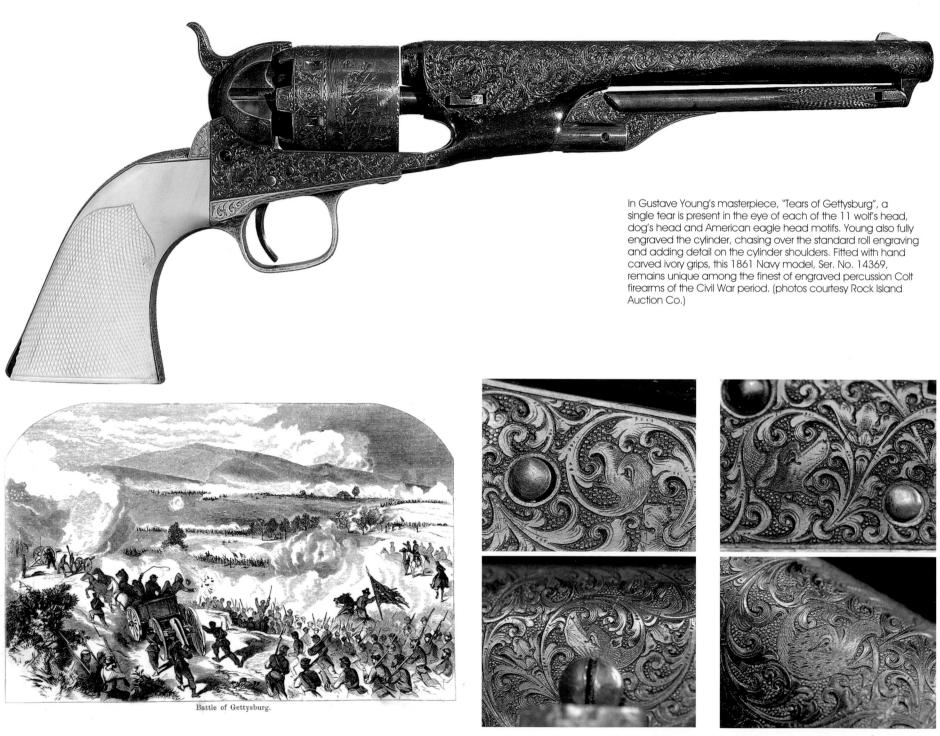

In Gustave Young's masterpiece, "Tears of Gettysburg", a single tear is present in the eye of each of the 11 wolf's head, dog's head and American eagle head motifs. Young also fully engraved the cylinder, chasing over the standard roll engraving and adding detail on the cylinder shoulders. Fitted with hand carved ivory grips, this 1861 Navy model, Ser. No. 14369, remains unique among the finest of engraved percussion Colt firearms of the Civil War period. (photos courtesy Rock Island Auction Co.)

Battle of Gettysburg.

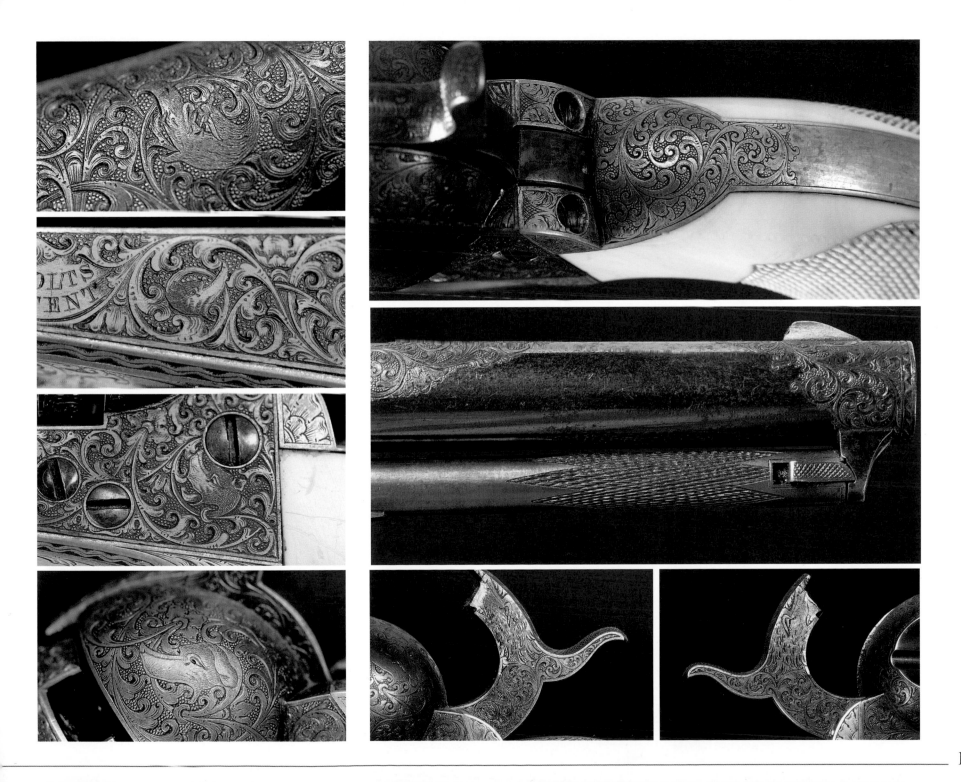

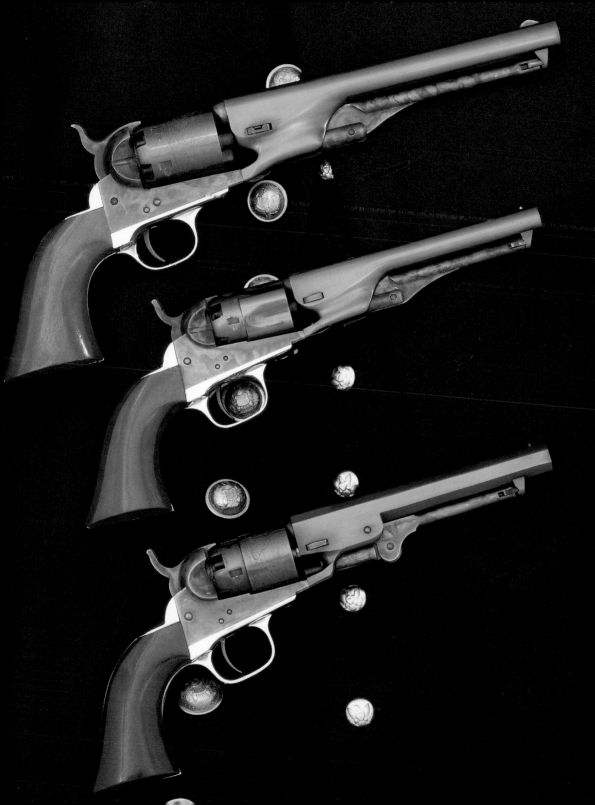

Remington was asked to begin manufacturing another 64,900 Army Models, of which the company delivered 57,003 by December 31, 1864, with the remainder carrying over into 1865. With the outcome of the war still in doubt, two months prior to fulfilling the 1863 order, the Ordnance Department contracted for another 20,000 Army revolvers to be received between January and March of 1865. Needless to say the Ilion, New York manufacturing facilities were kept bustling until the war ended. The net result was that Remington was second only to Colt's in arming the U.S. military. Final production totals showed 12,251 Navy and 115,557 Army revolvers of all model variations produced for the U.S. between 1861 and 1865. Including orders for "Harpers Ferry" model rifles with bayonets, Springfield rifled muskets, and Remington breech loading carbines, E. Remington & Sons earned over $2.8 million during the war.[2] [A complete breakdown of revolver models and the U.S. regiments to which they were issued can be found in *Civil War Pistols of the Union* by John D. McAulay].

Even with a war, Remington still had a thriving civilian market. Between 1860 and 1862 several thousand .44 caliber percussion Beals Army revolvers and 15,000 Navy (.36 caliber) models had been produced. Of those totals more than a 1,000 Army models were sold to the State of South Carolina. In addition, civilian sales of Remington Army and Navy models to retailers in the South certainly put many more into the hands of Confederate soldiers. With the eminent threat of a civil war following Abraham Lincoln's election in November 1860, Eliphalet Remington, Sr. decided to refuse any further orders from Southern states.[3]

Between 1858 and 1863 numerous improvements to the original Beals design were made, which finally resulted in the last and best rendition of the Remington Army and Navy revolvers used

Far left: The last models designed by Samuel Colt; from top to bottom, 1860 Army with fluted cylinder, 1860 Army with rebated cylinder, 1861 Navy, 1862 Police Model, and c.1865 Pocket Model of Navy Caliber. Though already designed, the latter was not put into production until three years after Samuel Colt had died. The fine examples pictured are all from Colt's superb 2nd Generation of historic percussion revolvers produced from 1971 through 1984. (Ser. Nos. 209155; 205933; 42446; 52016; and 50611, respectively)

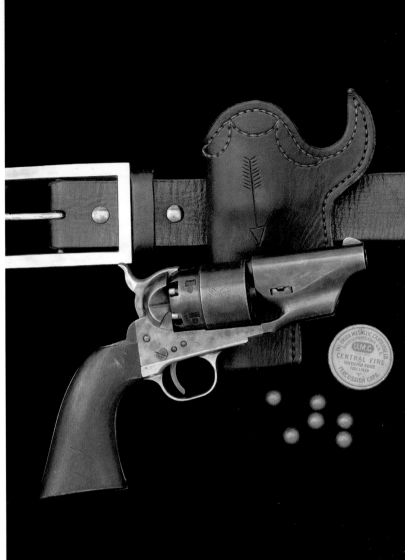

Belly guns, usually made from Colt 1860 Army and 1851 Navy revolvers were not uncommon. Though no such arms were ever issued to soldiers on either side, belly guns began to come into use toward the very end of the Civil War. This particular gun and holster were reproduced from an original 1860 Army belly gun and Slim Jim exhibited in the 1980s at the famous John Bianchi Frontier Museum in Temecula, California. Bianchi provided the reference photos for the gun to be duplicated by R. L. Millington of Armi Sport LLC and the holster by Alan and Donna Soellner of Chisholm's Trail Leather. The originals dated to the period just after the Civil War.

125

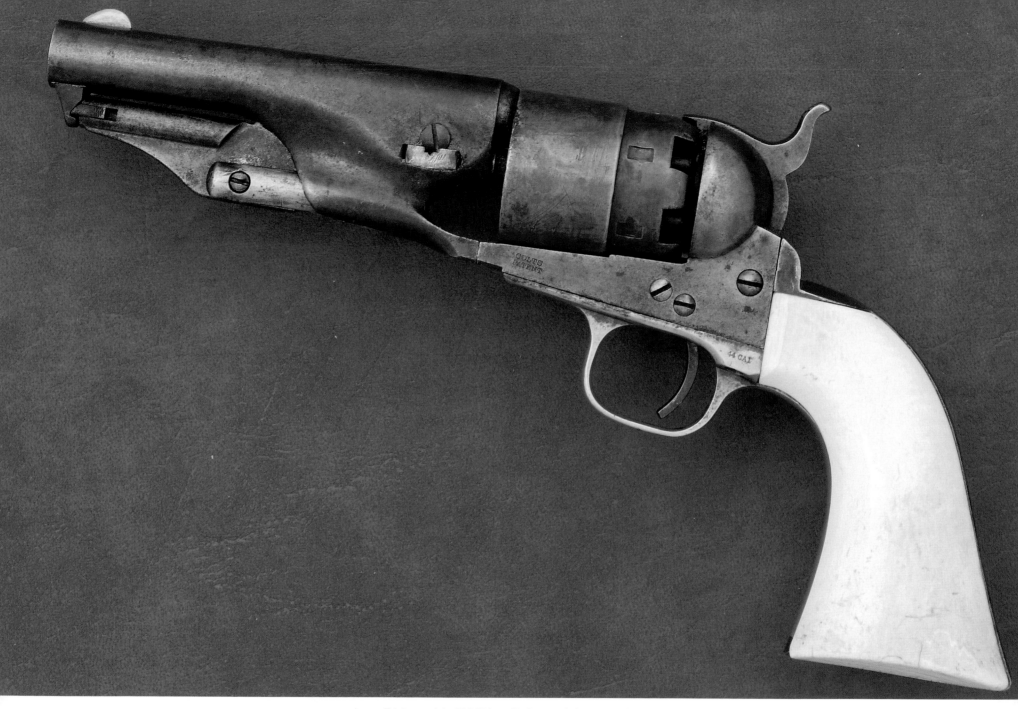

This is an original 1860 Army that was cut down sometime during the late 1860s. This is particularly notable as whoever did the work also shortened the loading lever so it could still be used. Most examples of cut down Army and Navy revolvers had the leaver removed and the loading channel filled. (Dennis LeVett Collection)

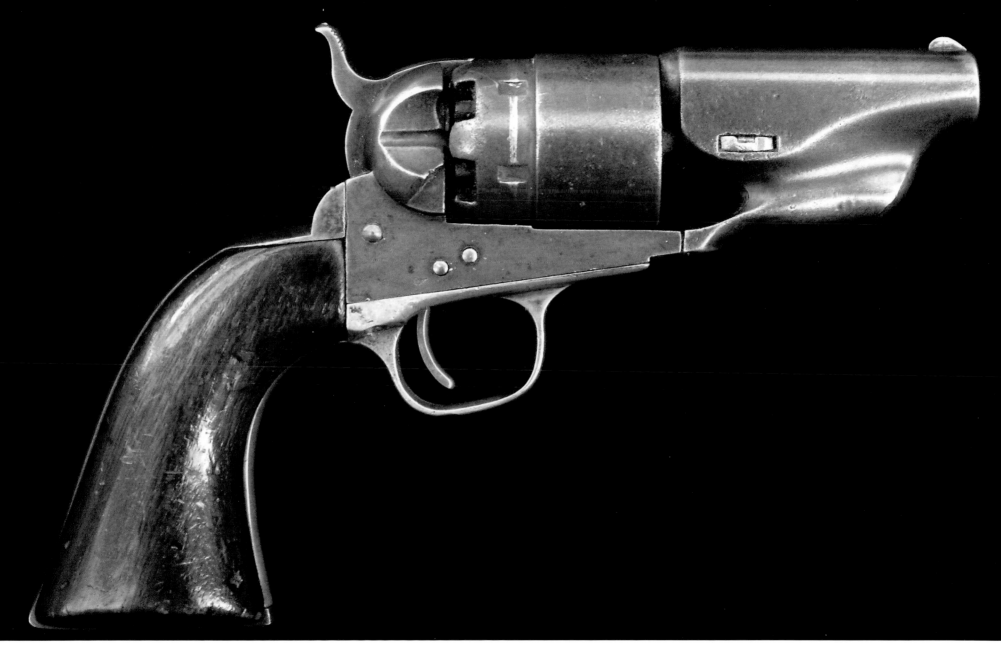

Another documented cut down 1860 Army done in the most commonly seen fashion of the late Civil War period. Guns like these were carried well into the 1870s by savvy lawmen who saw the advantages of a large caliber hideaway gun; unfortunately, so too did outlaws. Riverboat gamblers liked them too, and by the late 1860s the cut down Colts picked up the nickname "Natchez Specials". (Gerald E. Dickerson, Jr. Collection)

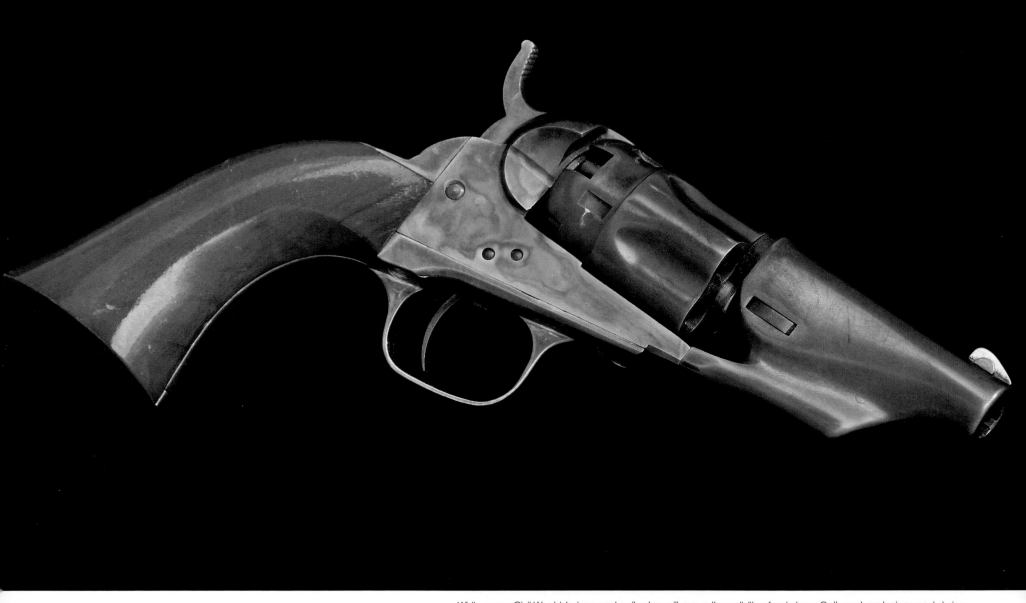

While many Civil War historians and collectors will argue the validity of cut down Colt revolvers being used during the Civil War, there is an indisputable precedent established in the early 1860s by none other than the Colt's Patent Fire-Arms Mfg. Company. It is known that anywhere from 25 to 50 Police Model revolvers were manufactured with cut down 2-inch or 2-1/2 inch barrels with crowned muzzles, dovetailed front blade or bead front sights, and filled plunger channels. They were all manufactured during the Civil War. The guns picked up the rather biblical sobriquet "Avenging Angel" from their known use by Mormon leader Brigham Young's bodyguards, including the infamous "Wild Bill" Hickman, and Orrin Porter Rockwell, who later became a U.S. Deputy Marshal.

throughout the Civil War, the Models of 1863. Several unique features distinguished the Remington from the Colt. Aside from the obvious use of a topstrap (which Sam Colt had previously done on a handful of prototype Colt revolvers and in the production 1855 Root's revolvers and rifles) was Beal's use of the loading lever as a means of securing the cylinder arbor. Dropping the lever fully, permitted the arbor to be extracted from the front, thus releasing the cylinder which was easily rolled out of the frame with the thumb and forefinger. This was vividly depicted in the Clint Eastwood western *Pale Rider* as he quickly changed out cylinders in the middle of a gunfight. In practice it wasn't much different. It was easy enough that a cavalryman could change cylinders on horseback. This was made even simpler with the Model of 1861 with modifications to loading lever design by William H. Elliot (another famous hyphen in Remington model designations), which allowed the base pin (cylinder arbor) to be extracted without lowering the loading lever. These are easily distinguished by the open channel between the bottom barrel flat and the top of the loading lever. The 1861 model had one fundamental drawback; the base pin could inadvertently move forward from vibration and cause the gun to jam. Thus, this was a short-lived model.

Among the most distinctive changes in the Remington revolver design of 1863, the "New Model" Army and Navy, was an iron blade front sight screwed into the barrel, rather than dovetailed. The sight had unique scooped sides, which have since come to be known as a "pinched" sight. Earlier models are distinguished by their dovetailed brass or German silver cone-shaped front sight, which in combat had proven harder to

One of the more interesting casings for the 1862 Police Model was the "book-style" casing. This particular design, there were several others, was titled on the spine, COLT/ON THE CONSTITUTION/HIGHER LAW & RESPONSIBLE CONFLICT... DEDICATED BY/THE AUTHOR/TO...with a blank space following the TO for the recipient's name. This beautifully engraved vine scroll pattern 1862 Police, accented with a rosette above the barrel wedge on both sides, was presented to a member of the Freemasons, and bears a Freemasons symbol, the key and scroll, on the grip strap. (Dr. Joseph A. Murphy collection)

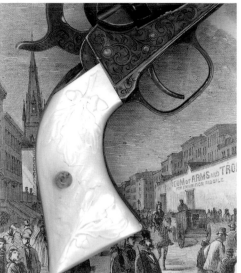

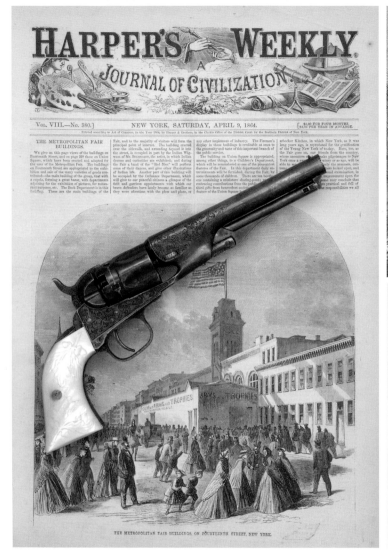

For the 1864 Metropolitan Fair in New York, a massive public trade show set up along Fourteenth Street and Union Square, Colt's created two special display guns, a handsomely engraved 1855 Sidehammer with ivory grips and this striking 1862 Police Model, both engraved by Gustave Young. The rare mother of pearl grips on the 1862 were carved in low relief with a patriotic stand of flags, liberty cap, musket and star devices on the left grip panel, and oak leaf motifs on the right. (Dr. Joseph A. Murphy collection)

One of the finest deluxe engraved and cased pairs of Colt 1862 Police models, consecutively serial numbered, 15859/I and 15860/I, were engraved by the Gustave Young shop and presented to Major General James B. McPherson in 1862. Pictured with the cased guns is an August issue of *Harper's Weekly* telling of the death of General McPherson. On July 22, 1864, Confederate General John Bell Hood launched an attack against Union forces in front of Atlanta. During the battle, a line of Confederate skirmishers shot and killed McPherson while he attempted to reach the headquarters of Commanding General William T. Sherman. Also shown is a portrait of McPherson alongside his Medal of Honor for the Vicksburg Campaign (commanding the 17th Corps) in May 1863, and Col. Elmer E. Ellsworth's own Zouave Medal from the 17th Corps. (Dr. Joseph A. Murphy collection)

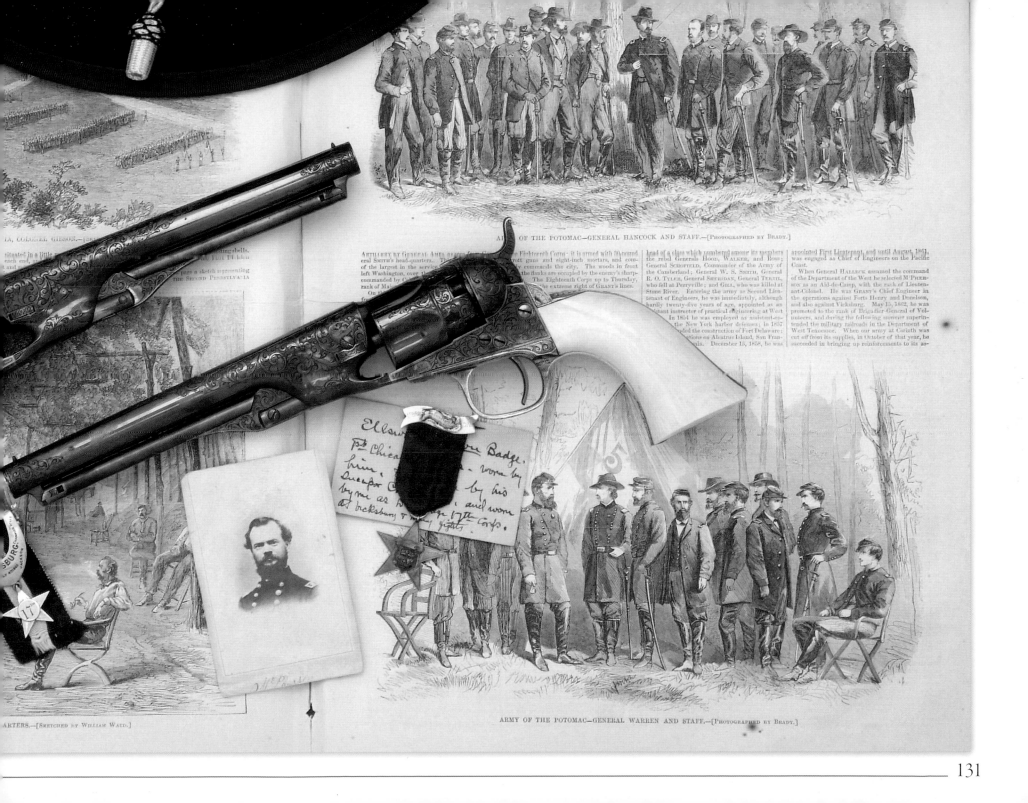

ARMY OF THE POTOMAC—GENERAL HANCOCK AND STAFF.—[PHOTOGRAPHED BY BRADY.]

ARMY OF THE POTOMAC—GENERAL WARREN AND STAFF.—[PHOTOGRAPHED BY BRADY.]

Sam Colt had pretty much ruled the roost among American arms makers from 1847 until his patent extension finally ran out. No sooner had the flood gates been opened than one of America's oldest gunmakers E. Remington & Sons in Ilion, New York introduced its first revolvers in 1857-1858. The Remington design was completely different from Colt's. After all they'd had plenty of time to develop their own version of the revolver. Their first large caliber models, chambered in .36 caliber (Navy) and .44 caliber (Army) were patented in 1858 and in production by the start of the Civil War. Pictured atop a map of the western states and territories between the Mississippi and Pacific Ocean c.1858 is a Remington Old Model Navy .36 caliber revolver c.1861 (top), and 1858 New Model Army .44 caliber c.1863. (Mike Clark/Collectors Firearms collection, map from the Carl Fogerty collection)

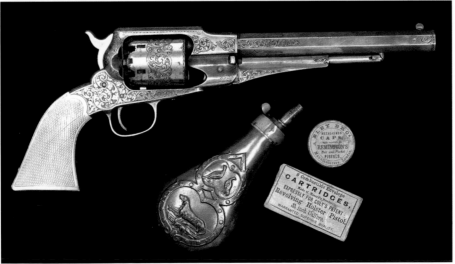

Like Colt's, Remington produced some exceptional engraved examples. Pictured is a factory engraved New Model Army cased with accessories. This model exhibits extra grade engraving to the cylinder and is silver and gold plated with checkered ivory grips. (Mike Clark/Collectors Firearms collection)

acquire when aiming the revolver. This is as interesting observation as in 1860 Colt's had gone from a brass bead front sight to a leaf front sight on the new Army models. This was carried on with the 1861 Navy, while the rest of the Colt's line continued with a brass bead.

Additional changes to the 1863 Remington were made to the loading lever which now rested almost in contact with the underside of the barrel to prevent the base pin from moving forward, unless the lever was dropped. The 1863 design also precluded the base pin from being entirely drawn out of the frame. These revisions were designed and patented in March 1863 by Samuel Remington, one of the "& Sons" who, along with brothers Philo and Eliphalet Jr., had taken the reins of the company following their father's death in August 1861.

Brig. Gen. G. A. Custer.
Comdg 1st Brigade.
1st Cavy. Division

Kindness
Capt. Coppinger

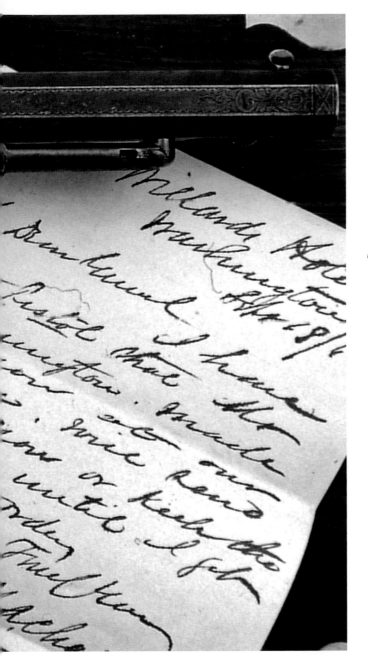

Following the Civil War Lieutenant Colonel George Armstrong Custer was presented with an engraved New Model Army revolver by E. Remington & Sons. (photo courtesy R.L Wilson, *The Peacemakers*)

One of approximately 7,000 Remington Model 1861 Navy Revolvers manufactured in 1862. Note the open channel under the bottom barrel flat and above the top edge of the loading lever. This variation was designed by William H. Elliot (another famous hyphen in Remington model designations), and allowed the base pin (cylinder arbor) to be extracted without lowering the loading lever. (Photo courtesy Rock Island Auction Co.)

Produced during the Civil War, this Remington New Model Army exhibits the final design evolution of the Remington percussion revolver. The guns were so successful that they remained in production until 1875. (Photo courtesy Rock Island Auction Co.)

Just as it would be with the Colt's Patent Fire-Arms Mfg. Co. after January 1862, the success of Remington had also fallen upon a younger generation.

While the Remington revolvers were neither as elegant in design, fit, or finish, though of no lesser quality than a Colt's 1860 Army or 1861 Navy, they had one endearing feature that appealed to the U.S. They were less expensive; the Navy coming down in price from the initial $15 each to $12, the same as most of the Army models, with the Model of 1863 Army reduced to $11.82 cents apiece. At the time Colt's was charging the government $14 each for its 1860 Army model. For 1864 the Ordnance Department contracted with Remington for the majority of its .44 caliber revolvers, resulting in the armsmaker's largest single order during the war, 64,900 guns.

A quality firearm, Remington Army and Navy revolvers were carried by ex-soldiers, Army scouts, cowboys, outlaws and lawmen as the nation began its Western Expansion after the Civil War. The 1863 versions were the last Remington percussion models, and in the decade to come would not only earn a reputation for their durability, but become the first American made cap-and-ball revolvers converted to fire metallic cartridges.

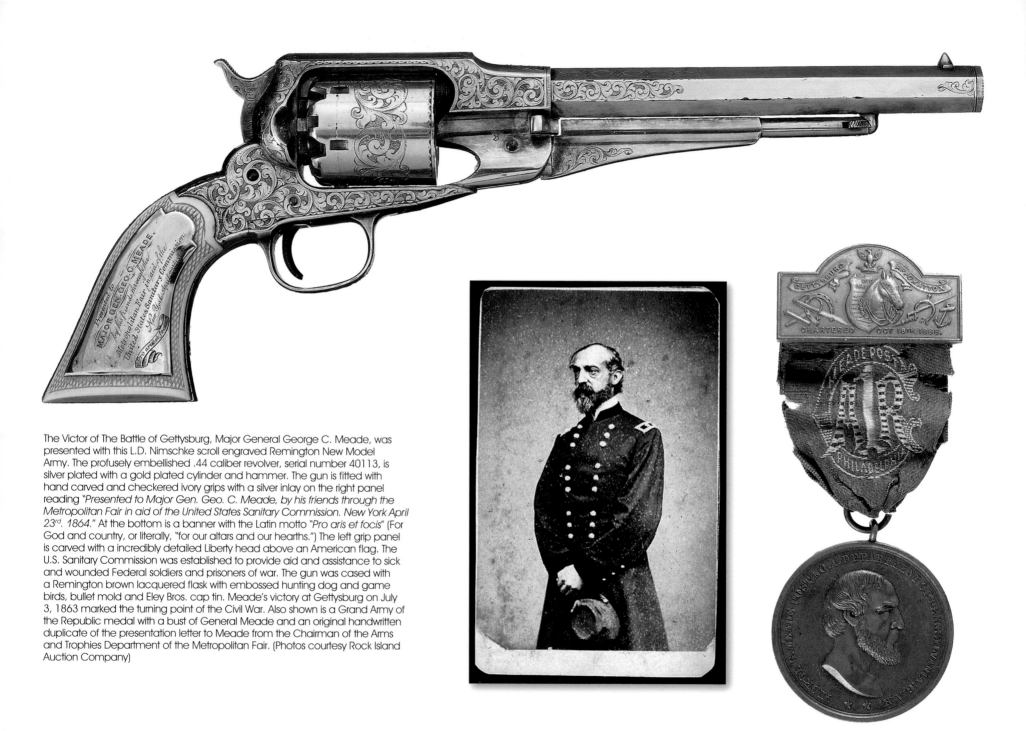

The Victor of The Battle of Gettysburg, Major General George C. Meade, was presented with this L.D. Nimschke scroll engraved Remington New Model Army. The profusely embellished .44 caliber revolver, serial number 40113, is silver plated with a gold plated cylinder and hammer. The gun is fitted with hand carved and checkered ivory grips with a silver inlay on the right panel reading *"Presented to Major Gen. Geo. C. Meade, by his friends through the Metropolitan Fair in aid of the United States Sanitary Commission. New York April 23rd. 1864."* At the bottom is a banner with the Latin motto *"Pro aris et focis"* (For God and country, or literally, "for our altars and our hearths.") The left grip panel is carved with an incredibly detailed Liberty head above an American flag. The U.S. Sanitary Commission was established to provide aid and assistance to sick and wounded Federal soldiers and prisoners of war. The gun was cased with a Remington brown lacquered flask with embossed hunting dog and game birds, bullet mold and Eley Bros. cap tin. Meade's victory at Gettysburg on July 3, 1863 marked the turning point of the Civil War. Also shown is a Grand Army of the Republic medal with a bust of General Meade and an original handwritten duplicate of the presentation letter to Meade from the Chairman of the Arms and Trophies Department of the Metropolitan Fair. (Photos courtesy Rock Island Auction Company)

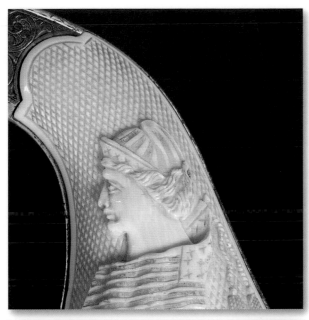

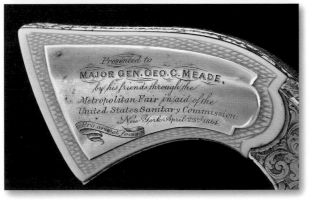

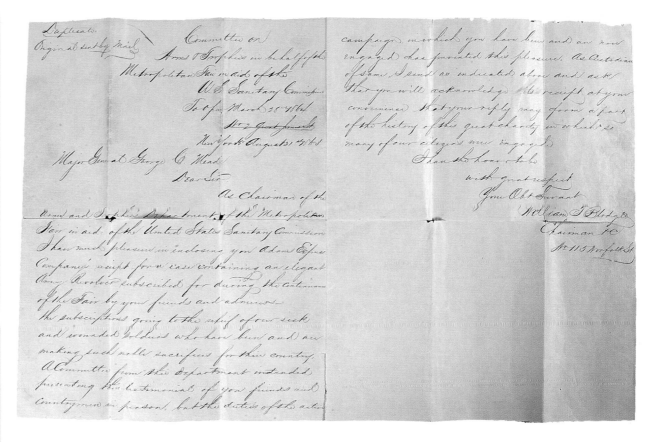

After Colt and Remington, the third most familiar revolver used during the Civil War was the Starr, a uniquely styled and highly innovative handgun patented in 1860. Literally years ahead of everyone else in America, Eben T. Starr's design was for a .36 caliber, double action, topbreak revolver. The Ordnance Department initially purchased 1,810 Navy models (.36 caliber percussion). By 1862 demand from the War Department brought about the addition of a .44 caliber (Army) version, resulting in the procurement of just over 21,000 guns by the end of 1864. The double action design, however, tended to confound some soldiers, as the trigger was actually a "lifter trigger" used to rotate the cylinder and cock the hammer. By pulling the lifter fully to the rear it struck the hammer release, which was a small, curved stub projecting outward from the frame. The idea was that the gun could be fired two ways; rapidly as a double action by pulling the lifter trigger all the way back, or with slightly less effort only cocking the gun for aiming with the hammer notch, after which the revolver could be touched off by lightly pressing the rear trigger. It was innovative, but soldiers unfamiliar with its operation could easily cause the guns to jam. One officer in the 12th Kentucky stated: "The man who sold these pistols to the government and the contractor who bought them ought to be hanged as traitors."[4]

In September 1863 the Ordnance Department requested that Starr build a second model, a more traditional single action version with a longer 8-inch barrel (the double action models had 6-inch barrels).

The third most carried sidearm on the Union side was the Starr revolver. Initially Eben T. Starr sold the Ordnance Department his innovative, top break, double action, .36 caliber percussion (Navy) revolver with 6-inch round barrel. With the beginning of the Civil War Starr added a .44 caliber double action, and later, at the request of the Ordnance Department, a single action version in 1863. (Collection of Dr. John Wells, bottom, and author's collection, top)

139

The single action Starr model was introduced in 1863. In addition to the single action design, the new revolvers had longer 8-inch barrels and were produced in far greater numbers than the double action Starr. The example pictured is a rarely seen engraved model executed in a remarkable floral motif with gold inlays. (Photos courtesy Rock Island Auction Co.)

In September 1863, the Ordnance Department requested that Starr Arms Co. build a traditional single action version of their revolver. This became the most prolific of the Civil War era Starr arms, with production of the single action reaching 25,000 by the end of 1864. (Photos courtesy Rock Island Auction Co.)

Pictured at top is a single action Starr compared to the original double action design. The double action, though highly innovative, tended to confound some soldiers, as the trigger was actually a "lifter trigger" used to rotate the cylinder and cock the hammer. By pulling the lifter fully to the rear it struck the hammer release, which is the small, curved stub projecting outward from the frame. The gun could thus be fired two ways; rapidly as a double action by pulling the lifter trigger all the way back, or with slightly less effort only cocking the gun for aiming with the hammer notch, (as shown) after which the revolver could be touched off by lightly pressing the rear trigger.

This photo shows a soldier, far right, posing with a Starr double action. (Civil War photo Library of Congress.)

This became the most prolific of the Civil War era Starr arms, with production of the single action reaching 25,000 by the end of 1864.

Another advantage of the Starr was its topbreak design. Although Eben Starr didn't patent the idea (Sam Colt had actually proposed such a design among his 1850 Dragoon patents) Starr made improvements to the concept by mortising the top strap to fit over the standing breech, thus giving his guns incredible strength. Starr revolvers were built to withstand the punishment of heavy use, yet by simply unscrewing the large knurled cross bolt that passed through the frame between the recoil shield and hammer, the barrel and

topstrap (hinged at the front of the frame) could be tilted down allowing replacement of an empty cylinder in a matter of seconds. The gun could also be loaded conventionally using the rammer and plunger.

The Starr's unique cylinder design did away with a conventional center arbor (around which both Colt and Remington cylinders revolved), and instead had a long ratchet shaft that seated well into the breech, and a conical bolt extending from the front of the cylinder that locked into a corresponding recess in the frame. Because of this design Starr revolvers were less apt to foul since they did not have to rotate around an arbor. Unfortunately, the innovative double action models proved easy to jam if not properly handled. Because of this weakness many were never issued and ended up in arsenal storage. The single action versions saw far greater use throughout the war.

As good a design as the Starr was, with its government contracts fulfilled by the end of 1864, the New York firm found that it could not be competitive with Colt and Remington in the civilian market. Two years after the end of the war, Ebenezer Townsend Starr ceased production of the guns; revolvers that had perhaps been too advanced for their time.

Outside of collectors and Civil War aficionados, the Starr's history and design was mostly overshadowed by Colt's and Remington's until Clint Eastwood used an old double action model as Civil War veteran and reformed gunfighter William Munny in his 1992 Academy

The big advantage of the Starr was its topbreak design. Although Eben Starr didn't patent the idea (Sam Colt beat him to it even though he never built any) Starr improved the concept by mortising the top strap to fit over the standing breech, thus giving his guns incredible strength. By simply unscrewing the large knurled cross bolt that passed through the frame between the recoil shield and hammer, the barrel and topstrap could be tilted down allowing replacement of an empty cylinder in a matter of seconds. The double action models were issued to Union soldiers beginning in 1861. The Starr cylinder (at far left) did away with the use of a conventional cylinder pin. Eben T. Starr's design used a long ratchet shaft at the back of the cylinder that seated well into the breech, while a conical bolt extending from the front of the cylinder locked into a corresponding recess in the frame. Because of this, Starr revolvers were less apt to foul since they did not have to rotate around an arbor. (Guns from the author's collection and John Wells Collection, respectively)

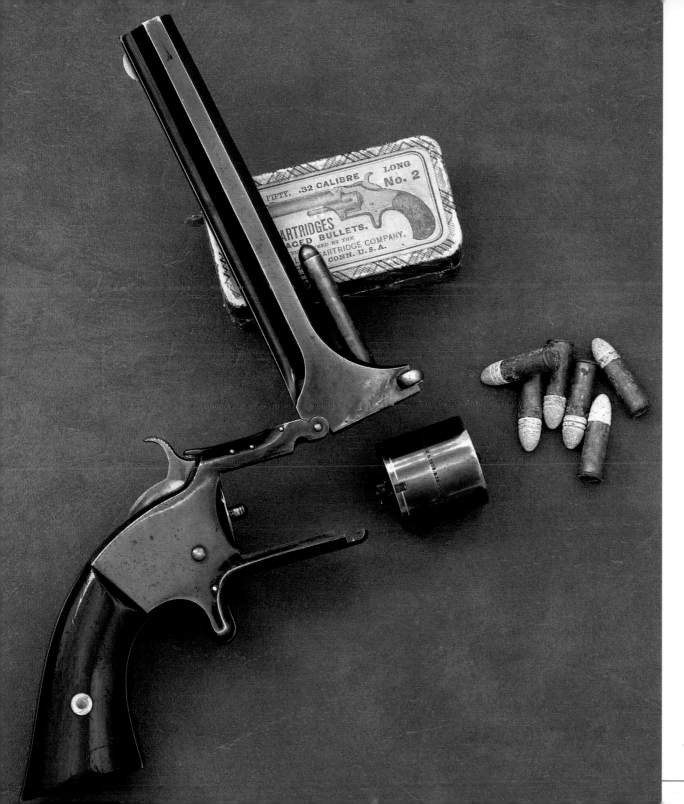

Smith & Wesson took a back seat to Colt and Remington during the Civil War, but through its ironclad patents and stringent enforcement thereof, was the only American arms maker allowed to manufacture a cartridge firing revolver. The large .32 caliber No. 2 model was the most popular among soldiers on both sides. Loading and reloading was easily accomplished by pressing up on the barrel latch at the bottom of the lug, which released the barrel and lug allowing it to "tip up" on its hinged top and expose the cylinder and short arbor. The cylinder was simply slipped out and reloaded, replaced, and the barrel dropped down into the locked position. An extra loaded cylinder could be changed out in a matter of seconds. (Mike Clark Collection/Collectors Firearms)

they could build. Orders were still being filled long after the war had ended.

The .22 was an anemic cartridge better suited for plinking, though close in even a .22 short can be deadly. With the beginning of hostilities in 1861 S&W added a more powerful .32 caliber version, the No.2, a small frame 6-shot, spur trigger revolver offered with barrel lengths up to 6-inches. Though there were no orders from the Ordnance Department for the No. 2, it became one of the most popular backup guns for both Confederate and Union officers and infantrymen with the money to purchase their own pistols. One known exception was the state of Kentucky, which procured 731

This handsomely engraved S&W No. 2 with ivory grips has the long 6-inch barrel. They were also offered with 4-inch and 5-inch barrel lengths. Introduced in 1861 they were manufactured through 1874. It is said that Wild Bill Hickok had one in his vest pocket the day he was murdered in Deadwood, North Dakota Territory. (Roger Muckerheide collection)

Whitney revolvers were manufactured by Eli Whitney, Jr. in New Haven, Connecticut, and were also known by the name Whitney Navy & Eagle Co. Revolvers. They were produced from the late 1850s to the early 1860s. The design was similar to other solid frame revolvers of the late 1850s and early 1860s, like the Remington, Roger & Spencer, Marston, and Freeman, but the Whitney was among the first to use this design. Most of the 1860s production was purchased by the Army and Navy during the Civil War. Pictured ensemble, at top is a .36 caliber 2nd Model with holster; middle, another 2nd Model; and bottom a 1st Model with inscribed grip "H. Noble". Note the notches! There were three Whitney Navy models all chambered in .36 caliber. Whitney also produced a Pocket Model variation in .31 caliber, and a spur trigger New Model Pocket Revolver in .28 caliber during the period of the Civil War. The single gun is a .31 caliber percussion Pocket Model with 6-inch barrel. This is the 2nd Type with the the round juncture of the grip to frame like a Remington. (Mike Clark Collection/Collectors Firearms and Rock Island Auction Co.)

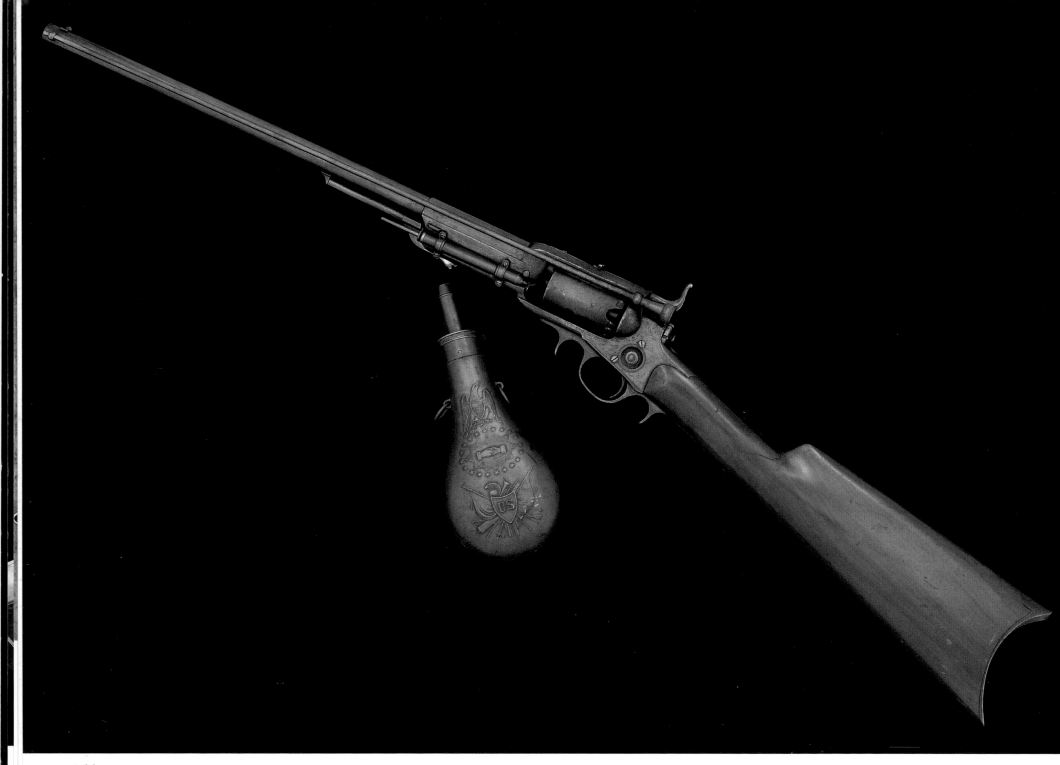

Civil War re-enactor Corporal Mark Anderson of the 145th Pennsylvania Volunteer Infantry, Company D, shows how the Roots Revolving Rifle was fired. This is the manner in which most soldiers held the Roots rifle; however, it was a risk, as there was always the chance for a chain fire, which could have devastating consequences to the fingers of the support hand. Anderson also demonstrates the safer way to handle a Roots rifle when it could not be rested or supported. Note the Roots pistol tucked in Anderson's waist belt.

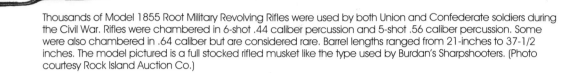

Thousands of Model 1855 Root Military Revolving Rifles were used by both Union and Confederate soldiers during the Civil War. Rifles were chambered in 6-shot .44 caliber percussion and 5-shot .56 caliber percussion. Some were also chambered in .64 caliber but are considered rare. Barrel lengths ranged from 21-inches to 37-1/2 inches. The model pictured is a full stocked rifled musket like the type used by Burdan's Sharpshooters. (Photo courtesy Rock Island Auction Co.)

At the very end of the Civil War, E. Remington & Sons introduced a revolving carbine based on its .44 caliber percussion Army and .36 caliber percussion Navy revolvers. The guns were manufactured though 1879 with total production not exceeding 1,000 examples. Barrels, with the Remington address and NEW MODEL stamp were offered in 24 inch and 28 inch lengths, almost all of which were octagonal, with some models having octagonal to round barrels. A small number were also converted to fire metallic cartridges in 1869 and 1870. Though based on the revolvers, the cylinders were 3/16 in. longer, triggerguards were handsomely styled, the buttstocks bore a nicely inset brass crescent buttplate, and both buckhorn (shown) or folding leaf sights were available. (Photos courtesy Rock Island Auction Co.)

Introduced in 1855, the Root Revolving Rifle, designed by E. K. Root (who took over management of the Colt's Patent Fire Arms Mfg. Co. following Samuel Colt's death in January 1862), was already integrated into the U.S. military by the start of the Civil War. Although generally outdated by more contemporary repeating rifles, the Ordnance Department purchased over 4,600 Colt Revolving Rifles during the war. This is an early 1855 Sporting model (shown at left and on page 164) distinguished by the triggerguard design and oiler device attached to the left side of the barrel lug. (Mike Clark/Collectors Firearms Collection)

PATENTED SEPT 14 1858
E. REMINGTON & SONS. ILION NEW YORK U.S.A.
NEW MODEL

Ordnance, General James Ripley, who had essentially snubbed Oliver Winchester when he first approached the Ordnance Department offering to sell the U.S. military his new repeating rifle. Ripley regarded Winchester's first model as less than ideal for combat, because the Henry used an open follower slot on the lower side of the magazine tube. Open to the elements it had a propensity to jam if not carefully maintained. What Ripley and government inspectors failed to realize was that in a fight, a properly functioning Henry was worth a dozen soldiers armed with single shot percussion U.S. Rifled Muskets. Gen. Ripley believed that no better weapon could be issued to infantry soldiers in the field than the rifled musket. Unfortunately no one in Washington ever asked the soldiers in the field for their opinions, and no one, except those soldiers in the field truly recognized the value of the 16-shot, .44 rimfire Henry repeater in fire-fight.

Yes the .44 cartridge had little more power than an Army model handgun, but fired by a trained marksman, a well cared for and smoothly operating Henry rifle could inflict more damage to an enemy line in less than a minute than 16 soldiers firing a single round each. Winchester's sales agents boldly claimed "a resolute man, armed with one of these rifles, particularly if on horseback, CANNOT BE CAPTURED."[1] While this bit of marketing hyperbole was a little optimistic, it wasn't too far fetched as Confederates on the receiving end of Henry repeaters began calling it that, "Damned Yankee rifle you can load on Sunday and shoot all week." During the War Between the States, soldiers armed with Henry lever-action rifles decided many a skirmish. Nevertheless, the prevailing military rifle round (single shot) was the .58 caliber; a large, stout lead bullet that, when it struck home, was capable of inflicting a devastating wound. Using a paper cartridge or lead ball rammed down the barrel of a Rifled Musket, it was as close to a standardized load as the U.S. could manage. B. Tyler Henry regarded the .58 caliber round as too large to be practical at the time for his lever action rifle, thus he had chosen to make a .44 caliber cartridge, which was an adequate enough bullet given that his rifle had proven capable of exceptional accuracy, and provided a soldier with 15 rounds ready in the magazine plus one in the chamber. Henry had wisely chosen capacity and sustained firepower over cartridge size.

Riding on the success of this single model, in 1865, B. Tyler Henry tried to oust financier Oliver Winchester and rename the company after himself. Winchester had

was little he could do with the existing guns. Henry started over, and three years later, in 1860, gave Oliver Winchester the repeater he had sought to build, a magazine-fed, breech-loading, lever-action rifle. Patented October 16, 1860, it was named the Henry after its inventor, as was the new .44 caliber rimfire cartridge it would fire.

To Oliver Winchester's fortune the start of the Civil War made the Henry rifle one of the most admired and feared weapons in the hands of U.S. troops, and one of the most coveted prizes for any Confederate soldier. Ironically, the U.S. War Department didn't purchase Henry rifles for Federal Troops in any significant number, instead individual soldiers and units purchased them at their own expense! This came much to the chagrin of Chief of

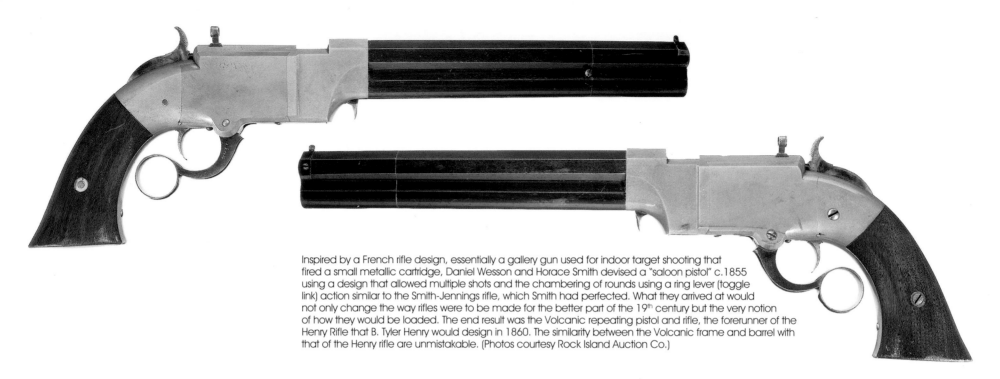

Inspired by a French rifle design, essentially a gallery gun used for indoor target shooting that fired a small metallic cartridge, Daniel Wesson and Horace Smith devised a "saloon pistol" c.1855 using a design that allowed multiple shots and the chambering of rounds using a ring lever (toggle link) action similar to the Smith-Jennings rifle, which Smith had perfected. What they arrived at would not only change the way rifles were to be made for the better part of the 19th century but the very notion of how they would be loaded. The end result was the Volcanic repeating pistol and rifle, the forerunner of the Henry Rifle that B. Tyler Henry would design in 1860. The similarity between the Volcanic frame and barrel with that of the Henry rifle are unmistakable. (Photos courtesy Rock Island Auction Co.)

been gracious enough to allow his brilliant plant superintendent to name the first model after himself, but when Henry succeeded in taking control of the company, Winchester simply withdrew, and in so doing took all of the New Haven Arms Co.'s assets with him. He immediately turned around and started the Winchester Repeating Arms Co. which introduced its first new model in 1866.

In open field combat the rules were simple. They hadn't changed a great deal in over 200 years. A foot soldier had one shot, reload and shoot again, reload, etc., and if the odds were in his favor he would live to fight another day. Benjamin Tyler Henry and Oliver Winchester changed those odds by setting into motion the wheels of industry that would lead to the adoption of the first lever action repeating rifle used in war, but two other men, both talented designers and industrialists, were to play an equally important role in the story of 19th century America and the War Between the States; Christian Sharps and Christopher M. Spencer. Because of the rifles that bore their names, the course of the Civil War turned in favor of the Union by the end of 1863.

Despite its fame today, during the war the Henry was eclipsed by the most successful repeating rifle of the 1860s, the Spencer, which was carried by thousands of Union troops and cavalrymen. It was designed by Christopher Spencer, a brilliant inventor whose mechanical interests went well beyond firearms. At the start of the Civil War he was only 32 years old, yet he had already applied for and received numerous patents. His

genius for invention was not unlike that of 16th century artist and visionary Leonardo da Vinci, who prophesied countless devices well ahead of their time. In Christopher Spencer's case, not only had he conceived of an automobile for personal transportation in 1861 but had constructed a steam-powered carriage that he tested and actually drove around Hartford, Connecticut! This was some 30 years after the first such devices were experimented with in England and France and long after the colossal French Cugnot steamer built in 1770 (about as unwieldy a contrivance as could be imagined), but for the United States in 1861, Spencer's steam carriage was extraordinarily unconventional. So too, was his 1860 patent for a lever-actuated repeating rifle that would evolve into one of the most successful and enduring longarms of the 19th century.

Like all of Spencer's designs, his 7-shot repeating rifle was over engineered, almost to a fault. He first conceived of the idea in 1857, a year later fashioned a prototype and in 1859 presented a working sample for his patent application for the C. M. Spencer Self-Loading Fire Arm. Simple in its operation, it was built to withstand heavy use. As many of his inventions had to do with textile machines, and in later years, machines for manufacturing screws (his last in 1907), the 1860 Spencer rifle was, pardon the pun, "bullet proof."

The heart of Spencer's repeating rifle was a rotating block which could feed a cartridge into the breech each time the lever was operated. The rounds were drawn from a

The Henry rifle, which Benjamin Tyler Henry created for Oliver Winchester's New Haven Arms Co. (which succeeded the Volcanic Repeating Arms Co. in 1857) was the first successful lever action repeater. Introduced in 1860 and chambered for the new .44 caliber rimfire cartridge, also created by B. Tyler Henry, the rifle gained great notoriety during the Civil War. Though very few Federal orders for the Henry were forthcoming, private purchases by soldiers and individual Union infantry and cavalry units put thousands into the hands of U.S. troops and a great deal of fear into the hearts of Confederates on the receiving end of a Henry's 16 round volley. (Photos courtesy Rock Island Auction Co.)

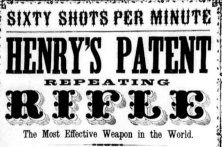

tubular magazine inserted through the buttstock. Each time a cartridge was fired and the action worked, the spent casing was extracted from the chamber and ejected, and a fresh one carried into the breech by closing the lever. The cartridges were pushed forward through the magazine by a spring within the magazine tube. All that remained was to fully cock the hammer, take aim and pull the trigger. While not as fast as Benjamin Tyler Henry and Oliver Winchester's lever action design, which automatically cocked the hammer on the backstroke of the bolt, the Spencer was neither as delicate nor as prone to jamming, as the cache of seven cartridges were safely carried inside the rifle's stock rather than exposed to the elements in an open magazine tube. Granted, the

Henry packed better than twice as many cartridges, but the Spencer's .56-56 rimfire rounds were nearly as powerful as a musket ball; .56 caliber (.550 in. diameter) vs. the .58 caliber (.570 in. diameter) conical lead bullet loaded in a Rifled Musket. By comparison, the Henry .44 rimfire was a considerably smaller cartridge than the Spencer, with a bullet diameter of .446 in.

Spencer also designed a number of variations; rifles, carbines, and sporting models in different calibers. For the military the primary cartridge used during the Civil War was .56-56 Spencer with a 350 grain lead bullet. Rifles were made to fill orders for both the Navy and Army and in both 30-inch barrels (with attachable bayonets) and carbines with 22-inch barrels and saddle rings for the U.S. Army. It was Spencer himself who secured the largest military orders by personally demonstrating the 1860 model to President Lincoln after Ordnance Department requisitions failed to meet Spencer's expectations.

Spencer had no financial interest in the company which bore his name. He was backed by financiers who paid him a royalty on every gun sold, so for Christopher Spencer marketing was fundamental to his financial wellbeing. He had successfully demonstrated the 7-shot repeater to the Navy Department in 1861, after which the company received an order for only 700 rifles with bayonets. The guns were so well made that when word got around to Army officers, they too wanted Spencer repeaters. Additional orders from the Ordnance Department came in 1862, and as more of the rifles and carbines got into the hands of military men, tales of the 7-shooter's tactical

This is an historical 23rd Illinois inscribed and identified Civil War New Haven Arms Co. Henry lever action rifle in .44 rimfire with standard 24-inch octagonal barrel. Manufactured in 1863, this example bears the inscription on the left receiver panel, Peter Church, Co. C. 23rd Ill. Vols in fancy script lettering. The 23rd Illinois Infantry (Irish Brigade) was organized in Chicago in June of 1861. After initial service in Missouri, the regiment was transferred to West Virginia and fought in the Shenandoah Valley Campaign during the summer of 1864. The Irish Brigade participated in the Appomattox Campaign and was present at Appomattox Court House on April 9th 1865 when General Robert E. Lee surrendered the Army of Northern Virginia to Ulysses S. Grant. (Photos courtesy Rock Island Auction Co.)

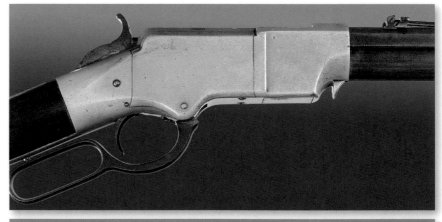

advantages continued to spread. Seizing on the opportunity, in August 1863, only one month after the pivotal Union victory at Gettysburg (fought from July 1st to July 3rd) Spencer went to Washington and asked to see the president. The always affable Commander in Chief met with Spencer on the 18th and again on the 19th, during which time Spencer went into detail about the gun's design and operation, disassembling and reassembling an example at Lincoln's request and then allowing the President to test fire it. Whether it was Lincoln's favorable impression of the Spencer rifle, after shooting it outside the White House (near the site where the Washington Monument is today), and striking the target well on the mark with seven rounds in less than half a minute, or the fact that officers and enlisted men were purchasing Spencer rifles with their own money in order to have one, late in 1863 the Ordnance Department placed substantial orders. The requisition was for Navy rifles with bayonets, and for the Army saddle ring carbines, 11,000 of the latter for the Cavalry. Spencer production during the Civil War totaled (ordered) 64,675 carbines, over 1,200 rifles for the Navy, and 11,471 for the Army and other government service. Total deliveries by 1866 amounted to over 76,000 for which Spencer received no less than $1 royalty per gun.

In order to keep the supply of Spencer rifles and carbines flowing during the war,

The Henry may have garnered more glory from its use during the Civil War than the Spencer repeating rifle and carbine, but unlike the Henry, the Spencer was formally adopted by the U.S. Army and Navy during the Civil War. Spencer production for the war totaled (ordered) 64,675 carbines, over 1,200 rifles for the Navy, and 11,471 for the Army and other government service. Total deliveries by 1866 amounted to over 76,000. In addition, the Burnside Rifle Co. was contracted to produce 30,496 Spencer carbines in 1865. The sling bar and ring on the left side of the receiver was used to attach the Spencer carbine to a cavalryman's snaffle hook on the cross-shoulder carbine sling. Carried this way, the carbine is inverted along the left side of the trooper when mounted, its muzzle down and forward underneath the leg, and the muzzle itself caught in a short leather socket to keep it from flopping around.[10]

171

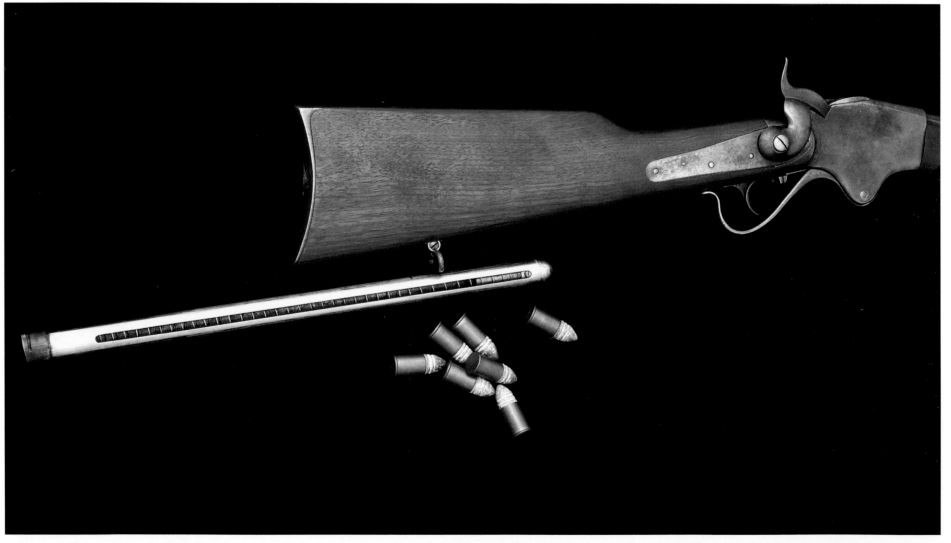

Although the 22-inch barrel length Spencer carbine was the primary model used by the U.S., the 30-inch barreled Spencer rifles proved their worth with greater range and accuracy combined with its 7-round capacity. Union Col. John S. Wilder wrote of the Spencer rifle: "My Brigade of Mounted Infantry have repeatedly routed and driven largely superior forces of rebels, in some instances five or six times our number and this result is mainly due to being armed with the Spencer Repeating Rifle."[11] (Photo courtesy Rock Island Auction Co.)

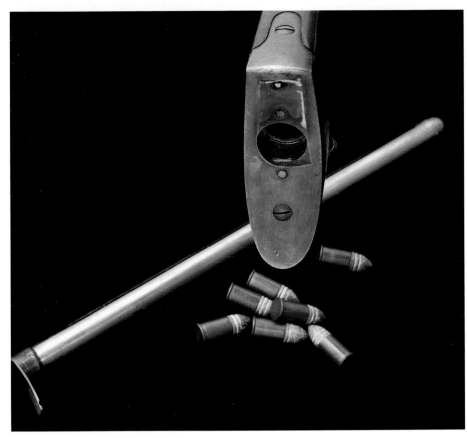

The heart of Spencer's repeating rifle was a rotating block which could feed a cartridge into the breech each time a lever was operated. Working the Spencer's combination action lever and triggerguard ejected a spent shell on the down stroke and chambered a fresh round when as it was raised into the closed position. You had to manually cock the hammer to fire the round. Cartridges were drawn from a tubular magazine inside the stock. Rounds were pushed forward through the magazine by a spring within the cartridge tube. The Spencer remained in use by the U.S. Army until 1873. Ironically the 7-shot repeater which had served so well in the War Between the States and in the early years of the Western Expansion, was replaced by the single shot Springfield Trapdoor rifle.

the Burnside Rifle Company in Providence, Rhode Island, was commissioned to produce 30,502 Spencer carbines c.1865. In addition, the new Model 1865 Spencer was also ordered by the Ordnance Department. Of this model, with a shorter 20-inch barrel, 18,959 were delivered to the Army and another 4,000 (approximately) to other government agencies.

Throughout the war Spencer had also filled orders from individual state militias, units in the field, and private individuals. Christopher Spencer had done well. Even after the war, when Spencer's military contracts were cancelled, there were substantial orders

remaining on the books, but as those were fulfilled the demand for Spencer rifles and carbines fell well short of the company's production capacity. By the late 1860s Spencer's wartime success was to have serious consequences. With the conflict over, war surplus Spencer rifles and carbines began to flood the market, (over 46,000 between 1866 and 1877), though as historian and noted Spencer authority Roy M. Marcot notes in his book *Spencer Repeating Firearms*, this was not a significant enough number to drive Spencer out of business. The majority of surplus sales actually took place after 1868. It was competition from other armsmakers, particularly Winchester (which had cured all of the Henry's ills by 1866) that drove Christopher Spencer out of the gun business.

Postwar sales of Spencer's sporting models were good but nothing in comparison to the military contracts he had enjoyed from 1862 to 1865. Sporting models were produced from 1864 to 1868 in various barrel lengths and configurations (round and octagonal) measuring 16, 28, and 30-inches in length and chambered in .56-46 Spencer, .56-50 and .56-52 Spencer. But there was simply too much competition. By the end of 1868 Spencer had decided to leave the company and pursue other interests. In December, all property of the Spencer Repeating Rifle Company was liquidated and sold to the Fogerty Repeating Rifle Co., a local Boston firearms manufacturer, which in turn sold everything to Oliver Winchester and the Winchester Repeating Arms Company. Winchester auctioned off the machinery, earning back most of its purchase price as well as permanently eliminating any future competition from Spencer, or so they thought. Winchester had in effect purchased the rights to the Spencer rifle design, but Christopher Spencer's prolific imagination hadn't been part of the deal, and would come back to haunt the New Haven armsmaker in later years when the inventor formed the Spencer Arms Company and introduced America's first successful slide action shotgun, a decade before the first Winchester!

In the late 1860s and throughout much of the 1870s, Spencer rifles, carbines, and sporting models were still used by the U.S. military (which had Civil War guns reconditioned at the Springfield Armory), and by thousands of men heading west, ex-soldiers, cowboys, cattle rustlers and highwaymen, adventurers, settlers, explorers, hunters, even Indians. General Ulysses S. Grant declared the Spencer "the best breech-loading arms" available. George Armstrong Custer, whose Michigan volunteers carried Spencer rifles and carbines, wrote: "Being in command of a Brigade of Cavalry which is armed throughout with Spencer Carbine and Rifle, I take pleasure in testifying to their superiority over all other weapons. I am firmly of the opinion that fifteen hundred men armed with the Spencer Carbine are more than a match for twenty-five hundred armed with any other fire-arm – I know this to be true from actual experiment."

For most of the Civil War the Spencer rifle and carbine had been a staple of the Union, a reliable, almost unbreakable repeater that remained a prized possession of everyone who ever worked the lever and pulled the trigger.

For Union and Confederate sharpshooters, sometimes one shot was enough, at least

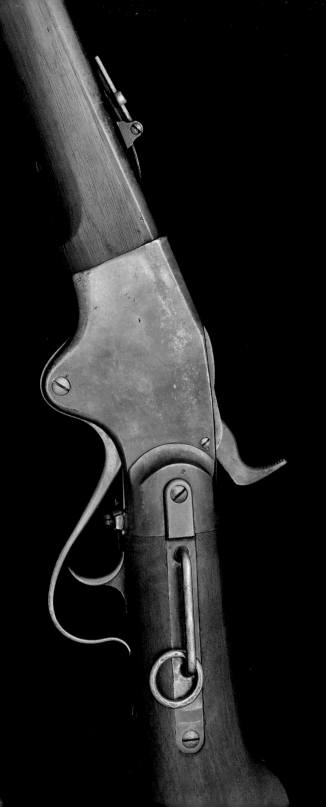

Toward the end of the Civil War many Spencer carbines were equipped with a device known as a Stabler Cut-Off. Inventor Edward Stabler had already patented a Spring Assist for the Spencer's blade ejector (cartridge ejector) in 1864. His second invention for the Spencer came in 1865. The Stabler Cut-Off was a device mounted forward of the trigger that limited the downward travel of the lever, thereby making the Spencer into a single shot rifle that could be easily loaded from the breech, while maintaining the cartridges in the rifle's magazine as a backup for quick loading. The Ordnance Department so liked Stabler's invention that all military orders were required to be so equipped from the factory. Stable was paid a royalty of 25 cents for very Spencer rifle to use his invention.

in the mind of Christian Sharps and the thousands of men who used his rifles in the War Between the States. If there is one gun that truly defines America's Western Expansion after the Civil War it is not the Colt revolver or Winchester repeater, but the single shot Sharps rifle.

Rifles and muskets fitted with a percussion lock had only been around for about 20 years, slowly, very slowly, replacing the time-honored flintlock rifles and muskets which had been a mainstay of Americans since the War of Independence and for a generation before. In fact, flintlocks had been in use since the early 17th century.

The advantages of a percussion lock were noteworthy. First and foremost, ignition was faster, sidestepping the momentary delay until the burning powder in the pan touched off the charge within the breech. Secondly, a percussion lock was far more resistant to the elements, heavy wind and pouring rain could make a flintlock into a very handsome club in a matter of moments, but a percussion lock was nearly waterproof and the only effect wind might have would be throwing off someone's aim. Still, there was one constant. Loading required the time-honored procedure of pouring a measure of powder down the barrel and following it with a patched lead ball driven home with the rifle's ramrod. Instead of adding priming powder to the pan, a percussion lock required only the application of a small brass cap containing a trace of fulminating mercury at its base, which was placed over a small, hollow tube leading into the breech. Drop the hammer, the cap ignited on impact sending a spark directly into the powder charge and your bullet was

on its way down the barrel. It was a faster, more efficient method, but Christian Sharps wanted to make loading and charging a rifle even faster, and his idea was to do it all from the breech end.

A former apprentice at the Harpers Ferry Arsenal under John Hall (who designed the first flintlock breechloader adopted by the U.S. military in 1824), Sharps received his patent in 1848 and introduced his first model a year later. The original Sharps breech-loading design, of which less than 100 were made, also incorporated an automatic capping device, but he abandoned this design in 1850, and by 1851 had advanced through two further improvements, neither of which utilized automatic capping. A March 9, 1850, article in *Scientific American* extolled the advantages of the Sharps breechloader stating that a man with no previous weapons experience could fire it up to nine times a minute and place every bullet within a six-inch circle forty yards away.[2] By 1852 the familiar Sharps rifle (first with slanting breech) and side hammer had come into being. Within three years Sharps had sold more than 5,000. In the interim he had also come up with several variations; the 1853 carbine, a breech-loading shotgun, and a long barrel military rifle. More than 10,000 of the 1853 models (mostly carbines) had been produced by 1857 and Sharps had set up his own manufacturing facilities in Hartford, Connecticut. Previously he had his rifles made by Robbins & Lawrence in Windsor, Vermont.

All of the early models used Sharps' patented "pellet primer" mounted in the lockplate. The only exceptions were the Model 1855 U.S. Carbine and British Carbine which were required to use the Maynard Tape Priming system. Sharps also improved upon the paper cartridge. The common version in use was a proper measure of

The Sharps Model 1852 carbine was Christian Sharps first slanting breech model and the gun which led to the company's incredible success in the decade to come. These first models were manufactured for Sharps by Robbins & Lawrence in Windsor, Vermont. This was the model that established the fundamental design of all Sharps rifles to come. (Mike Clark/Collectors Firearms Collection)

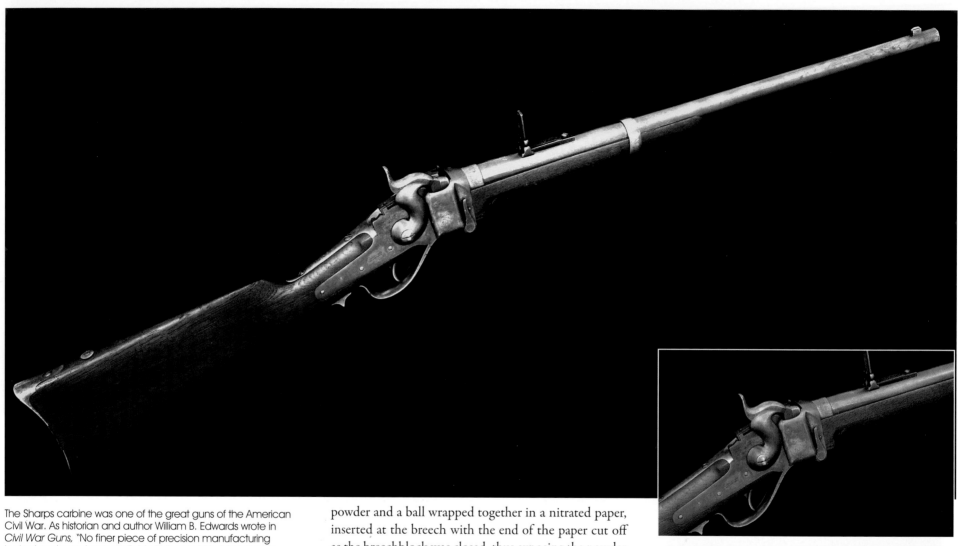

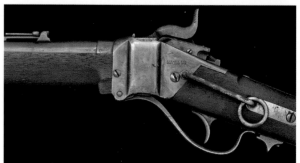

The Sharps carbine was one of the great guns of the American Civil War. As historian and author William B. Edwards wrote in *Civil War Guns,* "No finer piece of precision manufacturing in steel and wood was available in the world in 1861 than a U.S. contract carbine; and among the best of these was the Sharps." The carbine pictured is a Model 1863 manufactured by the Sharps Rifle Co. in Hartford, Connecticut. The New Models c.1859, 1863, and 1865 were manufactured through 1866 in carbine and rifle with production totaling more than 115,000. These are also known as the straight breech type Sharps, which became the design used throughout the remainder of Sharps production. The cavalry carbines, like this battle scared veteran, had the patented Lawrence folding leaf rear sight, and barrel lengths of 22 inches (rifles had 30 inch barrels) and were chambered in .52 caliber percussion. (Mike Clark/Collectors Firearms Collection)

powder and a ball wrapped together in a nitrated paper, inserted at the breech with the end of the paper cut off as the breechblock was closed, thus exposing the powder charge. The concept was actually much older with the paper having originally been torn open and the powder contents poured down the barrel and paper and ball rammed down afterward. Sharps new breech-loading linen cartridge was a self-contained fabric bullet. The linen cartridges loaded the same and the fabric was easily consumed by the powder's ignition.

By 1859 Christian Sharps had made his last major change in the percussion rifle's design with a new straight breech and three standard versions – carbine, military rifle, and sporting rifle. All Sharps percussion models had traditional brass patch boxes mounted on the right side of the stock. The U.S. military was the single largest purchaser of Sharps rifles and during the Civil War the Army and Navy procured more than 100,000 rifles and carbines. A sharpshooter armed with a 30-inch barreled Sharps rifle could knock an officer off his horse at 1,000 yards or more. Ironically, when abolitionist John Brown and his followers had attacked the armory at Harpers Ferry in 1859, the very same armory where Christian Sharps had apprenticed; Brown's entire raiding party had been armed with Sharps rifles!

When the Civil War ended in 1865 three rifles emerged as the most successful, the Spencer, Henry, and Sharps, yet the U.S. military regarded the traditional Army rifle as the Model 1861 U.S Percussion Rifle-Musket (and its successors) built in the hundreds of thousands during the war. In addition, toward the end of the war, Erskine S. Allen, the master armorer at the Springfield Armory, introduced the "First Model Allen" breech loading cartridge rifle chambered in .58 caliber rimfire. By 1868 it had evolved into the famous Springfield "Trapdoor" rifle, which became the standard, single shot, military rifle carried throughout much of 1870s by the U.S. Cavalry. A curious decision, given the recognized and proven in the field advantages of the Henry and Spencer repeaters! As historian Edward C. Ezell wrote in *Handguns of the World*, his influential 1981 treatise on handgun development, "With the advantages of hindsight, it is difficult to see the logic expressed by the military men of the 1860s and 1870s."

Other Breech Loading Rifles

There were numerous makes of rifles and carbines in use throughout the war, which was itself one of the biggest problems the Ordnance Department and U.S. military had to face in the early 1860s. At the start of the Civil War there were no fewer than 79 models of rifles, muskets, and rifle-muskets, 23 models of carbines and musketoons, and 19 models of pistols in use![3] This is an object lesson in why modern-day militaries the world over use one primary pistol and rifle cartridge. While there are other calibers and types of guns used for special operations, the majority of U.S. troops in the 21st century are armed with 9mm Beretta pistols and 5.56mm M16A2 rifles. The reason, simply enough, is the standardization of weapons and ammunition. During the Civil War standardization was a much greater problem because so many different guns, calibers, and types of ammunition were in use at the same time. The advent of early metallic cartridges at the beginning of the war complicated things even further. This was the principal reason why the U.S. did not rely on repeating rifles as primary weapons for the Army and Navy. Another was the cost of new arms and the ready supply of pre-Civil War muskets and rifled muskets in hand, most of which dated to the mid 1840s and early 1850s.

The New Model 1865 Sharps Percussion Carbine was the last model of the Civil War. The example shown is fitted with a Lawrence patent folding rear leaf sight graduated to 800 yards and the Lawrence patent pellet primer. The 22-inch barrel is roll-stamped "New Model 1865" between the rear sight and the receiver. This gun does not bear a military inspection mark and was probably manufactured after the end of the war in 1865 and sold commercially. This is a prime example of the last paper cartridge Sharps models. (Photos courtesy Rock Island Auction Co.)

Others were more than 20 years old, including outdated .69 caliber smoothbore muskets that had been converted from flintlock to caplock and put into storage. Thus the Union was at first armed with older guns, while U.S. arsenals and Northern armsmakers tooled up to produce new rifled muskets, carbines, and revolvers. The needs of the Ordnance Department and its Chief of Ordnance, Brigadier General James W. Ripley, was to standardize the guns and the ammunition in use and this proved to be as great a challenge in 1861 as the Confederacy was to the Union.

While muzzleloaders were the principal longarms of both the North and South, breech-loading, single shot rifles and carbines were also abundant in the early 1860s. In addition to the Sharps, arguably the best single shot breech loading rifle that money could buy; there were the old Merrill .54 caliber carbines, the U.S. Model 1843 Hall carbine chambered in .52 caliber, the .52 caliber Gwyn & Campbell carbine (a singularly unusual looking longarm as it had no forend), the equally peculiar looking 1863 Maynard chambered in .50 caliber, the break-action Smith percussion carbine in .50 caliber, and the legendary Burnside .54 caliber percussion carbine, invented by U.S. Major General Ambrose Everett Burnside, commander of the Rhode Island Volunteers.

Horse Soldiers

The demands of the U.S. Cavalry, the Army's elite corps descended from the Dragoons of Mexican-American War fame, were different from the infantry. The cavalry was easier to mobilize, quicker to alter its strategy, and en mass a formidable force. Brigadier General George Armstrong Custer proved this on the third day of fighting at Gettysburg when he led the 7th and 1st Michigan cavalry in two successive charges against Confederate General J.E.B. Stuart's position, thereby stalling Stuart's crucial offensive during Pickett's Charge. Though Custer's losses, 219 men, were severe, Civil War scholars have written that Custer's cavalry attacks contributed to the Confederate's defeat at Gettysburg on July 3rd.

Mounted troops needed lighter, easier to handle rifles; they needed carbines with shorter barrels and most of all they needed breechloaders. The first to be issued to the U.S. Cavalry was the Burnside Carbine. It was produced in five variations from the time of its introduction in 1855 until manufacturing ended in 1865. In total, the federal government ordered 55,567 Burnside carbines during the war.

An 1847 graduate of West Point, Ambrose E. Burnside resigned his commission in 1853 to pursue his interests in arms making. His original company, Bristol Firearms, was organized in 1855 at Bristol, Rhode Island. Burnside patented his own design for a breech loading rifle, which were initially (1st and 2nd models) distinguished by their tip-up breech and conspicuous absence of a wood forearm. Models ordered during the war (3rd, 4th, and 5th) were fitted with a wood forearm and single barrel band.

Burnside originally sold a quantity of 200 of the 1st model carbines to the government in 1856 when Jefferson Davis was U.S. Secretary of War. Another 709 were delivered in 1858. A major improvement in the gun came with the 2nd model, which introduced a new triggerguard release lever designed by G.P. Foster, manufacturing superintendent at Bristol. This is the most distinguishing feature as the Foster designed release lever rides inside the lower circumference of the triggerguard, and when pressed downward releases

the entire action allowing the inner receiver to "tip up" for loading or ejecting a spent shell case. The 1st Model release had been mounted on the side of the receiver.

Shortly after the 2nd model was introduced in 1861 Bristol Firearms relocated to Providence, Rhode Island, and was renamed the Burnside Rifle Company. With the Civil War only months old, Burnside had left the company and become commander of the Rhode Island Volunteers, armed with Burnside Carbines. Federal orders for Burnside models continued to pour in throughout the war and the new Providence works was turning out late 2nd model and new 3rd model (with wood forearm) carbines by the thousands. By 1863 the factory was delivering an average of 2,000 guns a month. Orders for the improved 4th model, introduced in October 1862 (the difference being a new hinged, double-pivoting breechblock), and 5th model, distinguished by the addition of a guide screw in the right side of the frame, totaled over 47,000 by the end of 1864. Another 3,800 Burnside Carbines were delivered in 1865, the last shipment being ordered in February.[4]

The Burnside was neither an austere nor elegant rifle but one that bore the mark of a military design, no nonsense, no frills or unnecessary expenditures in manufacturing, thus the first two models having been produced without a wood forearm under the barrel. Never mind the heat of the metal after several repeated shots, wear a gauntlet! The Ordnance Department thought better of it and required the 3rd and subsequent version to be fitted with a wood forend. As for the gun's general appearance, it was trim, with a narrow, handsomely color cased receiver, light weight, at just 7-1/2 pounds (approximately), and truly suited to the cavalry.

The .54 caliber metallic cartridge used in the Burnside had a drawn brass case with a small pinhole in the back. Although it appeared to be a rimfire cartridge, the Burnside still required a percussion cap, ignited by the hammer, to send a spark through the hole in the back of the cartridge case and ignite the powder. The foremost advantage of the Burnside's metallic case was its durability

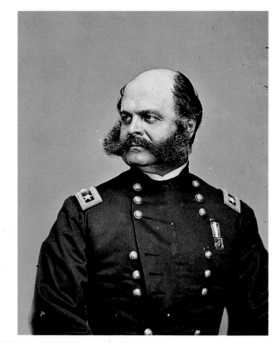

One of the most efficient and relied upon breech loading rifles carried by the U.S. Cavalry during the Civil War was designed by U.S. Major General Ambrose Everett Burnside (pictured above). His patented design for a breech loading rifle, distinguished by its tip-up breech and conspicuous absence of a wood forearm, was manufactured beginning in 1855 at the Bristol Firearms Co. in Bristol, Rhode Island. Although he left the company at the start of the Civil War to resume his military career, early (prewar) Burnside carbines had already been purchased by the Ordnance Department for issue to the cavalry. Later models (3rd through 5th) are easily distinguished by the addition of a wood forend requested by Ordnance in 1861. Pictured (facing page) are a late 5th Model (top) and a 2nd Model. (Mike Clark/ Collectors Firearms Collection and Library of Congress)

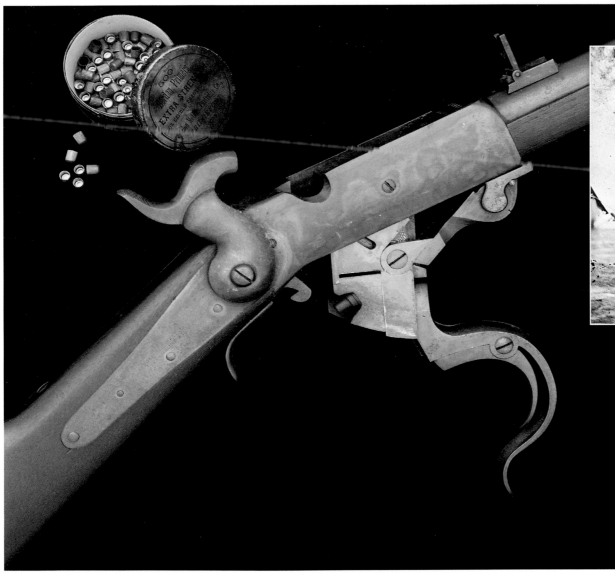

The Burnside action dropped down to allow loading and extracting a spent cartridge case. The lever that rests inside the triggerguard was pushed downward to release the action. The guns inventor, Major General Ambrose Burnside is pictured with two of his staff officers at an encampment in Warrenton, Virginia. (Mike Clark/Collectors Firearms Collection and Library of Congress)

Christian Sharps was a prolific inventor (including the Sharps Patent four-barrel, .32 caliber Pepperbox Derringer, one of the most successful small, multi-barrel pistols of the 1860s and 1870s) and he designed a second breech loading carbine in 1862, his first to use a metallic cartridge, the Sharps & Hankins Army Carbine.

This innovative rifle was the first to use a firing pin in the breechblock and the first longarm designed with an integral hammer safety to prevent an accidental discharge. Both the Army and Navy ordered Sharps & Hankins models between 1862 and 1865. The Navy purchased the majority, roughly 6,000 with special leather-cased barrels, with approximately another 1,200 delivered to the Army. Like several early breech loading models, the Sharps & Hankins was an austere design, but at least it had a wood forearm.

over more easily damaged paper and linen cartridges. Its unusual shape (a tapered case that bulged below the base of the bullet like an old fashioned ice cream cone) also served to seat the round firmly within the barrel breech and keep a tight gas seal.

During the war Burnside rose to the rank of Major General and would lead the Army of the Potomac during the Fredericksburg campaign of late 1862 and early 1863. Despite being the inventor, Ambrose Burnside never received any of the profits from the company's Civil War contracts. After the war he returned to Rhode Island and was elected Governor in 1866. In 1874, he was elected U.S. Senator and served as a representative from the State of Rhode Island until his death in 1881.

This extraordinary un-issued Burnside 5th Model Carbine with 21-inch barrel shows the original brilliant color casehardened receiver and hammer. The 5th Model is distinguished by the guide screw mounted in the right side of the frame, which allowed smoother operation of the breech as it rides in a corresponding curved groove in the breech block. This example clearly shows the two leaf folding rear sight on the barrel and the bright finished sling bar and ring. A remarkably well preserved gun even the three initial Ordnance final inspection stamp on the left side of the stock wrist is unmarred and clearly visible. The 5th Model was manufactured from 1863 to 1865. The largest quantity of Burnside Carbines purchased by the government was from the 5th series, which reached a total production of approximately 43,000. (Photos courtesy Rock Island Auction Co.)

Another 5th Model Burnside Carbine in excellent condition. Part of a Federal Cavalry purchase in 1864 this gun bears full inspectors markings but shows comparatively little wear, a testament to the quality of the Burnside. (Photos courtesy Rock Island Auction Co.)

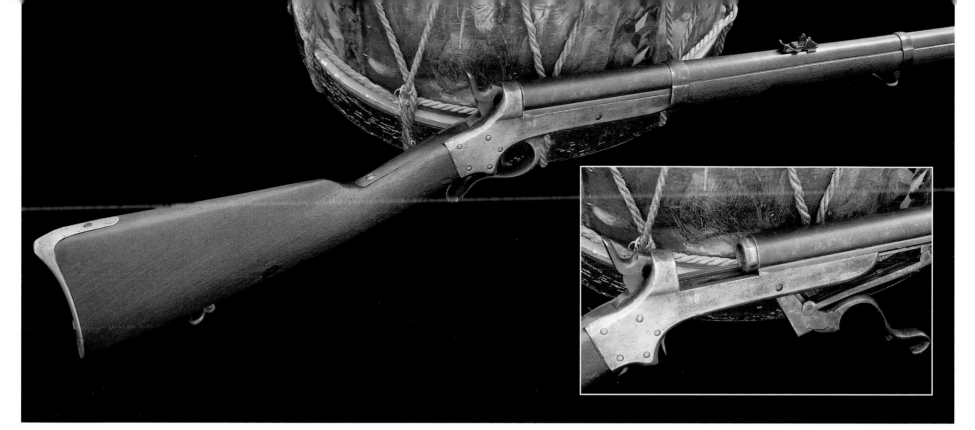

The first cartridge breechloader designed by Christian Sharps, the Sharps & Hankins Army Carbine patented July 9, 1861, was the first model to use a firing pin in the breechblock and the first longarm designed with an integral hammer safety to prevent an accidental discharge. Both the Army and Navy ordered Sharps & Hankins models between 1862 and 1865. Lowering the triggerguard allowed the entire barrel assembly to slide forward on the receiver for ease of loading and spent cartridge extraction. (Mike Clark/Collectors Firearms Collection)

The Hankins part of the name comes from one of Sharp's business partners William C. Hankins, who was also his superintendent of the works. When he became a full partner in 1863 the firm of Sharps & Hankins was established. The new rifle's operation differed from other breech loading models designed by Christian Sharps in that when the action lever was lowered the entire breech and barrel slid forward in unit, allowing the .52-56 caliber rimfire Sharps & Hankins cartridge to be easily chambered. Sharps had used a similar sliding breech design for his earlier four-barrel Pepperbox Derringer, which allowed the entire barrel assembly to slide forward on the frame exposing the chambers for quick loading and unloading.

The simple but efficient Sharps & Hankins carbine remains somewhat lost in the shadows cast by the vastly more successful and appealing Sharps Rifle Mfg. Co., and C. Sharps & Co. breech loading rifles and carbines, but the U.S. government managed to procure 1,468 Sharps & Hankins carbines for the Army and 6,336 for the Navy during the course of the Civil War.[5]

While best remembered for his innovative top break single and double action revolvers, Eben T. Starr also left his mark on the world of rifle making with an equally innovative breech loading carbine that he patented in September 1858. The Starr was a rather elegant looking rifle, though not as smooth of line as the Sharps. It was nevertheless a quality firearm at a time when the Union needed everything it could get. During the Civil War the Ordnance Department ordered 20,000 Starr carbines chambered in .54 caliber percussion and fitted with 21-inch barrels. Similar to other breech loading arms of the period, lowering the triggerguard allowed the split breechblock to swing down (much like a Sharps) exposing the chamber which could be loaded with a standard paper or linen cartridge. When the triggerguard was raised it closed the breech, and the action was ready to be fitted with a percussion cap. All that remained was to cock the hammer, take aim and fire.

By January of 1865 Starr had developed a rimfire cartridge version of the carbine chambered for the .56 caliber Spencer round and the Ordnance Department placed an order for 3,000 to be delivered on or before the 10th of April 1865. Another contract for 2,000 additional guns came in April on the heels of Starr's fulfillment of the first order. That, unfortunately was the last government contract Starr received for carbines or revolvers. With the war over and no further government requests, Starr was unable to compete with larger manufacturers like Winchester, Sharps, and Colt. After giving it a

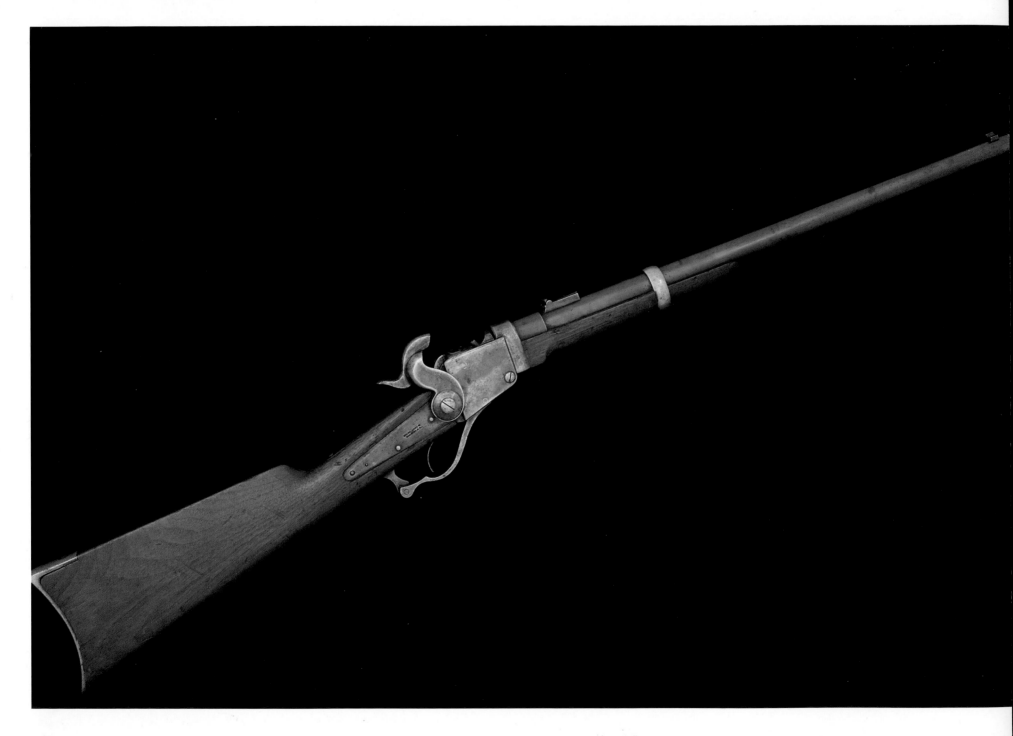

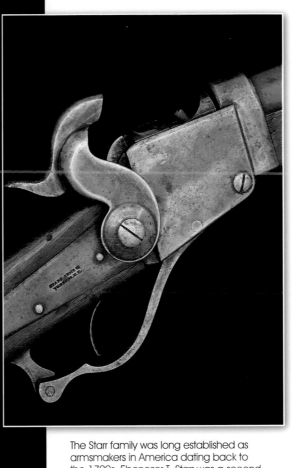

good go for two more years, Starr closed the doors to its Yonkers, New York, factory in 1867 bringing an end to one of the 19th century's most innovative arms makers.

While the Starr breech loading carbines may appear to be little more than a footnote in Civil War arms history, the company became the fifth largest supplier of carbines to the Union, and the third largest supplier of .44 caliber single action revolvers between 1861 and 1865.

The government's inventory of breech loading designs included some unusual rifles and carbines that took distinctive if not perplexing approaches to loading and firing. The most unusual was certainly the Jenks Navy Rifle. As noted by author John D. McAulay in his book *Civil War Breech Loading Rifles*, the Jenks had the distinction of being the only "mule-ear" side hammer rifle and carbine to be used by the Union. It was also the only one to have the percussion nipple mounted to the side of the lock plate rather than above. The Jenks design was originally a flintlock patented by inventor William Jenks in 1838.

After a military Board of Officers found the breech loading flintlock unimpressive in 1839, Jenks went ahead regardless and had them tooled up for manufacture by the Chicopee Falls Co. in Massachusetts. Only 100 were sold to the government, nearly all of which found disfavor with the military and were sent to storage at the Springfield Armory. A quantity of these were converted at Springfield to a percussion lock by then chief of the armory Major James Ripley, later to become Chief of the Ordnance Department during the Civil War.

The Starr family was long established as armsmakers in America dating back to the 1790s. Ebenezer T. Starr was a second generation armsmaker when he received his first patent in 1856 for a double action percussion revolver, a gun that was to become one of the most innovative sidearms of the Civil War. Two years later he patented a breech loading carbine, which was also adopted by the U.S. military during the war. The Starr carbine was similar in operation to the Sharps with the triggerguard used to work the action. The triggerguard was locked into place by a hooked catch at the back. When lowered and pushed forward it allowed the split breechblock to swing down and backward to inset a paper or linen cartridge. Raising the triggerguard to its locked position closed the breech. A standard percussion cap was seated and the hammer was cocked making the gun ready. (Mike Clark/Collectors Firearms Collection)

The Starr carbine was chambered in .54 caliber percussion. Barrel length was 21 inches. Sturdy construction and easy operation made the Starr the fifth most issued carbine carried by Federal troops. The Starr Arms Co. of Yonkers, New York, was established in 1862 to manufacture the guns with total production for the carbine exceeding 20,000 by 1865. (Photo courtesy Rock Island Auction Co.)

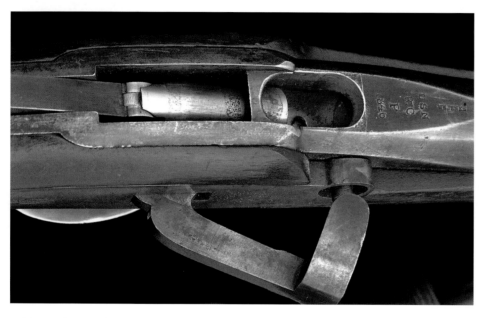

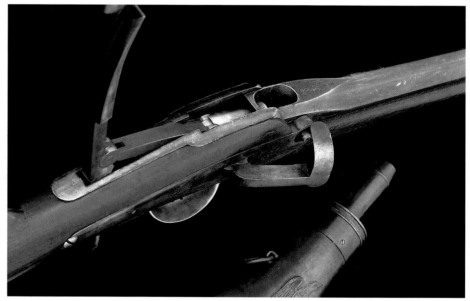

The Jenks was designed to load at the breech by pulling up on a lever inside the tang, which in turn slid the breech cover back allowing the insertion of a round ball and powder charge. The lever was then pushed down to close the breech behind the powder and ball. It is probable that William Jenks had been inspired by one of the first breech loading arms built, the British Fergusson rifle, which allowed loading at the breech by turning the triggerguard one revolution counter clockwise to lower a breech plug and allow the ball and powder charge to be inserted into the barrel. The lever was then turned clockwise to close the breech. Used by British troops during the Revolutionary War, the Fergusson could be loaded and fired three times faster than a muzzleloader. His other inspiration was no doubt the first Hall flintlock breechloaders designed by John Hall, assistant

armorer at the Harpers Ferry Arsenal. His 1811 patent for the Hall Rifle became the first breech loading longarm issued to the U.S. military c.1824-1828. The Hall flintlocks were succeeded by the Hall percussion lock in 1841, which became the government's first breech loading percussion rifle. They remained in use until 1862.

After William Jenks altered his original flintlock design to the "mule-ear" side hammer percussion lock, his rifles immediately had greater appeal, and in 1841 he was commissioned to have built 1,500 rifles with bayonets, and carbine versions in .54 caliber percussion for the U.S Navy. The rifles were to have 36-inch barrels and the carbines 24-inch barrels. Not having his own manufacturing facilities, Jenks had the guns built by the Ames Manufacturing Co. in Massachusetts. The government's foremost manufacturer of

Singularly distinctive, no other carbine of the Civil War era could be mistaken for a Jenks Navy. The Jenks breechloader was opened by raising a lever within the tang, which in turn slid the breech cover back allowing the insertion of a round ball and powder charge. The lever was then pushed down to close the breech behind the powder and ball. The most unusual feature, however, was the "mule-ear" side hammer which was pulled away from the lock plate to cock the action and allow a cap to be placed on the percussion nipple.

The Jenks carbine was also manufactured under contract by E. Remington & Sons in 1847-48 and fitted with a Maynard tape primer, which made the "mule-ear" design more practical as one did not have to maneuver a percussion cap around the set hammer. Only around 1,000 were produced. (Photo courtesy Rock Island Auction Co.)

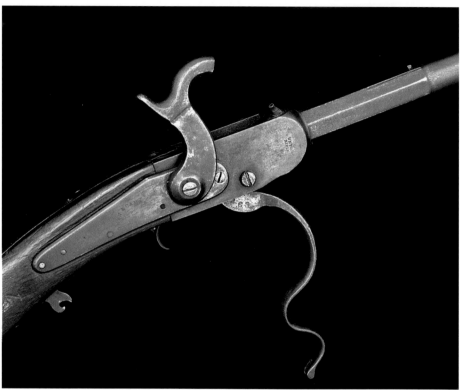

swords, Ames took over the Chicopee Falls Co. in order to build the guns for the Jenks Navy contract. The Jenks were stamped N.P. AMES/SPRINGFIELD/MASS, and had Wm JENKS stamped at the rear of the barrel. Ames manufactured another 4,200 Jenks carbines for the Navy by 1845. The Jenks "mule-ear" carbines and rifles have the distinction of being only the second breech loader to be adopted by the United States,[7] and certainly became the inspiration for other breech loading designs that followed in the 1850s and 1860s.

When the Civil War began the Jenks carbines and rifles were pressed into service by the Union, but like many other prewar arms, most were replaced by more modern rifles and carbines. A quantity of Jenks Navy carbines were captured by the Confederates early in the war and the guns were issued to the 2nd Virginia Cavalry Battalion,[6] which was somewhat ironic, as William Jenks was a Southerner by birth.

The simplest breech loading rifle of the war, both in design and use, was the Cosmopolitan or Gwyn & Campbell carbine. Built by the Cosmopolitan Arms Co. of Ohio, owned by Edward Gwyn and A. C. Campbell, the gun was designed by Henry Gross, who had received his patent on August 30, 1859. A second patent showing improvements was issued to Gwyn & Campbell on October 21, 1862, following an initial order from the Ordnance Department for 1,140 Cosmopolitan carbines in December of 1861. The .52 caliber models were austere in their design with 19-inch octagonal to round barrels and no forearm. Lowering the triggerguard opened the breech for loading of a paper or linen cartridge. Returning the lever closed the breech and the gun was ready to be capped and fired.

The guns proved durable ("fully satisfactory") and easy to work, thus additional orders were issued by the Ordnance Department, and by the end of the Civil War a total of 9,342 Cosmopolitan (and Type I and Type II Gwyn & Campbell) carbines had been delivered, with the final shipment sent on December 31, 1864.

Another breechloader that wasn't exactly a beauty to behold but proved to be one of the most accurate carbines of the war was the Maynard, designed by Dr. Edward Maynard, inventor of the Maynard tape self primer. The Maynard self priming device, patented in

1845, was adopted by the U.S. government on a wide variety of arms throughout the early 1850s and was still in use on guns produced through 1861.

The Maynard carbine was designed and patented in 1851 and a second patent was issued in December 1859. After passing Navy and Army test trials the Maynard carbine was adopted by the U.S. with the first deliveries in June 1864. Total orders through the end of the war amounted to 20,002.[8] Maynard carbines for U.S. government contracts were produced by the Massachusetts Arms Co.

Early style Maynard rifles and carbines (manufactured through 1859) and fitted with Dr. Maynard's self priming device were already in use by Southern States militias prior to

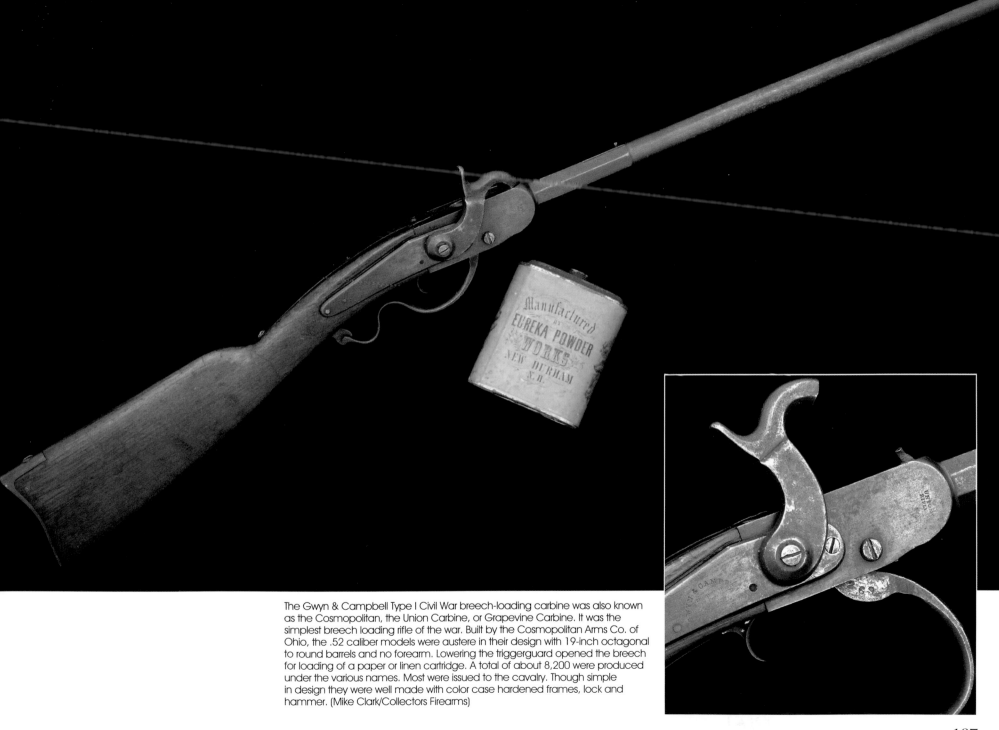

The Gwyn & Campbell Type I Civil War breech-loading carbine was also known as the Cosmopolitan, the Union Carbine, or Grapevine Carbine. It was the simplest breech loading rifle of the war. Built by the Cosmopolitan Arms Co. of Ohio, the .52 caliber models were austere in their design with 19-inch octagonal to round barrels and no forearm. Lowering the triggerguard opened the breech for loading of a paper or linen cartridge. A total of about 8,200 were produced under the various names. Most were issued to the cavalry. Though simple in design they were well made with color case hardened frames, lock and hammer. (Mike Clark/Collectors Firearms)

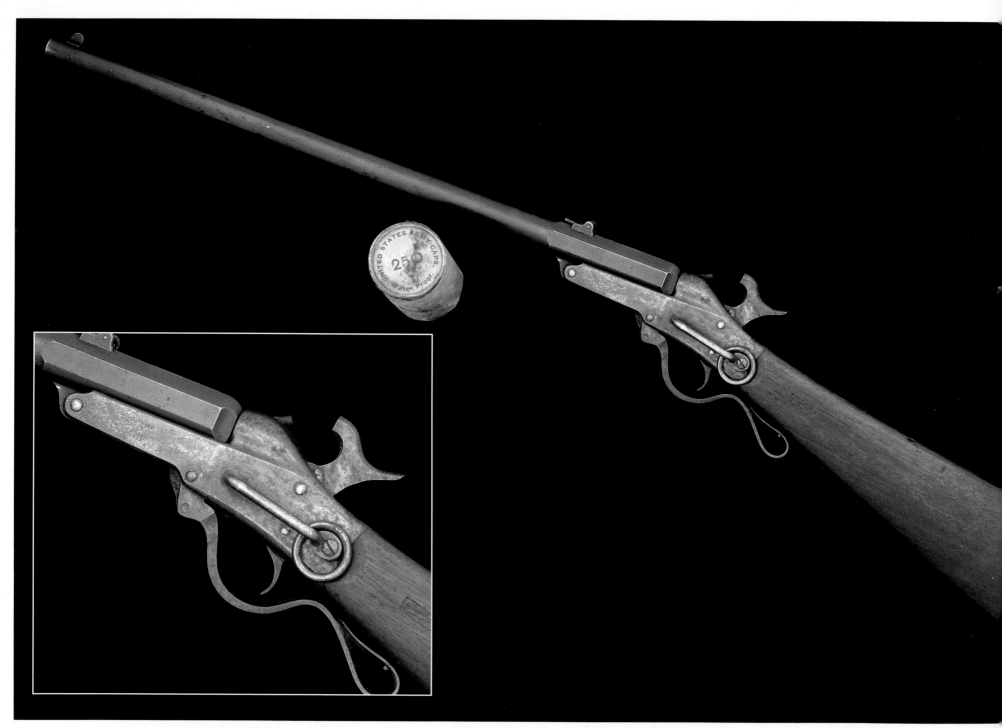

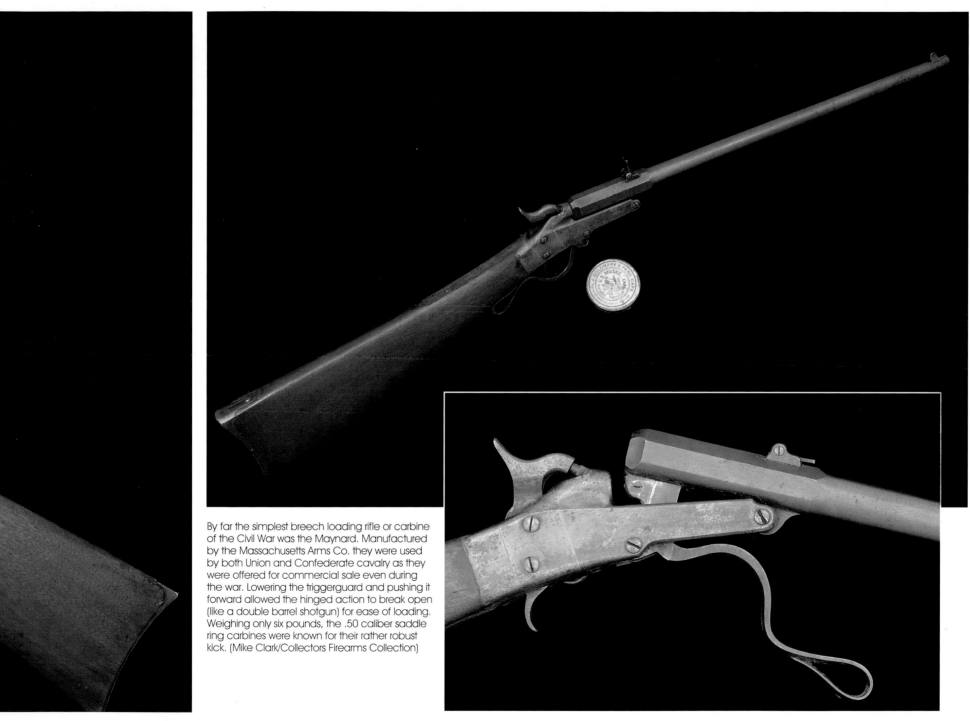

By far the simplest breech loading rifle or carbine of the Civil War was the Maynard. Manufactured by the Massachusetts Arms Co. they were used by both Union and Confederate cavalry as they were offered for commercial sale even during the war. Lowering the triggerguard and pushing it forward allowed the hinged action to break open (like a double barrel shotgun) for ease of loading. Weighing only six pounds, the .50 caliber saddle ring carbines were known for their rather robust kick. (Mike Clark/Collectors Firearms Collection)

A Massachusetts Arms Co. marked Maynard carbine in excellent condition shows the inherent quality of this rather austere breechloader. This example has nearly 96 percent of its original blue finish and 90 percent of the original case colors in the frame. (Photo courtesy Rock Island Auction Co.)

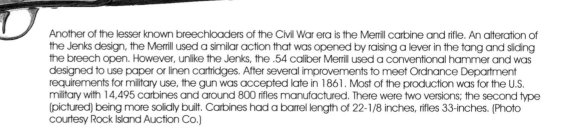

Another of the lesser known breechloaders of the Civil War era is the Merrill carbine and rifle. An alteration of the Jenks design, the Merrill used a similar action that was opened by raising a lever in the tang and sliding the breech open. However, unlike the Jenks, the .54 caliber Merrill used a conventional hammer and was designed to use paper or linen cartridges. After several improvements to meet Ordnance Department requirements for military use, the gun was accepted late in 1861. Most of the production was for the U.S. military with 14,495 carbines and around 800 rifles manufactured. There were two versions; the second type (pictured) being more solidly built. Carbines had a barrel length of 22-1/8 inches, rifles 33-inches. (Photo courtesy Rock Island Auction Co.)

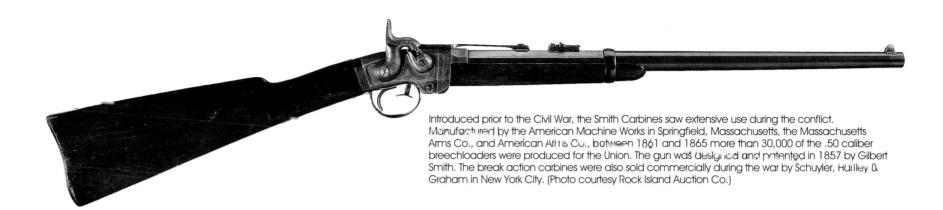

Introduced prior to the Civil War, the Smith Carbines saw extensive use during the conflict. Manufactured by the American Machine Works in Springfield, Massachusetts, the Massachusetts Arms Co., and American Arms Co., between 1861 and 1865 more than 30,000 of the .50 caliber breechloaders were produced for the Union. The gun was designed and patented in 1857 by Gilbert Smith. The break action carbines were also sold commercially during the war by Schuyler, Hartley & Graham in New York City. (Photo courtesy Rock Island Auction Co.)

the Civil War, to the extent that after 1861 the Maynard was listed as a standard issue rifle and carbine in Confederate Ordnance Manuals.[9] Additional guns were also taken by Confederate forces from arsenal storage at the start of the war, thus the Maynard was carried by both Union and Confederate cavalry throughout the conflict. The notable difference is that models produced under the Ordnance Department contracts from 1863 to 1865 were not equipped with the Maynard self priming device, as it had been judged unreliable by 1860 and its use discontinued in 1861. The early Maynard carbines were manufactured in both .35 and .50 caliber but 1863 contract models for the Union were only chambered in .50 caliber.

Of all the longarms used during the Civil War, the Maynard was the simplest breechloader to operate of any rifle or carbine. Lowering the triggerguard and pushing it forward allowed the entire barrel assembly to pivot down (like a side-by-side shotgun) exposing the chamber for easy extraction of a spent shell and reloading. The

Maynard cartridge was similar to the Burnside in that it had a small hole in its base and required the spark from a percussion cap to ignite the powder charge. Fitted with 20-inch octagonal to round barrels, the .50 caliber carbines were known for their hefty recoil because the guns only weighed six pounds.

The design was so successful that the Maynard remained in use long after the Civil War and with the addition of a centerfire cartridge model, continued to be manufactured until 1890.

The list of longarms used by the Union from 1861 to 1865 represents most of the major and secondary armsmakers in the Northern States, and includes such names as Gallager, Merrill, Joslyn, James Warner (who was Superintendent of the Springfield Arms Co.), Ballard, Gibbs, Lindner and Frank Wesson. In the end, every American armsmaker played a role in the War Between the States, and like the ideology of the Antebellum South, many failed to survive the conflict.

[1] Advertisement reproduced in *William B. Edward's Civil War Guns*, page 160.

[2] *Winchester An American Legend* by R. L. Wilson, 1991 Random House.

[3] *American Rifle* by Alexander Rose, Bantam Dell (A Division of Random House) 2008, page 135.

[4] Burnside production figures estimated from orders as published in *Carbines of the Civil War* by John D. McAulay, 1981, Pioneer Press.

[5] *Civil War Breech Loading Rifles – A survey of the innovative Infantry arms of the American Civil War*, by John D. McAulay, 1987, Andrew Mowbray Inc. Publishers.

[6] ibid

[7] ibid

[8] ibid

[9] *Flayderman's Guide to Antique American Firearms* by Norm Flayderman

[10] *Civil War Guns by William B. Edwards*, 962 The Stackpole Co.

[11] ibid

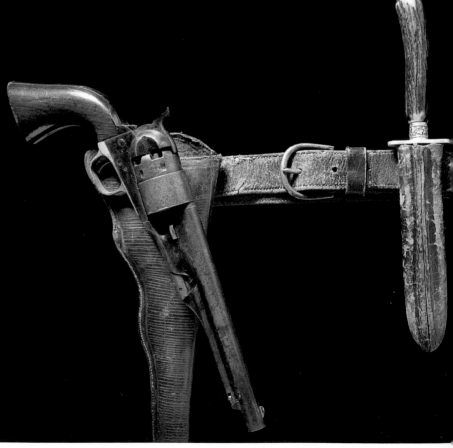

Chapter Four

Confederate Arms

Building an arsenal from church bells and anvils

It came as no surprise to Confederate President Jefferson Davis, the former U.S. Secretary of War, that with Colt's entire production allotted to the Union Army after General Beauregard's attack on Fort Sumter, and with the majority of U.S armsmakers situated in the North, that the South would have little choice but to build its own guns or import them from abroad.

In 1861 after North Carolina became the 11th state to join the Confederacy in May, the South was already engaged in the task of sizing up its armaments. As noted earlier, all of the revolvers, pistols and longarms in use by the Union were divided among the states and Southern states had a proportionate number of comparable arms to the North. Nearly all, however, were of older designs. As such, most Confederate officers and soldiers were carrying Colt 1851 Navy and early c.1858 Remington Army and Navy revolvers, as well as privately owned handguns that many Southerners already had. This is not to say that a considerable number of new Colt's 1860 Army revolvers weren't already in Southern hands by early 1861, Colt himself having shipped 500 just days after the attack upon Fort Sumter, but it was incumbent upon the Confederacy to acquire as many new arms as possibly by whatever means. Adding the new .44 caliber Colt Model 1860 Army to the Confederate arsenal meant capturing Union shipments and collecting guns from slain Federal troops in combat.

The Southern States secession from the Union had not been a simple task, as there were many "slave states" still in the North that had chosen to stand by President Lincoln and the federal government after the attack on Fort Sumter in April. Prior to Sumter, only seven Southern states had actually filed articles of secession; South Carolina on December 20, 1860, Mississippi on January 9th 1861, Florida on the 10th, followed by Alabama the next day, Georgia on the 19th, Louisiana on the 26th, and Texas on the 1st of February.

A Colt's Model 1860 Army was one of the more prized possessions of Confederate troops as all but a few thousand were in the hands of Federal soldiers by early 1861. Colt's had shipped 500 to the South within days of the attack on Fort Sumter, and others had been purchased by Confederate States early in 1861. The majority of 1860 Army models carried by Southerners, however, were captured guns. (Photos courtesy Rock Island Auction Co., Greg Martin Auction Co., and author)

President Lincoln called for troops to quell what was still regarded as a rebellion in April of 1861 following the Confederate assault on the Federal forts in Charleston Harbor. Faced with having to take up arms against fellow Southerners, the State of Virginia filed articles of secession on April 17th only three days after the surrender of Fort Sumter. With Robert E. Lee commanding the Army of Northern Virginia, the State's resolve was manifest, though it took the Virginia legislature until May 23rd to ratify the state's secession. The decision was hard fought as Virginia had been among the 13 Colonies which had fought for the nation's independence in 1776, and Robert E. Lee's father, "Light-Horse Henry Lee" (Henry Lee III) had been a hero of the Revolution. (Illustration Library of Congress)

Using the 1851 Navy as a model Griswold and Gunnison produced around 3,700 revolvers for the Confederacy between 1862 and 1864. A rough copy of the Colt, none of the fine attention to detail that had been the hallmark of the Hartford percussion pistols was evident in the hastily manufactured Griswold and Gunnison .36 caliber revolvers. Though "based" on the Colt Navy revolver with a 7-1/2 inch barrel, the Griswold and Gunnison used a brass frame, rather than steel, an octagonal to round barrel, and featured a rounded trigger guard. (Photos courtesy Rock Island Auction Co.)

Following South Carolina's assault on the Federal forts in Charleston Harbor, President Lincoln called for troops to quell what was still regarded as a rebellion, but faced with taking up arms against fellow Southerners, Virginia filed articles of secession on April 17th only three days after the surrender of Fort Sumter, and the beginning of the Civil War. It took the Virginia legislature until May 23rd to ratify the state's secession. Arkansas followed on May 6th, Tennessee the following day (though the state legislature did not ratify secession until June 8), and North Carolina became the last state to formally withdraw from the Union on May 20th, 1861.

These decisions were hard fought in parts of the South, as Virginia, North and South Carolina, and Georgia had been among the 13 Colonies which had fought for the nation's independence in 1776. Further complicating the division between the Union and Confederacy were Kentucky and Missouri, which had declared themselves neural on the issues of slavery and secession. Though Kentucky eventually took up arms in defense of the North, Missouri was always a state divided by slavery, even with its legislature's loyalty to the Union. Yet, so questionable were their allegiances to the Union, that the South regarded Kentucky and Missouri as the disputed 12th and 13th Confederate states.

Volunteers

While the Southern States had their own militias along with former Federal troops, the odds were simply not in the South's favor. The Confederacy was comprised of 11 mostly agricultural states, many of which were approachable from the sea (either by the Gulf of Mexico or along the Atlantic coast) up against a superior force better than twice its number. One could argue the 13 Colonies had stood against an entire nation and prevailed, but this was the heart of those very same Colonies taking up arms and turning them on themselves. The greater issue in 1861 was that there simply were not enough arms or soldiers in the South to fight a war.

In 1862 the government of Jefferson Davis, and the Confederate States of America, appealed to the patriotism of anyone who could contribute in the production of guns. Among a handful that came to the aid of the Confederacy was Samuel Griswold, owner

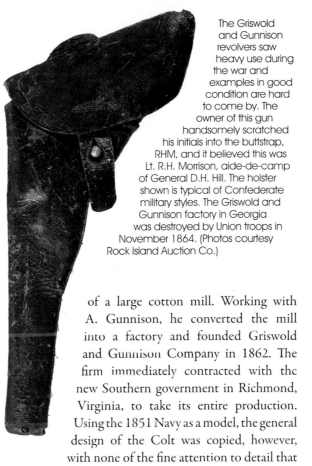

of a large cotton mill. Working with A. Gunnison, he converted the mill into a factory and founded Griswold and Gunnison Company in 1862. The firm immediately contracted with the new Southern government in Richmond, Virginia, to take its entire production. Using the 1851 Navy as a model, the general design of the Colt was copied, however, with none of the fine attention to detail that had been the hallmark of the Hartford percussion pistols. The Griswold and Gunnison frame was made of brass rather than steel, and featured a round trigger guard, and octagonal to round barrel.

Griswold and Gunnison, like many arms makers during the war, was plagued with material shortages and appealed for help. The Confederacy asked that churches donate their steeple bells for arsenal purposes. The bells allowed the company and other gunmakers to continue production in the early years of the war.

In the winter of 1861-62, J.H. Dance and Brothers, located east of Columbia (first capital of Texas), and 10 miles away from Angleton, Texas, also started production of revolvers. The prototype was presented on April 22,

1862 and a few months later the .44 caliber Dance was in production. Again the design was based on the Colt 1851 Navy, but Dance further simplified the revolver by eliminating the recoil shield, thus creating a flat sided frame. The Navy's octagonal barrel was also replaced by a simpler half round half octagonal design similar to that of the 1848 Colt Dragoon. Following the same lines, the Dance also used a square back trigger guard. The guns were produced in both .44 and .36 caliber models, the .44 with an 8-inch barrel length, and the .36 with a 7-3/8 inch barrel.

Among the handful of revolvers produced in the South during the war, the Dance was considered one of the finest arms of the period. The guns remained popular following the war, and famous owners included Geronimo (at least he was pictured with one), and infamous highwayman Bill Longley, who is said to have killed his first man with an 1862 Dance.

The company's location on the Gulf Coast of Texas put it within range of Union gunboats and in 1863 the factory was burned by the federals after the battle of Velasco, which enabled the Union gunboats to go up the Brazos River to Columbia. Approximately 500 guns were produced before the factory was razed. Dance was relocated to Anderson, Texas, but gun making was not resumed after 1863.[1]

Another of the more unusual looking Southern revolvers was the 1862 Spiller & Burr. A true hybrid design, the Spiller & Burr was again a soup kitchen recipe for making a handgun combining Whitney and Remington-style solid frames with a Colt mechanism. The gun was designed by Edward Spiller, nephew of James Henry Burton, lieutenant colonel of the Army, and David Burr, a respected Richmond, Virginia, industrial engineer. Together they formed Spiller & Burr, receiving a contact to produce 15,000 revolvers in a period of two and one half years. In 1862 a production facility was set up in a government-owned factory in Atlanta, but manufacturing the guns proved to be more difficult than either Messrs. Spiller or Burr expected.

From the very start, the company fell well behind schedule, essentially violating the terms of their contract. The entire arrangement was founded on a premise that the money advanced by the Confederacy to establish operations would be earned back by deducting 20 percent of the billed cost of each gun delivered. It was estimated that the money advanced to build the factory and produce the guns would be thusly recouped within two years based on original orders for 15,000 "Navy size" (.36 caliber) guns at a price of $30 each for the first 5,000, $27 each for the second, and $25 apiece for the final 5,000. There was continued negotiations, multiple contracts, changes in price, and very little actually accomplished in the manufacturing of guns throughout 1863. By then the course of the war had changed, the Confederacy had suffered a great setback at Gettysburg and Vicksburg, and in desperation, on January 7, 1864, the Confederate government purchased the entire Spiller & Burr company, patents, and tooling for $125,000 and moved production to Macon, Georgia, for the duration of the war. The guns were also known as the "Whitney" model because of their similarity to the 2nd Model revolvers made by Eli Whitney, Jr. at the Whitneyville armory in Connecticut.

In the winter of 1861-62, J.H. Dance and Brothers, located east of Columbia (first capital of Texas) began manufacturing .36 and .44 caliber revolvers. The prototype was presented on April 22, 1862 and a few months later the .44 caliber Dance was in production. The design was again based on the Colt 1851 Navy, but Dance used a simpler half round half octagonal barrel design similar to that of the earlier Colt Dragoons. The company further simplified the design on later .36 and .44 caliber models by eliminating the recoil shield from the frame, thus requiring less work and material. The down side was without a recoil shield the percussion nipples were more exposed, as was the shooter's hand to back flash. The Dance was a ruggedly built gun and many examples still exist. This is one of the few surviving early guns with a recoil shield. The holster appears to be original to the gun. The history of the Dance pictured was authenticated by Gary Wiggins, researcher of the Dance factory and author of the book *Dance & Brothers Texas Gunmakers of the Confederacy.* (Photos courtesy Rock Island Auction Co.)

196

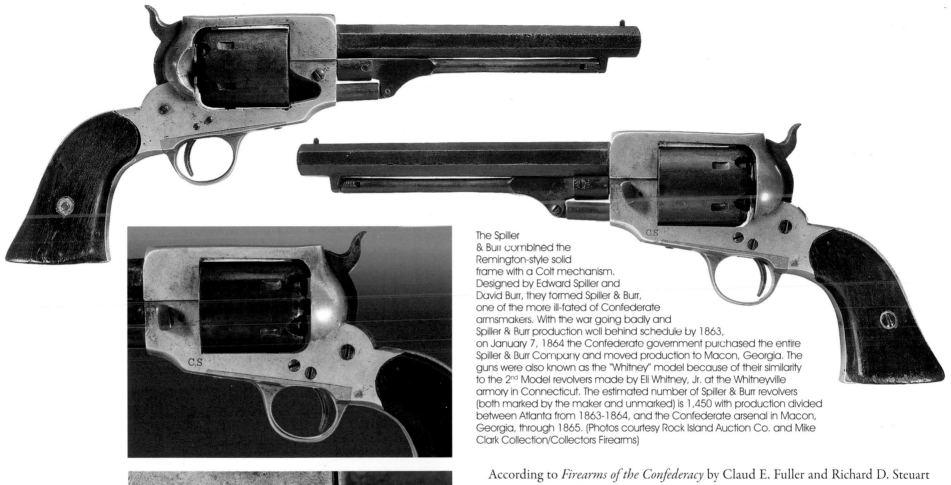

The Spiller & Burr combined the Remington-style solid frame with a Colt mechanism. Designed by Edward Spiller and David Burr, they formed Spiller & Burr, one of the more ill-fated of Confederate armsmakers. With the war going badly and Spiller & Burr production well behind schedule by 1863, on January 7, 1864 the Confederate government purchased the entire Spiller & Burr Company and moved production to Macon, Georgia. The guns were also known as the "Whitney" model because of their similarity to the 2nd Model revolvers made by Eli Whitney, Jr. at the Whitneyville armory in Connecticut. The estimated number of Spiller & Burr revolvers (both marked by the maker and unmarked) is 1,450 with production divided between Atlanta from 1863-1864, and the Confederate arsenal in Macon, Georgia, through 1865. (Photos courtesy Rock Island Auction Co. and Mike Clark Collection/Collectors Firearms)

According to *Firearms of the Confederacy* by Claud E. Fuller and Richard D. Steuart and notations in *Flayderman's Guide to Antique American Arms* there were minor variations of the Spiller & Burr revolvers but the number of guns manufactured never even approached the total due in the first delivery order from 1863. The estimated number of Spiller & Burr revolvers (both marked by the maker and unmarked) is 1,450 with production divided between Atlanta from 1863-1864, and the Confederate arsenal in Macon, Georgia, through 1865.

There were hundreds of individual revolvers of varying designs manufactured in the South during the war and it is literally "hundreds" because many small companies never managed to make more than a couple of hundred guns before ending production. Among the smaller but memorable makes were Colt 1851 Navy style revolvers made by the Augusta Machine Works in Augusta, Georgia, and the Columbus Fire Arms Mfg. Co. in Columbus, Georgia which built fewer than 100 guns. A handful of other

The Colt's Model 1851 Navy was one of the most commonly carried handguns of the Confederacy because so many were already in circulation before the war. Engraved examples were often carried in the war despite their greater value. This beautiful 1851 from the Mike Clark collection at Collectors Firearms in Houston, Texas, is shown atop the styles of Confederate currency that was probably used to purchase it for the war effort.

Southern makes contributed fewer than 100 guns apiece, again mostly copied from the Colt's 1851 Navy design which was still the most prevalent revolver in use by the South. Leech and Rigdon, with manufacturing in Columbus, Mississippi and Greensboro, Georgia, added another 1,500 revolvers in .36 caliber percussion to the Confederate effort between 1863 and 1864. Afterward, another 1,000 models were produced by Rigdon, Ansley & Co. in Augusta, Georgia, before General William T. Sherman and the Union Army's historic March to the

Sea in November and December of 1864, which left everything from Atlanta to the Savannah coastline under Federal control. Thus was the end of the Leech and Rigdon revolver.

Not every Confederate made handgun looked like an 1851 Navy, Remington or Whitney Navy & Eagle Co. revolver, the Leech and Rigdon models resembled scaled down .36 caliber versions of the massive .44 caliber Colt 3rd Model Dragoon with octagonal to round barrel, and round triggerguard. Of all the various gunmakers who answered the South's call to arms, Rigdon and his associates, wrote Civil War arms historian William B. Edwards, "...were probably the best-manufactured mass-production revolvers of the South." These were sturdy, well crafted firearms, but like most produced in the South too few in numbers.

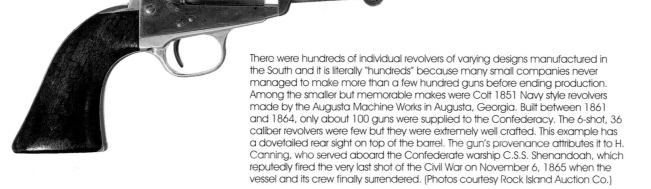

There were hundreds of individual revolvers of varying designs manufactured in the South and it is literally "hundreds" because many small companies never managed to make more than a few hundred guns before ending production. Among the smaller but memorable makes were Colt 1851 Navy style revolvers made by the Augusta Machine Works in Augusta, Georgia. Built between 1861 and 1864, only about 100 guns were supplied to the Confederacy. The 6-shot, 36 caliber revolvers were few but they were extremely well crafted. This example has a dovetailed rear sight on top of the barrel. The gun's provenance attributes it to H. Canning, who served aboard the Confederate warship C.S.S. Shenandoah, which reputedly fired the very last shot of the Civil War on November 6, 1865 when the vessel and its crew finally surrendered. (Photos courtesy Rock Island Auction Co.)

There was one truly original Southern revolver produced during the Civil War, a gun that has become synonymous with the Confederacy, the LeMat. It is the only percussion revolver of the mid 19th century that rivaled the 1847 Walker Colt for sheer audacity of size and power.

The LeMat was a unique firearm, bold in its design, and more so in its presentation, a 9-shot .42 caliber revolver with a secondary lower "shotgun" barrel chambered for a grapeshot paper cartridge – the *coup de grace*. This masterpiece of firearms design was the work of a medical doctor, Jean Alexandre Francois LeMat who, at age 22, having completed his medical training and residency as a surgeon and assistant medical officer at the military hospital in Bordeaux, moved to the United States in 1843 to further his study of medicine. After establishing

Another exceptional engraved Colt old enough to have been used in the War Between the States, an elegant 5-shot .31 caliber Colt's Model 1849 with 4-inch barrel. In addition to engraving, the gun was also refitted with a new dovetailed German silver blade-type front sight replacing the original brass bead used by Colt's on that model. (Mike Clark Collection/Collectors Firearms)

After Leech and Rigdon production ended in 1864, another 1,000 similar models were produced by Rigdon, Ansley & Co. in Augusta, Georgia. Production might have been more but the Augusta works were lost during General William Tecumseh Sherman's historic March to the Sea in November and December of 1864. The .36 caliber percussion Rigdon, Ansley & Co. revolvers had 7-1/2 inch octagonal to round barrels, 12-stop cylinders (which distinguish them from the Leech and Rigdon revolvers), color casehardened frames, with brass triggerguards and grip straps. The top barrel flats were stamped C.S.A. Production ceased in January 1865. (Photos courtesy Rock Island Auction Co.)

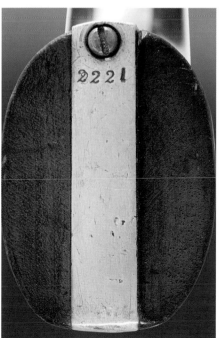

Not every Confederate made handgun looked like an 1851 Navy, Remington or Whitney Navy & Eagle Co. revolver, the Leech and Rigdon models resembled scaled down .36 caliber versions of the massive .44 caliber Colt 3rd Model Dragoon with octagonal to round barrel, and round triggerguard. Of all the various gunmakers who answered the South's call to arms, Rigdon and his associates, wrote Civil War arms historian William B. Edwards, "…were probably the best-manufactured mass-production revolvers of the South." These were sturdy, well crafted firearms, but like most produced in the South too few in numbers.

a practice in New Orleans, in 1849 he married Justine Sophie LePretre, the cousin of U.S. Army Major Pierre-Gustave Toutant Beauregard. The very same Beauregard would lead the bombardment of Fort Sumter in Charleston Harbor in 1861.

Though a practicing physician, LeMat was also an avid inventor, and his ideas intrigued Beauregard, who not only encouraged but often financed some of LeMat's most daring ideas in fields as diverse as medicine, navigation, and firearms. Among young Dr. LeMat's inventions was the tracheal speculum, an instrument for spreading and opening the trachea (the airway to the lungs) during surgery; an interesting contrast to his patent for rifling cannon barrels and the innovative revolver he developed with Beauregard's assistance in 1856. Three years later the very first examples of the LeMat Grapeshot revolver were

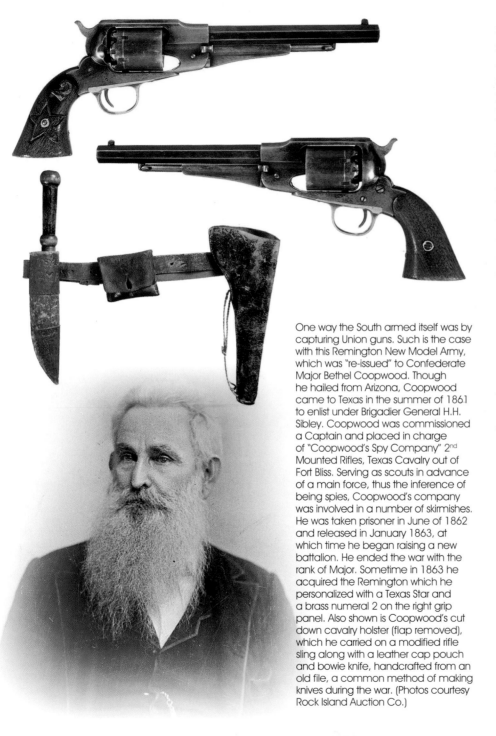

One way the South armed itself was by capturing Union guns. Such is the case with this Remington New Model Army, which was "re-issued" to Confederate Major Bethel Coopwood. Though he hailed from Arizona, Coopwood came to Texas in the summer of 1861 to enlist under Brigadier General H.H. Sibley. Coopwood was commissioned a Captain and placed in charge of "Coopwood's Spy Company" 2nd Mounted Rifles, Texas Cavalry out of Fort Bliss. Serving as scouts in advance of a main force, thus the inference of being spies, Coopwood's company was involved in a number of skirmishes. He was taken prisoner in June of 1862 and released in January 1863, at which time he began raising a new battalion. He ended the war with the rank of Major. Sometime in 1863 he acquired the Remington which he personalized with a Texas Star and a brass numeral 2 on the right grip panel. Also shown is Coopwood's cut down cavalry holster (flap removed), which he carried on a modified rifle sling along with a leather cap pouch and bowie knife, handcrafted from an old file, a common method of making knives during the war. (Photos courtesy Rock Island Auction Co.)

manufactured in Philadelphia, Pennsylvania, by gunmaker John H. Krider. The original invoice for the prototype revolver, dated Philadelphia, Oct 24, 1859 in the amount of $208.80 can be found at the University of Louisiana. Though designed and prototyped in America, and initially represented to the U.S. military for evaluation by Major Beauregard, events of the year to come would lead to the LeMat being manufactured in Europe as a gun intended to support the Confederate States of America after 1861.

Having seen the earliest examples of the "grapeshot" revolver the Governor of Louisiana was so impressed with LeMat that he commissioned him a colonel of the State Militia and his aide-de-camp. With the expectation that orders for his new revolver would be forthcoming in July of 1860 the freshly anointed Col. LeMat went into partnership with Charles Frederic Girard, former Assistant Secretary at the Smithsonian Institution. Like LeMat, Girard had also immigrated to the United States from France and was himself a firearms designer having received a French patent in 1858 for a breech-loading rifle. After the Civil War began Girard quietly left the country and returned to France as LeMat's European agent, establishing Girard & Cie. in Paris in 1862, which would see to the production of the LeMat revolvers in Liège (Belgium), then the biggest arms-making center in the world. LeMats were also made in Paris in 1864, while others were shipped in the white and completed in London, and bear British proof marks. The Paris LeMats consisted principally of those models regarded as the Navy variation with round triggerguard.

Never produced in large quantities, LeMats were shipped to the South by freighters, which often had to run Union blockades at night in order to make deliveries of the arm "formidable" to Southern seaports. And not every freighter made it through, some were captured, others rammed and sunk. Shipments were usually limited to four or five cases of guns destined for the Confederate capital in Richmond, where LeMat spent much of his time. He also made several voyages to France during the war on behalf of the Confederacy to purchase and import rifles (Enfield Rifled-Muskets) and military supplies; once even being intercepted by a Union frigate when en route.

There were two principal LeMat models produced for the Confederate military: the Cavalry or C.S. Army version with spur trigger guard, lever-type barrel release, cross pin barrel selector (primary 9-shot cylinder or lower grapeshot barrel), and swiveling lanyard ring (manufactured in Belgium); and the Navy variation with knurled pin barrel release, spur barrel selector and round triggerguard. There were also a handful of very rare LeMat carbines built late in the war. In addition, some 2000 Baby LeMats with 4-1/2 inch barrels chambered in .32 percussion (and .41 caliber grapeshot barrel) were ordered for the Confederate Navy in 1865. Only around 100 were completed before the war ended. Pinfire LeMats were also built at the Mariette factory in Liège between 1863 and 1865. The guns were modified with new cylinders, loading gates, and hammers to load and fire the French Lefaucheux 12mm pinfire cartridge.[2] Roughly 1,000 were delivered to the Confederacy. The pinfire guns remained in production for only a short time after the Civil War ended.

This is a rare Navy inspected 2nd Model LeMat revolver with 6-5/8 inch octagonal barrel and 4-inch smoothbore grapeshot barrel. This particular gun bears British proofs (note stamps on cylinder) indicating that the French-built revolver was assembled and proofed in England before being shipped to the South. (Photos courtesy Rock Island Auction Co.)

barrel); Second Type First Model with the loading lever moved to left side of the barrel, new finger-type pivoting barrel latch, revised hammer contour, and first use of full octagonal barrels (7-inch); the Second Model with full octagonal barrels (6-7/8 inches), round triggerguard, integral buttcap lanyard hole (knuckle) and a new knurled screw barrel latch; and the final variation, Second Model, Second Type, with revised loading lever design, (a flat arm) thus eliminating the removable grapeshot rammer previously retained inside the hollow round lever.

While the intent had been to build LeMat revolvers for the Confederacy in the thousands, the actual numbers were far less. Of the First Model fewer than 450, the Second Model a little over 2,000 not all of which were delivered to the military. LeMat revolvers were also sold commercially during the war by Richmond arms dealer Kent, Paine & Co., as well as in Europe.[3] Nevertheless the LeMat remains the most prominent sidearm of the Confederacy, carried by many of the South's most famous generals, including Pierre Gustave Toutant Beauregard, the dashing James Ewell Brown "J.E.B." Stuart, officers of the Confederate States Navy, and the famed 18th Georgia Regiment.

After the war LeMat decided to continue his career as an arms and armament designer, returning to France in 1868. Doctor, inventor and later French diplomat, Col. Jean Alexandre Francois LeMat died on July 28, 1895 at age 74. Like Samuel Colt, his name has been immortalized by the guns bearing the *Col. LeMat's Patent* trademark atop their barrels.

The LeMat design did not, however, fade away. By the late 1860s Col. Jean LeMat had perfected a centerfire cartridge model covered by 11 different patents in France, England, Belgium and the United States. The last cartridge LeMats were produced in the early 1880's.

All of the various percussion models produced during the Civil War (and essentially all LeMats, including pinfire and cartridge models) shared the same patented design, which used the grapeshot barrel as the center arbor for the revolver barrel and cylinder. The back of the grapeshot barrel was threaded to secure the revolver barrel, and once treaded together the entire mechanism was locked (to prevent the inadvertent unscrewing of the barrel) by a latch device mounted at the lower front of the frame. This device changed in design numerous times eventually becoming a knurled screw that threaded into the frame once the barrel assembly was aligned.

Despite the innovative design, the guns were not as successful as Dr. LeMat and his associates had hoped. There were numerous manufacturing problems at Liège and issues with military inspectors who found the construction of the guns at times too delicate for the heavy use they would receive, the cylinders prone to go out of time, and the firing mechanisms too easily damaged. Most of these issues were assuaged when manufacturing was moved to Paris.

LeMat revolvers can be divided into early First Type with half octagonal barrel, spur triggerguard, and early loading lever design (mounted on the right side of the

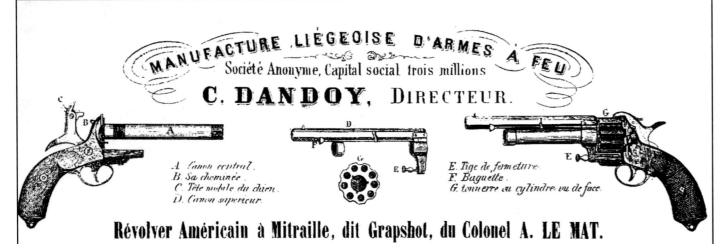

The most famous Confederate sidearm of the Civil War, the LeMat was an imposing 9-shot, .42 caliber revolver with a single grapeshot barrel (approximately 18ga.) underneath. The lower barrel was fired by flipping the firing pin lever into the downward position (shown with cocked gun). Though designed in America the guns were produced in Liège, Paris, and London between 1862 and 1865. (Mike Clark/Collectors Firearms collection, Civil War photos from the Carl Fogarty collection)

Pictured is a cased 2nd Model LeMat and Girard's Patent London marked revolver. Birmingham (England) proof marks are stamped on the upper left barrel flat and the barrel is marked **LEMAT & GIRARD'S PATENT LONDON.** The grapeshot barrel is noted as being 16ga. (16-inch smoothbore). The LeMat grapeshot barrel is generally a 20ga., however, they were also chambered in 18ga. and 28ga. (Photos courtesy Rock Island Auction Co.)

The Issue of Longarms

Every working flintlock and percussion rifle, musket, and shotgun made prior to 1861 was, in one way or another, a longarm of the Confederacy, though most surviving examples are hard to authenticate. At the start of the war the South had the same military issue longarms as the North, only in far smaller numbers. Each state, prior to the war, had its quota of government issued arms for state's militias, thus in 1861 Confederate State militias and former U.S. soldiers in the South were well enough armed, (in 1860 Southern arsenals had received an additional 115,000 assorted military arms, including many of the latest pattern rifled-muskets[4] but the issue that faced newly elected Confederate President Jefferson Davis and his Generals in 1861 was too few trained men, and too few guns to arm 11 Confederate states against a numerically superior force.

It is interesting to note that of 21 arsenals and armories throughout the United States prior to the start of the Civil War, eight were located in Southern States: Harpers Ferry

and North, the latter as late as April 19, 1861.

While the South was unable to manufacture the U.S. Model 1861 rifled-musket or its later iterations of 1863 and 1864, captured arms added considerably to the South's inventory. Wrote authors Claud E. Fuller and Richard D. Steuart in their seminal work *Firearms of the Confederacy*, "It has been estimated on good authority that the Battle of the Wilderness netted 35,000 small arms, Second Manassas 20,000, Harper's Ferry 11,000, Fredericksburg 9,000, Antietam and Shiloh 15,000 and the Tennessee campaign of late 1862 netted them around 27,500 small arms, totaling around 117,000 arms. Chancellorsville and Chickamauga added another 35,000 to this so that by the middle of 1863 there were quite likely more arms of this model [1861 rifled-muskets] in Confederate service than any other kind."

Even with this there was still an imbalance in the number of arms available to the South. By 1862 it had become apparent that the Confederacy would need to build its own guns, and while many small manufacturers answered the call to make revolvers, the manufacturing of longarms was a far greater task.

At the forefront was the C.S. Richmond Armory in Richmond, Virginia. The armory was charged with building new .58 caliber percussion muzzleloaders of the U.S. Model 1855 configuration and later Model 1861 variation, as well as reconditioning and rebuilding older muskets. The tooling for the Richmond Armory had been

taken from the old Harpers Ferry arsenal captured by Virginia militia on April 18, 1861, and modified to produce a more contemporary rifled-musket (the Harpers Ferry Model 1855 had been fitted with the Maynard tape priming device). More Confederate rifled-muskets came out of the Richmond Armory than all other Southern manufacturers combined. [5] Both .58 caliber rifled-muskets with 40-inch barrels, .62 caliber smoothbore muskatoons with 30-inch barrels, and .58 caliber carbines with 25-inch barrels were manufactured. The majority of lockplates were stamped *C.S. RICHMOND, VA* and marked with the date of manufacture between *1861* and *1865*.

and Fort Monroe in Virginia; the Fayetteville Arsenal in North Carolina, Charleston Arsenal in South Carolina, Mount Vernon Arsenal in Alabama, the Baton Rouge Arsenal in Louisiana, the San Antonio Arsenal in Texas, and Little Rock Arsenal in Arkansas. All of these U.S. Arsenals were taken over by the Confederacy and their respective inventories put into the hands of Southern troops. The estimated total of arms secured from these arsenals exceeded 159,000 smoothbore muskets, most in .69 caliber, rifled-muskets in .58 caliber (for the Minie bullet), .69 caliber muskatoons, carbines in varying calibers, and pistols, nearly all of which were seized by Southern states prior to the attack on Fort Sumter in April 1861!

If one were to set aside the military arms at the disposal of the Confederate States in 1861, comprised of rifled muskets, pistols, and revolvers issued c.1855 to 1860, the demands to arm tens of thousands of volunteers still easily outstripped the South's inventory. Thus volunteers brought their own handguns, rifles and muskets, and the combination of varied styles and calibers carried into battle laid the grounds for a logistical nightmare. Muskets were by far the weapon of choice for volunteers as they were easiest to load. Rifled Muskets were much more demanding of proper caliber rounds. Revolvers were, for the most part, mostly .36 or .44 caliber and presented less of an issue. In time captured Union revolvers (Colt 1860 Army and Remington 1863 Army models the most prized) and longarms such as the Henry repeater, and most importantly, U.S. Model 1861 and Model 1863 rifled-muskets added to the Confederacy's arsenal, as did privately purchased guns manufactured prior to the war and available through various retailers in both the South

Whether captured or purchased, the Starr single and double action .44 caliber revolvers were carried by Confederates. The unique topbreak design allowed the guns to be quickly opened to change out cylinders. There was, however, always the risk of dropping and loosing the knurled crossbolt that secured the topstrap to the frame. The Starr was never overly popular with the Union, especially the quirky double action models, but as the sign in the background notes, the South wasn't that picky. To Arms! (Mike Clark Collection/Collectors Firearms)

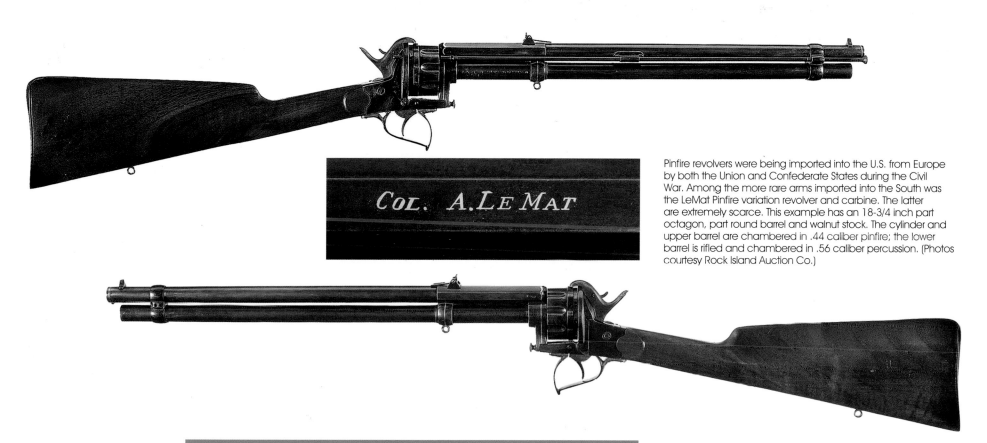

COL. A. LE MAT

Pinfire revolvers were being imported into the U.S. from Europe by both the Union and Confederate States during the Civil War. Among the more rare arms imported into the South was the LeMat Pinfire variation revolver and carbine. The latter are extremely scarce. This example has an 18-3/4 inch part octagon, part round barrel and walnut stock. The cylinder and upper barrel are chambered in .44 caliber pinfire; the lower barrel is rifled and chambered in .56 caliber percussion. (Photos courtesy Rock Island Auction Co.)

Utilizing the early LeMat design, a single nipple threaded into the back of the under barrel and fitted with a percussion cap was struck by switching the hammer setting to the lower barrel. The pinfire literally contained the firing pin for each bullet. The pin was vertical to the cartridge casing and extended through a small slot at the back of each chamber. When struck by the hammer, the pin impacted a percussion cap contained in the cartridge thus discharging the round. One was careful not to drop pinfire cartridges!

Cavalry. All of Baker's work was done between 1862 and 1863.

Another prolific Southern armsmaker was the Fayetteville Armory in North Carolina, which produced copies of the U.S. Model 1855 rifle. Here again parts and tooling was being used that had been taken from the U.S. Arsenals at Harpers Ferry and Fayetteville at the start of the war. Fayetteville had been one of the largest U.S. arsenals in the South and when taken by the Confederacy had an inventory of 20,000 muskets and 2,000 rifles. It is estimated that more than 8,000 rifles were assembled at Fayetteville between 1862 and 1865.[6]

While Richmond and Fayetteville were a wellspring of arms for the South, most of the other Southern armsmakers doing conversion work of old militia flintlocks, muskatoons, early Halls flintlock breechloaders, and assorted sporting arms, were

While there is little supporting documentation of cut down Colt's Navy and Army revolvers being carried by soldiers during the Civil War as backup or hideaway guns, Colt did produce a number of cut down .36 caliber Police models during the war, while others were likely made in the field. The fact that so many exist today lends some support to the theory that they were being used. This example is of particular interest as it is fitted with shield device to prevent percussion caps from falling off as the cylinder rotates. The shield extends around the cylinder leaving open the capping cutout on the right side of the recoil shield. (Mike Clark Collection/Collectors Firearms)

Richmond was also home to the C.S. Robinson Arms Manufacturing Co., which produced a very accurate copy of the Sharps Model 1859 carbine. Chambered in .52 caliber the 21-inch barreled breechloaders were manufactured through 1865. The company had been purchased by the Confederate government in March of 1863 in the hopes of increasing production. The previous year Robinson had manufactured around 1,900 guns.

From 1863 to 1864 another 3,000 were built with the primary distinction being a change in barrel stamping from *S.C. ROBINSON./ ARMS MANUFACTORY./ RICHMOND, VA./1862* to simply *RICHMOND, VA.* Though the Richmond Sharps look similar to those built in Hartford, Connecticut, for the Union, the fit, finish and subtle changes in the sights and lock work easily set them apart.

One of the most promising war time enterprises in the South was converting old flintlock muskets to percussion locks. Unfortunately much of the work was crudely done and a lot of truly great handcrafted late 18th century flintlocks were lost in the process. Among Southern armsmakers who manufactured replacement percussion locks and converted U.S. Model 1816 Muskets and 1817 Rifles to flintlocks was M.A. Baker in Fayetteville, North Carolina. Baker was contracted to make 500 rifle locks. As is noted in *Flayderman's Guide* it is not known if Baker only produced the locks or actually made rifles. The company is known to have manufactured 100 cut off double barrel shotguns with swivels ordered by North Carolina for the C.S.

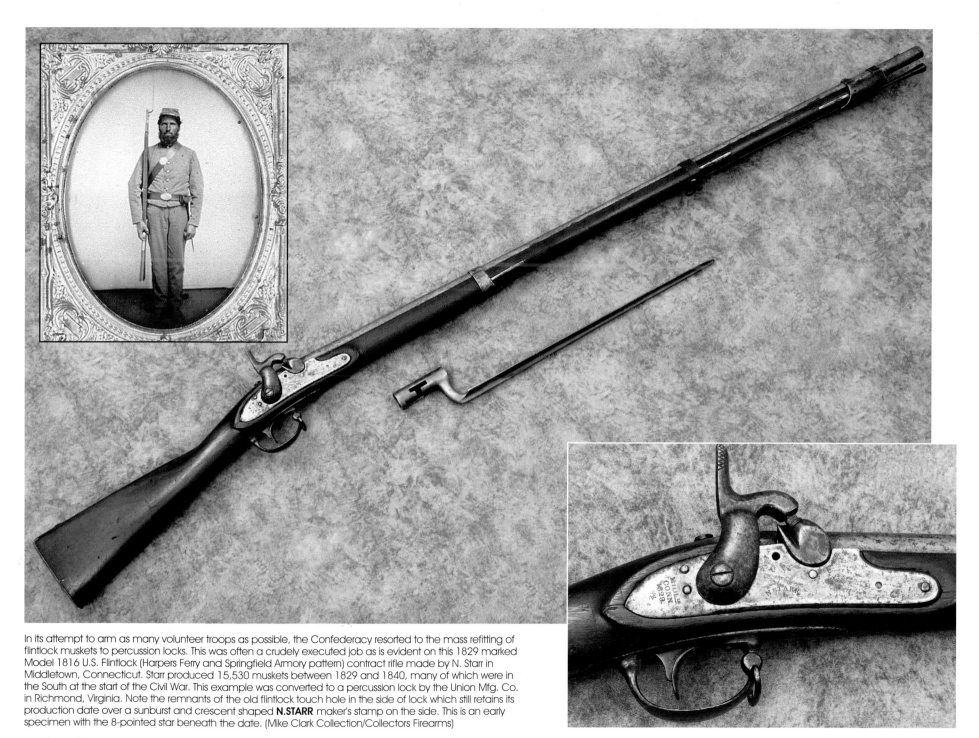

In its attempt to arm as many volunteer troops as possible, the Confederacy resorted to the mass refitting of flintlock muskets to percussion locks. This was often a crudely executed job as is evident on this 1829 marked Model 1816 U.S. Flintlock (Harpers Ferry and Springfield Armory pattern) contract rifle made by N. Starr in Middletown, Connecticut. Starr produced 15,530 muskets between 1829 and 1840, many of which were in the South at the start of the Civil War. This example was converted to a percussion lock by the Union Mfg. Co. in Richmond, Virginia. Note the remnants of the old flintlock touch hole in the side of lock which still retains its production date over a sunburst and crescent shaped **N.STARR** maker's stamp on the side. This is an early specimen with the 8-pointed star beneath the date. (Mike Clark Collection/Collectors Firearms)

Getting more than one shot out of a rifle had been a goal as far back as the mid 1850s. Colt's was the first to perfect the revolving rifle in 1847, an 8-shot, shoulder-stocked Dragoon with a 30-inch barrel. By 1855 the sidehammer revolving rifle had been developed and was well along in production by the start of the Civil War. They were used more so by Confederate troops throughout the conflict as Southern volunteers had limited options in longarms compared to their Union counterparts. Colt's sidehammer revolving rifles were produced in a variety of calibers and versions including military rifles like this example with 31-5/8ths inch barrel chambered in .56 caliber percussion. (Mike Clark Collection/Collectors Firearms)

only able to manufacture a few hundred examples each during the war.

Another among the handful of exceptions was Cook & Brother, originally of New Orleans, and later Athens, Georgia, which produced at few thousand .58 caliber muzzleloading rifles, mustkatoons, and carbines from 1861 to 1864. *Flayderman's* notes that brothers Ferdinand W.C. and Francis Cook had emigrated from England and settled in New Orleans, though there is no record of guns bearing their name prior to the Civil War. The longarms they manufactured

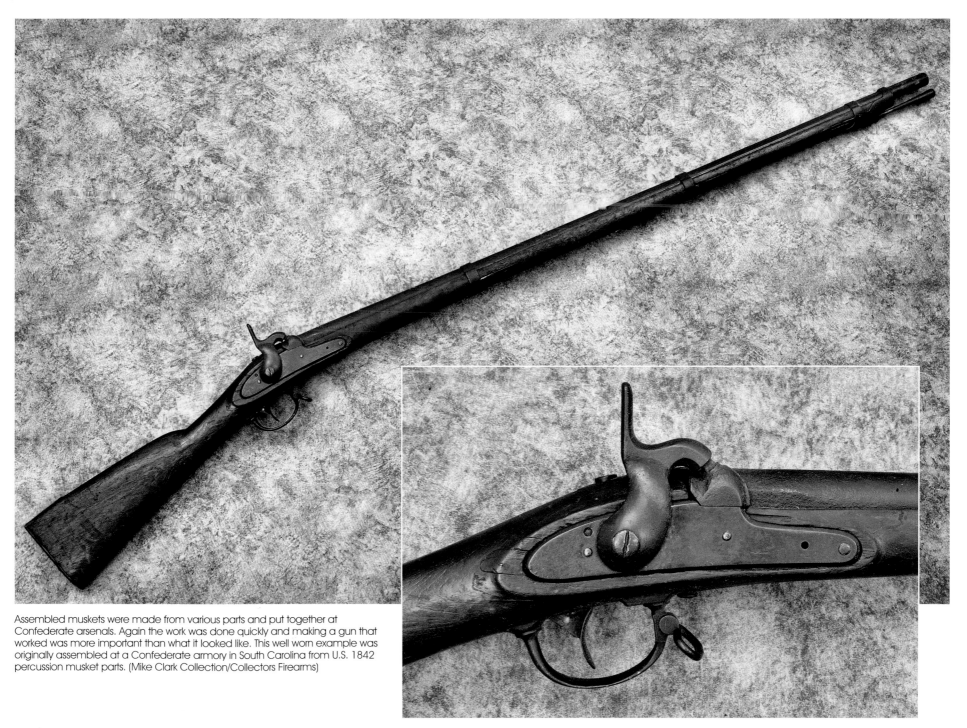

Assembled muskets were made from various parts and put together at Confederate arsenals. Again the work was done quickly and making a gun that worked was more important than what it looked like. This well worn example was originally assembled at a Confederate armory in South Carolina from U.S. 1842 percussion musket parts. (Mike Clark Collection/Collectors Firearms)

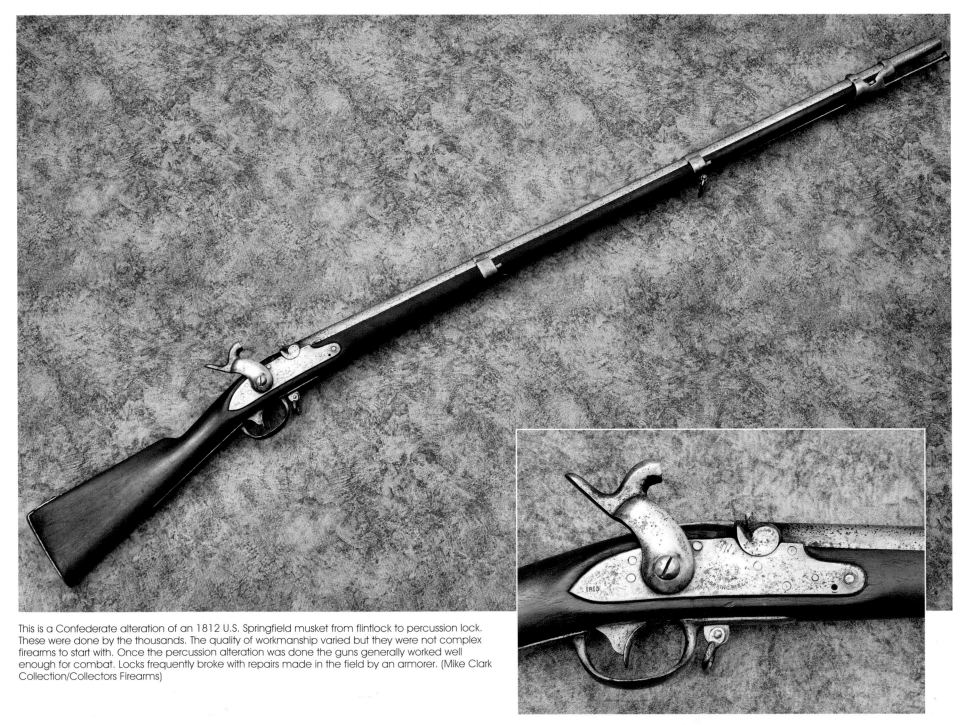

This is a Confederate alteration of an 1812 U.S. Springfield musket from flintlock to percussion lock. These were done by the thousands. The quality of workmanship varied but they were not complex firearms to start with. Once the percussion alteration was done the guns generally worked well enough for combat. Locks frequently broke with repairs made in the field by an armorer. (Mike Clark Collection/Collectors Firearms)

Battle of Gettysburg.

Before the Battle of Gettysburg, the noose was already tightening around the South. The Union's siege of New Orleans from April 25th to May 1st 1862 was another significant turning point in the Civil War, as the Confederacy lost its largest city, a vital seaport for bringing in arms from Europe, and access to the lower Mississippi River, which was now under Federal control. (Illustration, Library of Congress)

were based on the British Enfield rifle. Arms produced in New Orleans bore only *COOK & BROTHER NO 1862* stamped on the barrel, whereas models made between 1863 and 1864 have *COOK & BROTHER ATHENS GA/1864* stamped on the lockplate with a Confederate flag design. Models included an artillery rifle in .58 caliber percussion with a 24-inch barrel, and muskatoon with short 21-inch barrel.

The Cook brothers had been forced to relocate their factory to Athens in 1862, ahead of a Union advance. Between April 25th and May 1st, Northern forces approaching from both land and sea (the Gulf of Mexico and Mississippi River), captured and occupied the cities

A fine example of a Confederate Richmond manufactured carbine. The Richmond Armory produced carbines, muskatoons (essentially a carbine variation) and rifled-muskets. Though the total quantity of arms that came from the great Richmond Armory is unknown, it is likely that the variety of .58 caliber longarms produced numbered in the thousands between 1861 and 1865. Most of these arms were made with machinery taken by the South after its raid of the Federal Arsenal at Harpers Ferry, Virginia at the start of the war. The locks were stamped **C.S. RICHMOND, VA** on two lines. (Photo courtesy Rock Island Auction Co.)

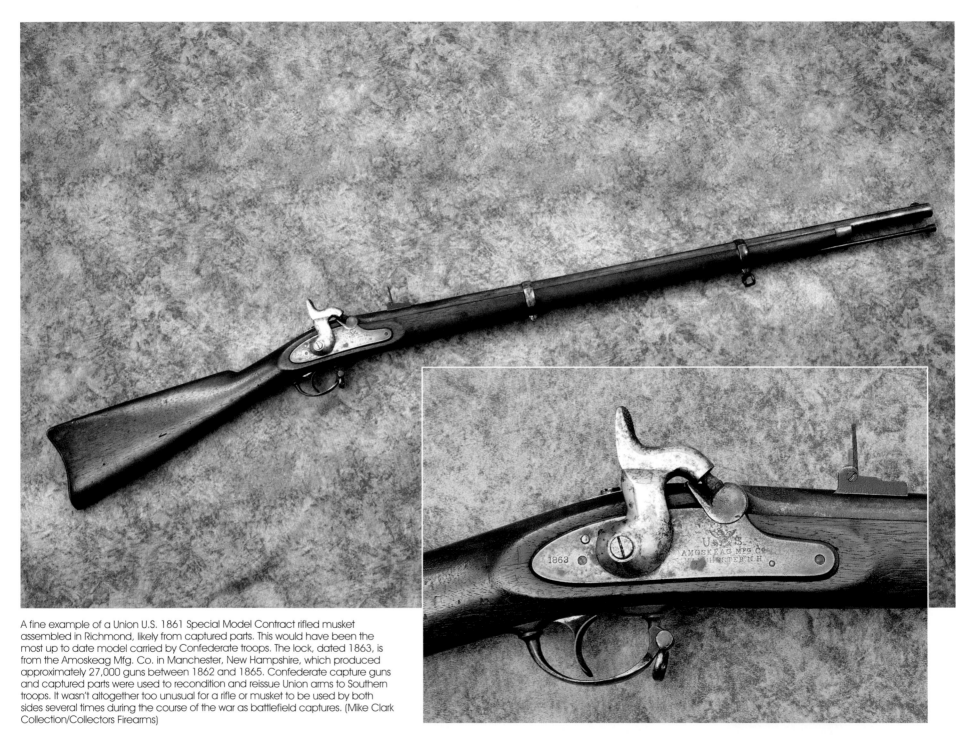

A fine example of a Union U.S. 1861 Special Model Contract rifled musket assembled in Richmond, likely from captured parts. This would have been the most up to date model carried by Confederate troops. The lock, dated 1863, is from the Amoskeag Mfg. Co. in Manchester, New Hampshire, which produced approximately 27,000 guns between 1862 and 1865. Confederate capture guns and captured parts were used to recondition and reissue Union arms to Southern troops. It wasn't altogether too unusual for a rifle or musket to be used by both sides several times during the course of the war as battlefield captures. (Mike Clark Collection/Collectors Firearms)

R. Whitechurch Sc.

U.S. Grant

Co. Production was, however, minor with only around 280 Maynard or Perry-style, brass frame .52 caliber tilting breech carbines built. A variety of breech loading carbines were produced in small numbers by other Southern firms such as the Tarpley, built c.1863 in North Carolina. Production was believed to have been only a few hundred.[7]

The capture of Union rifles, Henry rifles and cartridges, Sharps, and 1861 rifled-muskets in particular, was critical to any battle. In the end, it was a hodgepodge of arms from many sources that came into the hands of Confederate volunteers. As for the regular Army, the arms that had been in hand at the start of the war were still being used. The true secret weapon of the South, to as great a degree as could be managed, was the importation of guns from France and England. Even this was curtailed to a great extent by Union naval blockades and the North's own significant purchases of foreign-made handguns and longarms throughout the war.

Perhaps no other Army of the 19th century knew better than the Confederacy the true meaning of the words "make do."

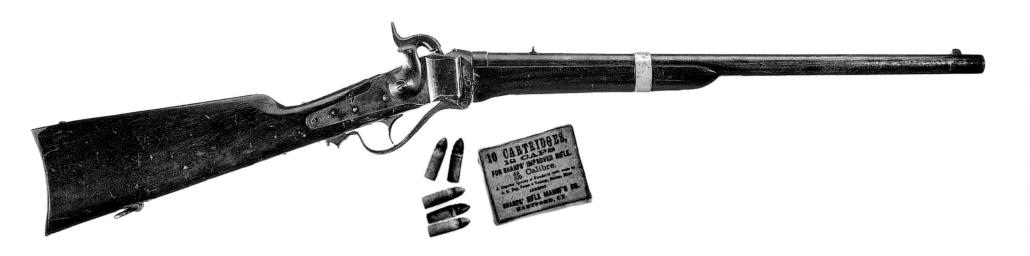

of New Orleans and St. Bernard Parish. In order to prevent the South's largest city from being destroyed by the Union siege, the arrival of 5,000 Federal troops into New Orleans on May 1st went unopposed, a marked turning point in the course of the war as the Confederacy had lost both a major seaport and access to the lower Mississippi River.

A significant number of rifled-muskets and carbines were also produced in Georgia by Dickson, Nelson & Co. It was quite literally a company on the move. Organized in 1861 to supply arms to the Confederacy, the factory was going to set up in Dickson, Alabama, but as the tide of the war changed a hasty move was made to Rome, Georgia. That facility was burned to the ground forcing them to relocate to Adairsville, Georgia. Dickson, Nelson & Co. remained in Adairsville up until the battle of Chicamauga in September 1863 at which time a hasty retreat with as much machinery as possible was made to a new facility in Dawson, Georgia for the remainder of the war. Originally named the Shakanoosa Arms Company, it was founded by William Dickerson, Owen O. Nelson, and L.H. Sadler. Despite their having to relocate several times, the company managed to supply the Confederacy with over 3,500 rifles and carbines. The Dixon, Nelson & Co. models were chambered in .58 caliber percussion and based on the U.S. Model 1842 and Model 1855 patterns, combining features from both.

Contract rifles, copies of the U.S. Model 1861 rifled-musket, were also made in modest quantities during the war but numbers were never great enough to be of any major consequence. A handful of breechloaders (aside from the Richmond Sharps) were manufactured in the South as well, one in particular, a variation of the Maynard design carbine for the C.S. cavalry was manufactured in Danville, Virginia, by Keen, Walker &

One of the most important longarms produced in the South was the Richmond variation of the C. Sharps breech loading carbine. Approximately 5,000 guns, copied from the c.1859 Hartford model, were produced in two variations, both chambered in .52 caliber with 21-inch barrels. The first type was manufactured by the S.C. Robinson Arms manufactory in Richmond from 1862. After the Confederate government purchased the factory production continued through 1864. Like the example shown, guns were simply stamped **RICHMOND, VA** on top of the barrels. (Photos courtesy Rock Island Auction Co.)

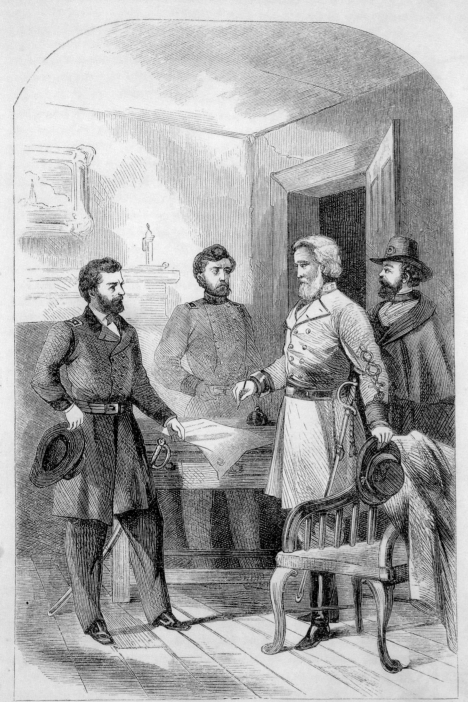

Surrender of General Lee.

Although the Civil War would last until almost the end of 1865, with small skirmishes between Union forces and Confederate troops either unaware that the war was over or simply unwilling to surrender, for the Confederate States of America and General Robert E. Lee's Army of Northern Virginia, the conflict concluded at Appomattox on April 9, 1865 when Lee sat across from U.S. General Ulysses S. Grant in the sitting room of Wilmer McLean's home and affixed his signature to a document surrendering the Army of Northern Virginia and fundamentally ending the War Between the States. Shown are period illustrations of the document signing at Appomattox, a daguerreotype of Appomattox Court House, Virginia surrounded by Union troops, an illustration of General grant made in 1865, and two portraits of Robert E. Lee following the surrender. (Photos Library of Congress, Grant portrait from *The History of the Civil War*, 1865.)

[1] *Firearms of the Confederacy* by Claud E. Fuller and Richard D. Steuart, 1996, The National Rifle Association, Odysseus Editions, Inc.

[2] The 12mm Pinfire cartridge was roughly the equivalent of a .45 caliber round.

[3] *LeMat The Man, The Gun* by Valmore J. Forgett and Alain F. & Marie-Antoinette Sepette, 1996 Val Forgett, Ridgefield, New Jersey.

[4] *Firearms of the Confederacy* by Claud E. Fuller and Richard D. Steuart

[5] ibid

[6] Flayderman's Guide to Antique American Firearms.

[7] *Firearms of the Confederacy* by Claud E. Fuller and Richard D. Steuart

Chapter Five

A Litany of Foreign Arms

European guns and their role in the war between North and South

A s early as December 1861 it had become manifest to both Abraham Lincoln and Jefferson Davis that the Union and the Confederacy would need to import longarms and revolvers from Europe in order to equip the tens of thousands of volunteers fighting on both sides of the Mason Dixon line. This demand was much greater in the South, where arms making was not a widespread industry.

In 1862 President Abraham Lincoln commissioned Marcellus Hartley, a partner in the New York firearms importing firm of Schuyler, Hartley & Graham, to supply the Union with French Lefaucheux (pronounced lue-foe-sho) pistols and pinfire ammunition. The early cartridge-firing Lefaucheux were the fourth most commonly used revolver in the American Civil War, surpassed only by the Colt, Remington, and Starr percussion pistols.

Although cap and ball revolvers were regarded as contemporary firearms in the U.S., in Europe pistols designed to fire metallic cartridges had been in use since the 1840s. During the Civil War tens of thousands of European cartridge revolvers and millions of metallic cartridges would be imported to arm Union and Confederate forces, and in so doing would change the very nature of the American firearms industry in the postwar 1860s.

More Than a Decade Ahead of America

By the mid 1840s rimfire cartridges were already in use throughout Europe, and by 1854 the first centerfire ammunition had been developed, thus the Europeans were more than a decade ahead of American armsmakers.

The first records of a metallic cartridge actually date back to 1812, when Swiss inventor Jean Samuel Pauley received a patent for a self-contained, self-primed, centerfire metallic cartridge. Four years earlier Pauley had applied for another patent, this covering the design for the first in-line rifle, which he improved upon in 1812 with the introduction of a

Cartridge firing guns were not as uncommon as one might think during the Civil War. Thousands were imported from England, France, Belgium, and even Germany, by the Confederate States and Federal Government. Pictured are Belgian, French, and German Pinfire revolvers. At top, a Belgian 10mm pinfire with gold and silver inlays and ivory grips; middle, a French 8mm pinfire w/British proofs; and bottom, a German 10mm with folding trigger, engraved receiver and cylinder. The side lever on this model releases the barrel from the arbor for loading. Note the firing pins in the top of each round. It was never advisable to drop a pinfire cartridge! (Guns and photo of Union sergeant from Mike Clark/Collectors Firearms collection)

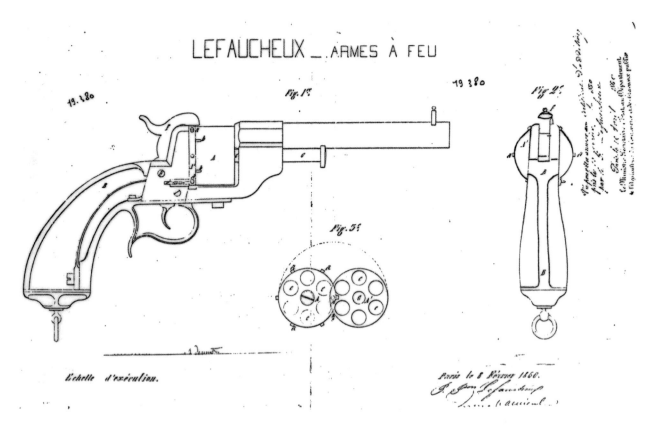

LEFAUCHEUX — ARMES À FEU

Fig. 1.

Fig. 2.

Fig. 3.

Echelle d'exécution.

Paris le 8 Février 1860.

Eugene Lefaucheux continued his father's work and made improvements to the pinfire design, including the invention of the bored through cylinder, which he patented in France on April 15, 1854. Shown is an 1860 patent by Eugene Lefaucheux for a pinfire revolver. (Patent reproduced from The Pinfire System with the permission of Chris Curtis)

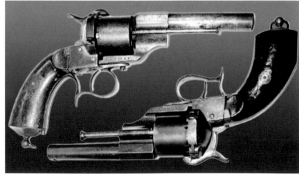

Two pairs of fine 12mm Le.faucheux pinfire revolvers show the various changes in designs. (Photo by Terry Tremewan from the Larry Compeau collection)

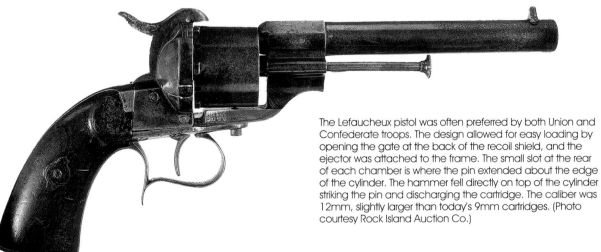

The Lefaucheux pistol was often preferred by both Union and Confederate troops. The design allowed for easy loading by opening the gate at the back of the recoil shield, and the ejector was attached to the frame. The small slot at the rear of each chamber is where the pin extended about the edge of the cylinder. The hammer fell directly on top of the cylinder striking the pin and discharging the cartridge. The caliber was 12mm, slightly larger than today's 9mm cartridges. (Photo courtesy Rock Island Auction Co.)

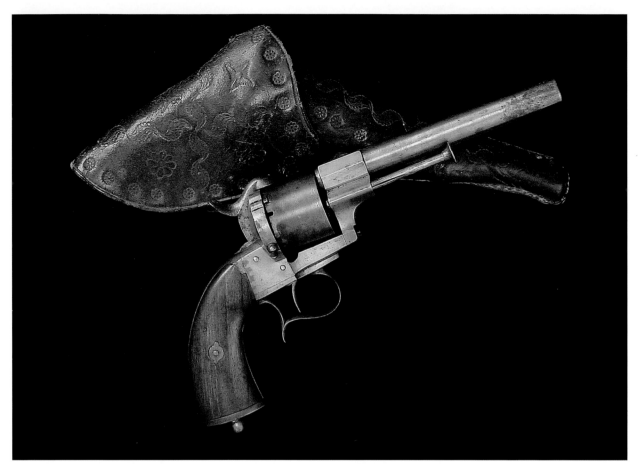

A fine example of a French pinfire revolver carried during the period of the Civil War. This model was manufactured in 1854. (Gun and holster courtesy of The Horse Soldier/Gettysburg, PA)

This is a finely crafted Belgian 10mm pinfire revolver with gold and silver inlays and ivory grips. It is resting on a fitted, velour lined pipe casing. Pinfire revolvers were favored by Southern officers. Each individual cartridge had its own internal firing pin, which projected through a slot in the chamber. When struck by the hammer the pin hit a primer discharging the round. (Mike Clark/Collectors Firearms collection)

breechloader. A gunmaker named Johann Niklaus von Dreyse, who apprenticed under Pauley from 1808 to 1814, further improved the in-line concept with his 1838 patent for the turnbolt rifle, which evolved into the well-known Prussian Needlegun a decade later. It was this design upon which German gunmaker Paul Mauser based his celebrated Model 1868 turnbolt cartridge rifle. The pioneering Mauser design was adopted by the German military in 1871, and provided the foundation for the celebrated 1903 Springfield.

A third type of cartridge was invented by French gunmaker Casimir Lefaucheux in 1843, the pinfire. Lefaucheux had actually been developing the design since 1835. His innovative pinfire cartridge was so well received across Europe that by the 1840s armsmakers were manufacturing revolvers, rifles, and even shotguns to work with the Lefaucheux pinfire. The pinfire was an ingenious design, and they could be reloaded. Although Casimir died in 1852, his son Eugene continued his father's work and made improvements, including the invention of the bored through cylinder, which he patented in France on April 15, 1854, a full year before Rollin White's U.S. patent for the same design. By the time of the Civil War breech loading pinfire revolvers, rifles, carbines, and shotguns had already been in common use for more than six years.

Between 1862 and 1865 the warring governments in Washington, D.C., and Richmond, Virginia, had purchased thousands of Lefaucheux revolvers. The Union Army received 1,900 pinfire revolvers through Hartley, and purchased another 10,000 under direct contract during the war. The Confederacy followed suit, as well as purchasing pinfire versions of the South's most potent revolver, the 9-shot .44 caliber LeMat manufactured in France and Belgium. By 1865 the Confederate States of America had purchased as many as 2,500 Lefaucheux revolvers.

Marcellus Hartley handled the majority of Union requisitions for imported firearms. A key figure in American industry (importing pinfire arms and ammunition before, during, and after the war), he was also responsible for establishing the Union Metallic Cartridge Co., one of only three American firms known to have manufactured and marketed pinfire ammunition in any quantity. UMC eventually became one of America's most important ammunition manufacturers.

Immediately after the attack on Fort Sumter, Jefferson Davis made a decision similar to Lincoln's, first sending Captain Caleb Huse to Europe to evaluate the purchase and importation of arms to the South. Huse was joined in May by a Major Anderson. As the war escalated into summer, Davis issued orders for the importation of as many revolvers and muskets as possible, of the latter even flintlocks, if such were available, would be acceptable.

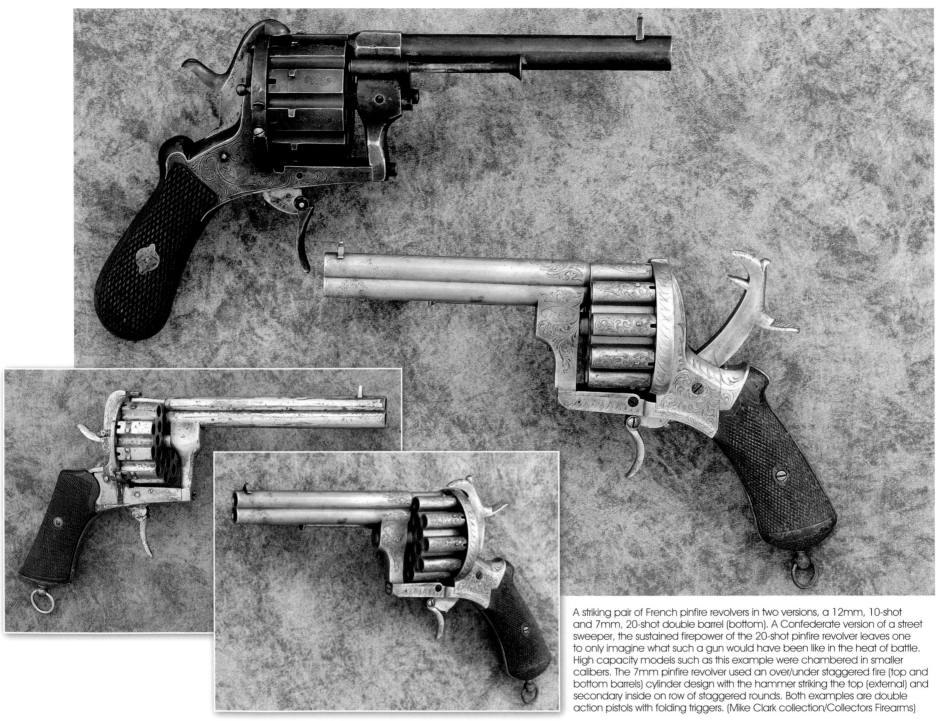

A striking pair of French pinfire revolvers in two versions, a 12mm, 10-shot and 7mm, 20-shot double barrel (bottom). A Confederate version of a street sweeper, the sustained firepower of the 20-shot pinfire revolver leaves one to only imagine what such a gun would have been like in the heat of battle. High capacity models such as this example were chambered in smaller calibers. The 7mm pinfire revolver used an over/under staggered fire (top and bottom barrels) cylinder design with the hammer striking the top (external) and secondary inside on row of staggered rounds. Both examples are double action pistols with folding triggers. (Mike Clark collection/Collectors Firearms)

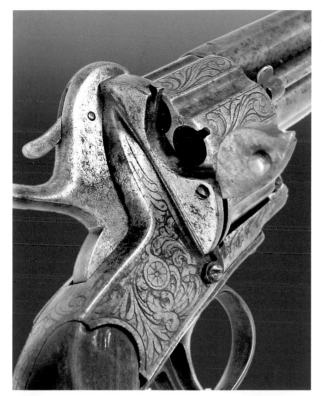

A close-up look at the business end of a 10-shot, 12mm Lufacheux pinfire. (Photo by Terry Tremewan)

The Lefaucheux design allowed for easy loading by opening the gate at the back of the recoil shield. The spent shell ejector was attached to the frame. The small slot at the rear of each chamber is where the pin extended above the edge of the cylinder. The hammer fell directly on top of the cylinder striking the pin and discharging the cartridge. (Photos by Terry Tremewan from the Larry Compeau collection)

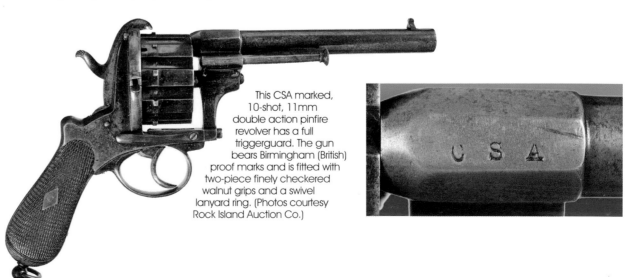

This CSA marked, 10-shot, 11mm double action pinfire revolver has a full triggerguard. The gun bears Birmingham (British) proof marks and is fitted with two-piece finely checkered walnut grips and a swivel lanyard ring. (Photos courtesy Rock Island Auction Co.)

Pinfire Arms

The majority of pinfire arms imported by the North and South were manufactured in Belgium. Being European guns, cartridge calibers were metric, another issue for the U.S. Ordnance Department and General Ripley to sort out as the war continued. The French and Belgian made guns were chambered in an assortment of calibers, 7mm, 10mm, 12mm and 15mm. The 12mm (roughly a .44) was among the most commonly used revolver calibers, although the more exotic Belgian pinfire revolvers with as many as 20 chambers in a massive double stacked cylinder were chambered in 7mm and 10mm.

While revolvers were profoundly important to the war, the importation of rifled muskets was paramount, particularly to Jefferson Davis and the Confederacy. The majority of quality imported longarms came into Southern hands from England. British Enfield, Tower of London, and London Armoury Company manufactured muskets, though mostly outdated in Great Britain, were purchased in large quantities. Shipments, however, were difficult as Union blockades of the waters leading to Southern ports had proven very effective.

It is interesting to note that payments for guns procured in England by the Confederacy were often made in trade for cotton, because Confederate currency had so little value outside of the Southern States. Cotton, however, was a badly needed commodity in Great Britain, which gave the South an advantage in purchase negotiations.[1]

The British Tower (Tower of London) musket was among those purchased in number by the South. These were considerably dated by the Civil War having been the first percussion muskets used by British Troops c.1836 to c.1842. The Tower muskets were chambered in .753 caliber (.670 diameter bullet weighing 490 grains and backed by a powder charge of 70 grains) and were

The 10-shot, 12mm Lefaucheux pinfire (roughly a .44 caliber cartridge) was a potent sidearm and given a capacity of 10 rounds, four better than any American made revolver of the time had to offer (unless one considers the bizarre Welch revolver) the Lefaucheux was a formidable weapon. Most were sold to the Confederacy.

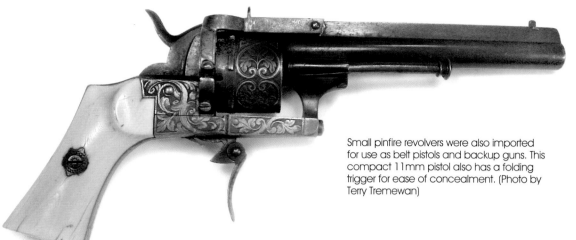

Small pinfire revolvers were also imported for use as belt pistols and backup guns. This compact 11mm pistol also has a folding trigger for ease of concealment. (Photo by Terry Tremewan)

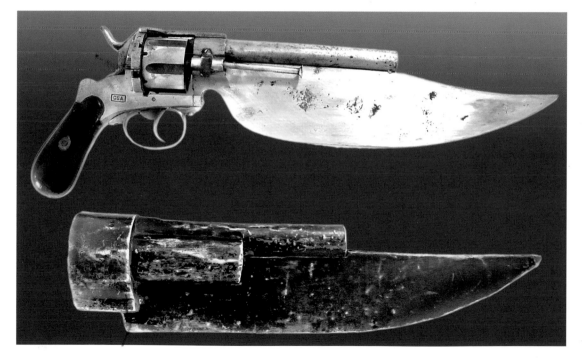

Suited to use by the Confederate Navy, large blade cutlass or knife blade pinfire revolvers were a double threat in close quarters combat. The rare matching holster kept the gun and blade protected, not to mention the person wearing it. (Larry Compeau collection)

A very important Confederate presentation French pinfire revolving carbine inscribed to Confederate Ordnance Officer Major Caleb Huse, who was responsible for importing arms from France and England to the South. The elegantly engraved 12mm pinfire carbine has a 25-1/8 inch octagonal barrel, a walnut stock, checkered at the wrist, and an ornate, inlaid silver presentation plaque. Note the swiveling cartridge ejector rod mounted on the right side of the frame along the barrel. This model was designed and manufactured by J. Chaineux and was a gift from the armsmaker to Huse. Chaineux ceased operation at the beginning of the Franco-Prussian War (1870-1871). Huse, pictured in the late 1890s was founder of the Highland Falls Military Academy in New York. (Photos courtesy Rock Island Auction Co.)

The LeMat (top) was the South's most recognized handgun. It was also the inspiration for modified French pinfire variations imported to support the Confederate cause. The exact number of pinfire LeMats is not known but surviving examples such as the 10-shot model are generally found in very good condition which tends to suggest many arrived too late and saw little use. The LeMat pinfire conversion shown was done on a late Navy-style percussion revolver. The grapeshot barrel was still loaded as before and fired with a percussion cap by rotating the firing pin lever (above hammer) to its secondary lower position. The loading lever has been removed from this gun but a rammer is still used (mounted on the right side) for charging the grapeshot barrel.

The Tower Armory in England became one of the principal arms suppliers to the Confederacy. This is a fine example of a c.1861 Tower percussion musket. The general construction of this arm followed that of the traditional British Brown Bess flintlock dating back to the Revolutionary War. The Tower Muskets used by the Confederacy were chambered in .753 caliber. Barrel lengths were usually 39 inches and the muskets measured 54-1/2 inches in length. (Photos by Terry Tremewan)

comparable to U.S. muskets of the same period. By early 1863, Huse, who had been promoted to the rank of Major, had shipped over 21,000 British Tower muskets to the South.

Huse was a pivotal figure in the Civil War. An 1851 graduate of West Point (7th in his class), he served at West Point from 1852 to 1860 when he was appointed Commander of Cadets at the University of Alabama. At the start of the Civil War he resigned his position to join his former West Point Commandant Robert E. Lee in support of the Confederate cause. Though he first served in the Army, his knowledge of arms made him a perfect choice for Ordnance and he was sent to England in May of 1861 to begin arranging for the procurement and delivery of arms to the South. Huse was one of the oldest Civil War veterans. Living until age 74, he died on March 12, 1905 at his home in Highland Falls, New York. After the war he had founded the Highland Falls Academy, also known as "The Rocks," a military preparatory school designed for young men who planned to attend West Point. Among his early students was a young man named John J. Pershing.

The most important longarm imported to the Confederacy was the Model 1858 British Enfield rifled musket. Compatible with U.S. government loads, the Enfield was chambered in .577 caliber and resembled many of the U.S. rifled muskets then in use by Confederate infantry. Barrel length was 39 inches, and when fitted with bayonet weighed 8 pounds, 14-1/2 ounces. More than 70,000 were purchased by the Confederate government.[2] Additionally, short barrel models with a

Though Huse initally failed to establish a relationship with the London Armoury in 1861 the British armsmaker eventually become a major supplier to the Confederacy. This is a typical percussion lock musket c.1862. (Photos by Terry Tremewan)

The very elegant British Kerr revolver was one of the more prized guns of the Civil War. Pictured are .44 caliber Kerr revolvers with engraving and gold inlays. The model at lower right is chambered in .36 caliber percussion, as is the cased pair. The ohers are chambered in .45 caliber percussion. Designed by James Kerr, the guns were an improvement of the British Adams patent revolver and were first produced in April 1859 at the London Armoury Company. The United States military and the Confederacy began purchasing arms in Britain early in 1861. By November, 1,600 revolvers were ordered by the Union army at $18.00 apiece. Soon after Confederate arms buyers Major Caleb Huse and Captain James D. Bulloch contracted for all the rifles and revolvers the Armoury could produce. The London Armoury Company delivered nearly 11,000 Kerr revolvers to the Confederacy. (Mike Clark.Collectors Firearms)

A later Tower version musket c.1863. (Photos by Terry Tremewan)

barrel length of 33 inches were also imported, as well as Enfield carbines with a barrel length of 21 inches for use by the cavalry. Roughly 9,715 short barrel arms and 354 carbines were procured and shipped in 1863.

Arming Confederate sharpshooters with British rifles was another task that had to be undertaken as Southern manufacture of such arms was extremely limited. The South relied heavily on captured Sharps rifles and other

Union arms used by Federal sharpshooters. Among the examples imported from England was the Whitworth Rifle, which was reported to have reliable accuracy up to half a mile! Chambered in .45 caliber, the percussion longarms had a barrel length of 33 inches and were equipped to have telescopic or globe sights mounted. Only a hundred or so were procured and shipped to the South, most going to the Army of Northern Virginia

and regiments in Georgia, including the Sharpshooters of Gordon's Brigade (Fourth Georgia regiment), which made headlines with their amazing accuracy during an engagement fought across the Tennessee River in November 1863. The Whitworth rifles were mentioned by name in the *Richmond Daily Examiner* article of November 10.

Other rifles and carbines purchased by the South included the Austrian Rifle, (an arm of lesser quality to the Enfield but suitable for infantry use) of which some 27,000 were procured; the English Terry breech loading, bolt-action rifle; Wilson breech loading rifle, LeMat revolving carbine, and the British Kerr rifle, the latter chambered in .44 caliber and used by Confederate sharpshooters.

Kerr was also one of the most popular imported British revolvers used by both the North and South. The elegantly-styled sidehammer Kerr revolver was one of the more prized guns of the Civil War. Designed by James Kerr, the guns were an improvement of the British Adams patent revolver and were first produced in April 1859 at the London Armoury Company. The United States military and the Confederacy began purchasing Kerr models early in 1861. By November, 1,600 revolvers were ordered by the Union army at $18.00 apiece. Soon after Confederate arms buyers Major Caleb Huse and Captain James D. Bulloch contracted for all the rifles and revolvers the Armoury could produce. The London Armoury Company eventually become a major arms supplier to the Confederacy, delivering nearly 11,000 Kerr revolvers.

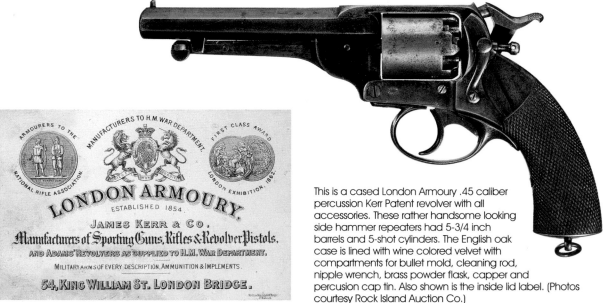

This is a cased London Armoury .45 caliber percussion Kerr Patent revolver with all accessories. These rather handsome looking side hammer repeaters had 5-3/4 inch barrels and 5-shot cylinders. The English oak case is lined with wine colored velvet with compartments for bullet mold, cleaning rod, nipple wrench, brass powder flask, capper and percussion cap tin. Also shown is the inside lid label. (Photos courtesy Rock Island Auction Co.)

Although the Kerr looked like a double action revolver, it was not. The side-mounted hammer had to be manually cocked; pulling the trigger with the hammer down only rotated the cylinder to the next chamber. One of the more interesting characteristics of the design was the cylinder arbor, which was extracted from the rear (protruding below hammer) to remove the cylinder. Unlike other revolvers of the day, the Kerr's lock mechanism was identical to that of the Kerr back-action rifle. The 5-shot revolvers were chambered in approximately .36 caliber and .44 caliber and Southern purchases were primarily issued to the Confederate Navy. Kerr revolvers were also carried by the 7th, 11th, 12, 18th, 35th Battalion Virginia, 24th Battalion Georgia, and 8th Texas cavalry regiments.[3]

The Kerr Revolver featured a side-mounted hammer on a back-action lockplate. Unlike other revolvers of the day, the lock mechanism of the Kerr revolver was identical to that of back-action rifle and single shot percussion pistol locks of the era. (Mike Clark/Collectors Firearms collection)

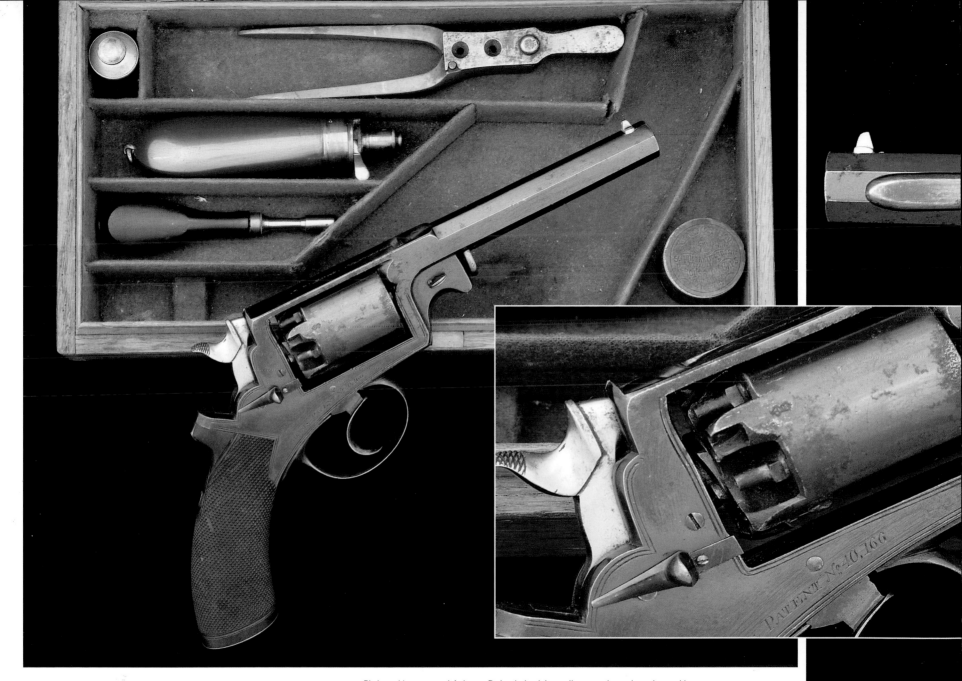

Pictured is a cased Adams Patent double action revolver chambered in .45 caliber percussion and fitted with a 5-3/4 inch barrel. A later variation of the Adams patent design, this is an Adams-Beaumont model, patented by Adams and Lieutenant F.E.B. Beaumont in 1855. The new models added a thumb spur to the hammer and an altered mechanism to allow the guns to be cocked and fired single action.

Less common during the Civil War were double action Kerr percussion revolvers. This rare example is serial number 1 and is chambered in .450 caliber, with a 5-3/4 inch octagonal barrel. The guns could also be cocked and fired single action. (Photos courtesy Rock Island Auction Co.)

Cased .36 caliber percussion engraved Kerr with presentation box and cased combination hat badge for bell crowned helmet and corresponding small badge for a Shako (small brimmed hat) both from Duke of Cornwall's Regiment. Deluxe presentation models of the Kerr were less common and few were imported during the Civil War except as presentation guns to officers. (Mike Clark/Collectors Firearms collection)

Kerr also manufactured a true double action model revolver but most guns purchased by the Confederacy were of the single action type.

The British Adams Patent Repeating Pistol was a true double action (self cocking) percussion revolver. The design was manufactured by Adams (designer Robert Adams), Beaumont-Adams, Deane, Adams & Deane, Adams & Tranter and other Adams Patent licensees in London, Birmingham, Wolverhampton, England and Liège, Belgium.

Like other British revolvers of the period, the Adams was a five shot pistol, quite a contrast to the LeMat, which was a nine shot, or even a Colt 1860 Army with six. The original Adams Patent revolvers had two other disadvantages, they could not be cocked or fired single action, and there was no loading rammer. Both issues were addressed with the Adams-Beaumont model patented by Adams and Lieutenant F.E.B. Beaumont in 1855. The new models added a thumb spur to the hammer and an altered mechanism to allow the guns to be cocked and fired single action. A Kerr-style bullet rammer was also added on the left side of the barrel.[4] These represent the majority of Adams Patent revolvers imported during the Civil War.

The Southern Condition

At the start of the Civil War thousands of Southerners went into battle with little more than an issued musket, if one was available, and a single shot flintlock or percussion pistol. Thousands of Confederate troops went to the front armed with weapons that had been out of date since the Mexican American War. The Virginia Armory issued both flintlock and altered percussion pistols to its volunteers.[5]

This is not to say that Southern States did not manufacture guns; quite the contrary. Southern gunmakers were very skilled but more accustomed to handcrafting sporting rifles, fowling pieces, and dueling pistols. They were not inclined toward mass production; that had always been the work of Northern manufacturers like Colt's and Remington. The closest the South came to mass production had been the federal armory at Harpers Ferry.

Before the war there had been many retailers such as Mitchell & Tyler, Kent, Paine & Co., and Samuel Sutherland in Richmond, Virginia; Hyde & Goodrich in New Orleans, and other prestigious firms across the South that imported fine pistols and longarms from Europe, thus the South was, by nature, more accustomed to foreign made arms.

The guns imported from England and France, both before and during the war, played a significant role in arming the Confederacy. Pistols like the two magnificent British Doubles pictured are excellent examples of c.1850's handguns that might have been carried into battle by Southern officers as a backup sidearm or pocket pistol.

There were also "brevet" models of Colt's pistols made in Belgium, most loosely based on the 1851 Navy. These too were imported by the South as they were chambered

Two shots were better than one. Though a traditionally British gun in the 1850s, roughly the period in which this handsome .52 caliber over/under percussion pistol was sold by Wilkinson & Son, London, many British, French and Belgian made firearms were exported to the United States and found their way into the hands of explorers, gunmen, soldiers, and lawmen in the mid 19th century, especially during the Civil War when any gun, made anywhere was in high demand. This example has a spring steel clip along the left side allowing it to be easily secured on a soldier's waist belt for quick access. It is also small enough to be carried in a pocket. According to noted gun collector and *Man At Arms* publisher and editor Stuart Mowbray, any British pistol bearing the Wilkinson & Son, London name was top drawer armament. (Author's collection)

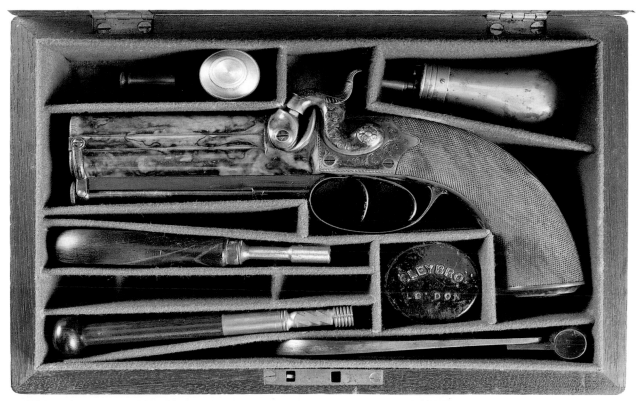

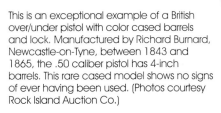

This is an exceptional example of a British over/under pistol with color cased barrels and lock. Manufactured by Richard Burnard, Newcastle-on-Tyne, between 1843 and 1865, the .50 caliber pistol has 4-inch barrels. This rare cased model shows no signs of ever having been used. (Photos courtesy Rock Island Auction Co.)

The Wilkison & Son over/under model has hammers that are slightly staggered to strike the percussion caps for upper and lower barrels. An attached swiveling rammer with tulip tip was used for loading and stowed beneath the barrels. The butt was hollow to permit the storage of extra percussion caps and rounds.

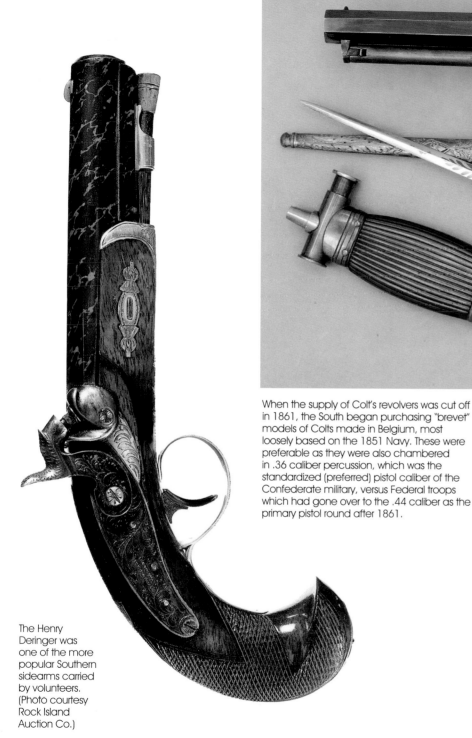

The Henry Deringer was one of the more popular Southern sidearms carried by volunteers. (Photo courtesy Rock Island Auction Co.)

When the supply of Colt's revolvers was cut off in 1861, the South began purchasing "brevet" models of Colts made in Belgium, most loosely based on the 1851 Navy. These were preferable as they were also chambered in .36 caliber percussion, which was the standardized (preferred) pistol caliber of the Confederate military, versus Federal troops which had gone over to the .44 caliber as the primary pistol round after 1861.

in .36 caliber, the Confederacy's standardized (preferred) pistol caliber, versus Federal troops which had gone over to the .44 caliber as the primary pistol round after 1861.

Before the war, Southerners who carried sidearms generally preferred small but powerful pocket pistols like the Colt's model 1849, or one of the many variations of the Philadelphia Deringer. So when the call to arms came, old Colt Dragoons came out of their oiled clothes, guns carried by many former U.S. soldiers who had served in the 1840 and 1850s. Most, however, had little choice but to bring what they had or what they could buy as the war escalated and the South's volunteer force increased in numbers.

In conclusion, one could say that the Europeans (the British and the French) were dispassionate, openly selling arms to both sides. While that is certainly one view, Samuel Colt would have simply considered it Europe's contribution to "moral reform."

[1] Firearms of the Confederacy by Claud E. Fuller and Richard D. Steuart

[2] ibid

[3] Civil War Pistols of the Union by John D. McAulay

[4] Handguns of the World by Edward C. Ezell

[5] Firearms of the Confederacy by Claud E. Fuller and Richard D. Steuart

Southern gunmakers were very skilled but more accustomed to handcrafting sporting rifles, fowling pieces, (like the example shown), and dueling pistols. They were not inclined toward mass production, thus many handcrafted arms were carried into battle by Southern volunteers. Other finely crafted flintlocks, muskets and fowling pieces were refitted for percussion locks and reissued to volunteers. (The .62 caliber English Fowler pictured is a handmade copy created for the author by Pennsylvania gunmaker Gary Rummell)

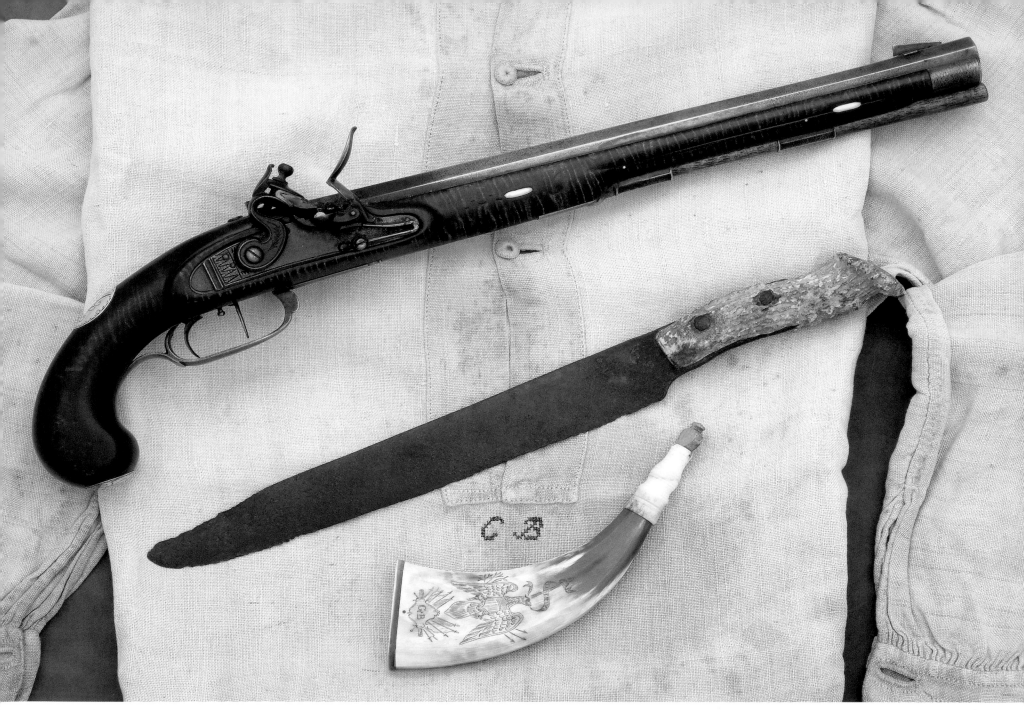

Though many Confederate volunteers were issued a musket, flintlock pistols were not uncommon in the waist belts of Southern soldiers throughout the Civil War. Examples like this long barreled Kentucky Pistol are exemplary of southern craftsmanship long before the Civil War.

Chapter Six

Modern Reproductions and Replicas

Tributes to American History

For nearly five centuries one of the finest gifts that a military officer, government official, or aristocrat could receive was a finely engraved presentation pistol. These devices of otherwise fierce power and destruction were tamed and ennobled when touched by the hands of artisans practicing the time-honored craft of fine engraving. These handsomely cased and accessorized presentation guns were often used as an olive branch, extended from the leader of one nation to another, either upon first meeting or at the conclusion of negotiations. Presentation pistols were also a means of engendering gratitude from a recipient; a tactic that Samuel Colt used to his advantage in promoting business relations for better than 20 years.

The traditional symbol of the "presentation piece" has survived to call forth outstanding qualities of craftsmanship in modern day artisans. "Fine weapons, and the accessories connected with them," explained British art historian and author Graham Hood, "are frequently beautiful and important, and deserve an integral place in any collection that attempts to reveal, through objects, the culture of an earlier age."

In the United States, rifles, pistols, and revolvers produced throughout the settling of the American West and Civil War era are the most coveted today among antique arms collectors. "During Samuel Colt's lifetime approximately 600,000 Colt percussion pistols of all types were manufactured, and only a fraction of those were engraved presentation models," notes Colt authority, author and historian R. L. Wilson. "In his entire career, Colt may have given away as many as 3,500 presentation pistols to military officers, foreign dignitaries, and heads of state." These 19th-century arms have become the most prized Colts of the 20th and 21st centuries, with many cased, engraved models valued today at well over $1 million.

Commissioned under the Tiffany & Co. name in 1992 and designed by Tom Watts of Tiffany & Co., this pair of handcrafted 2nd Generation Colt 1860 Army revolvers took master engraver Andrew Bourbon six months to complete. These were the last guns built under the Tiffany name.

Engraver John J. Adams, Sr. working on the Tiffany style grips for the 1851 Navy revolvers. Each pair of grips has to be cast, hand fitted and then detailed. Grips are usually silver plated, though guns were also done in the period in gold plate. Adams has done both.

Among the most impressive of all Colt presentation pistols were those sold by Tiffany & Co. during the Civil War. It surprises many people to find out that Tiffany was one of the oldest and most respected names in firearms embellishment in the mid 19th century.

In his book *Steel Canvas*, which chronicles the history of engraved firearms, R. L. Wilson noted that Tiffany produced a significant number of engraved Colt pistols. The New York firm continued to produce presentation pistols from the Civil War to the early 1900s, and catalogs for 1900 through 1909 advertised *Revolvers of the most improved types, mounted in silver, carved ivory, gold, etc., with rich and elaborate decorations.* Wilson, who was president of American Master Engravers, Inc., also noted that Tiffany & Co. still produced a limited number of engraved and embellished pistols each year well into the late 20th century. Tiffany briefly revived their exclusive art of engraving fine pistols in the early 1980s, much through the efforts of George A. Strichman, then chairman of Colt Industries, who commissioned three, gold and silver mounted Tiffany Colts. "That really marked the revival of the Tiffany tradition," said Wilson.

Although modern-day firearms are offered with gold inlay and engraving and feature gold and silver Tiffany stocks, many of the firm's most extraordinary examples have been based on the Colt 2nd Generation reproductions of Civil War era percussion pistols produced from the early 1970s until the early 21st century; guns which have themselves become collectable over the years.

Sometimes it's hard to tell the real thing. This handsome pair of Tiffany gripped 1851 Navy Models are handcrafted reproductions done by master engraver John J. Adams, Sr. in the 1990s. Both guns are now in a private collection. Though worth far less than an original pair, their appearance and the quality of the workmanship differs little from those sold by Schuyler, Hartley and Graham in the 1860s.

Pictured on top of R. L. Wilson's book *Steel Canvas* is the last Tiffany gripped 3rd Generation Colt produced. Known as the Heirloom 1860 Army, this was a limited edition created by Colt Blackpowder Arms between 1998 and 2000. The gun was engraved with 100 percent coverage in the L. D. Nimschke style, silver plated and accented with a 24-kt.Gold plated cylinder, loading lever, hammer, and trigger. The guns currently demand upwards of $6,000 on the secondary market. The Civil War battle scene Tiffany-style grips are typical of original guns marketed by the New York firm of Schuyler, Hartley and Graham during the Civil War era. The 3rd Generation Colt was so accurately reproduced, that if you look closely at the cylinder engraving you can read the W.L. Ormsby signature!

Wrote Wilson, "One of the most important developments in 20th century gun engraving occurred in 1971, when Colt returned black powder pistols to their product line through an arrangement with, among others, noted gunmakers Lou and Anthony Imperato, in New York. As a result, some of the finest antique Colts ever made have been produced in the last 40 years." There remains a great interest in embellished guns today, and the production of Colt Blackpowder Arms, which ended in 2002, was like a return to the golden age of gun making. That work continues to the present day either through engraving 2nd and 3rd Generation Colt Blackpowder revolvers or finely crafted Italian reproductions of Colt models. These, though still costly, are generally affordable, whereas the original antiques continue to hit record prices at auction and therefore become extremely difficult to purchase without paying a substantial price, and far too valuable to shoot.

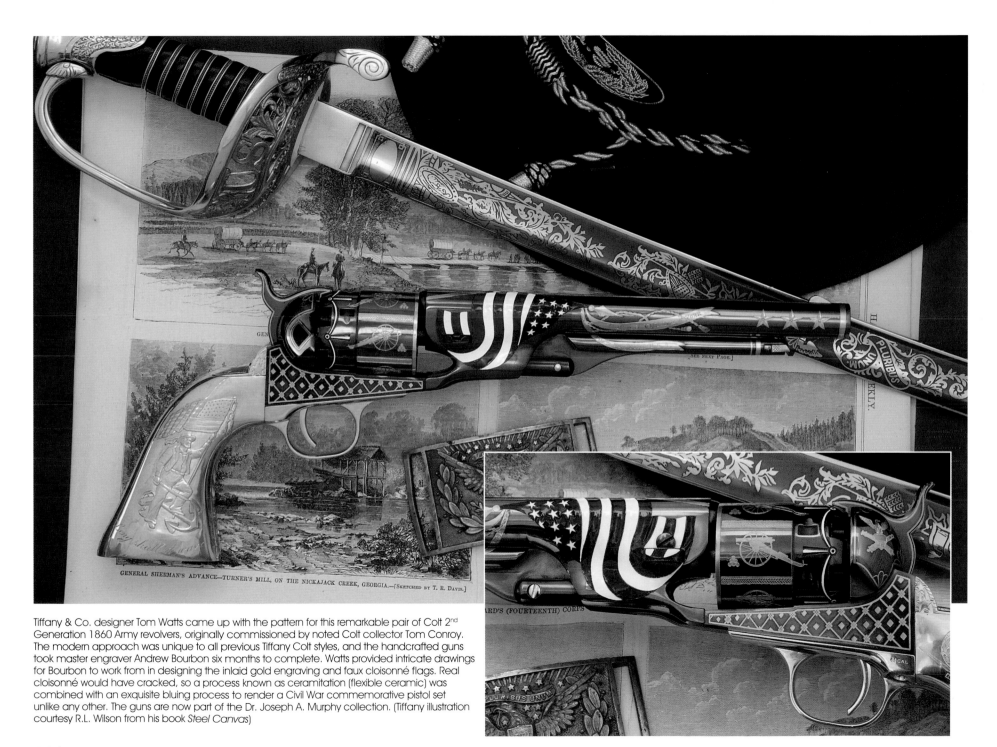

Tiffany & Co. designer Tom Watts came up with the pattern for this remarkable pair of Colt 2nd Generation 1860 Army revolvers, originally commissioned by noted Colt collector Tom Conroy. The modern approach was unique to all previous Tiffany Colt styles, and the handcrafted guns took master engraver Andrew Bourbon six months to complete. Watts provided intricate drawings for Bourbon to work from in designing the inlaid gold engraving and faux cloisonné flags. Real cloisonné would have cracked, so a process known as ceramitation (flexible ceramic) was combined with an exquisite bluing process to render a Civil War commemorative pistol set unlike any other. The guns are now part of the Dr. Joseph A. Murphy collection. (Tiffany illustration courtesy R.L. Wilson from his book *Steel Canvas*)

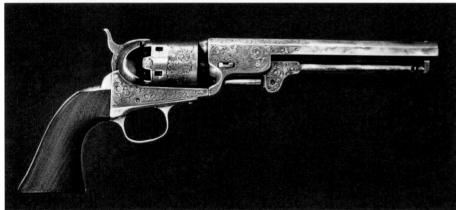

Adams also produced a pair of 1851 Confederate Navy revolvers, one of which bears an anchor amongst the intricate period-style engraving of the left barrel lug.

While the majority of Colt reproductions are of the commercial style – those sold to the general public in the late 19th century – and used today for movies, Civil War reenactments, and competition in Single Action Shooting Society events, modern-day Colt presentation pieces are still being handcrafted. The amazing thing is, that in over four hundred years the skills of the gunmaker and gun engraved have never died out.

A number of superb examples were produced through the Colt Custom Shop over the years, a few even by Tiffany & Co. Handcrafted firearms were also commissioned

through American Master Engravers in Hadlyme, Connecticut – the renowned firm headed by the late A.A. White – which for many years assisted Tiffany & Co. with highly exclusive presentation pistols.

Others have been masterfully created over the years by America Remembers (formerly the United States Historical Society) and The American Historical Foundation, through the craftsmanship of master engravers such as John J. Adams, Sr. and John Adams, Jr. of Adams & Adams in Vershire, Vermont. Engraving of good quality is reasonably priced, and the firearm when completed is worth more than the combined cost of the gun and its decoration.

This is also a time-honored practice in Italy, where the skilled artisans in Gardone and Brescia have recreated some of the most beautiful 19th century arms in the world. Companies like A. Uberti and F.lli Pietta have produced superbly hand-crafted, engraved Civil War era revolvers for more than two decades. Pietta currently has more engraved models available than any percussion gunmaker in Italy, including a striking LeMat, variations of the 1860 Army, 1851 Navy, 1858 Remington, and Starr, among others.

Contemporary artisans like Adams & Adams still use the same fundamental hand tools and venerable skills as 19th century engravers like Gustave Young, Louis Nimschke, and Cuno A. Helfricht, all of whom created some of the most outstanding presentation engraved firearms in the world.

A. A. White, who continued to engrave almost up until the time of his death, was a modern day Gustave Young. "In the annals of firearms engravers," wrote Wilson, "he was one of the greatest in history. He probably did more guns for famous people than any other American engraver of the 20th century." White created engraved pistols for Tiffany & Co., heads of state, and U.S. Presidents John F. Kennedy, Lyndon B. Johnson, Gerald Ford, and Ronald Reagan.

Over the decades since Colt's began remanufacturing models from the 19th century, thousands of extraordinary guns have been produced. Many of the finest were crafted in the mid to late 20th century by White, his protégé Andrew Bourbon, engravers Winston Churchill, Howard Dove, Ken Hurst, George Spring, Denise Thirion, Leonard Francolini, and K. C. Hunt. To watch engravers like John J. Adams, Sr., (who was one of the principal engravers for A. A. White,) work is an experience.

In a way it is harder for engravers today because of changes in metallurgy, use of investment castings, and the hardness and toughness of steel. In the days of the Old West the steel was dead soft and it was relatively easy to cut with an engraver's tool. "In order to do engravings today," wrote Wilson, "you need to have real expertise in metallurgy to soften and then re-harden metal, otherwise you can compromise the integrity of the firearm, and fundamentally, all of these engraved guns are supposed to be functional first."

The variety of engraved black powder pistols available today truly rivals those

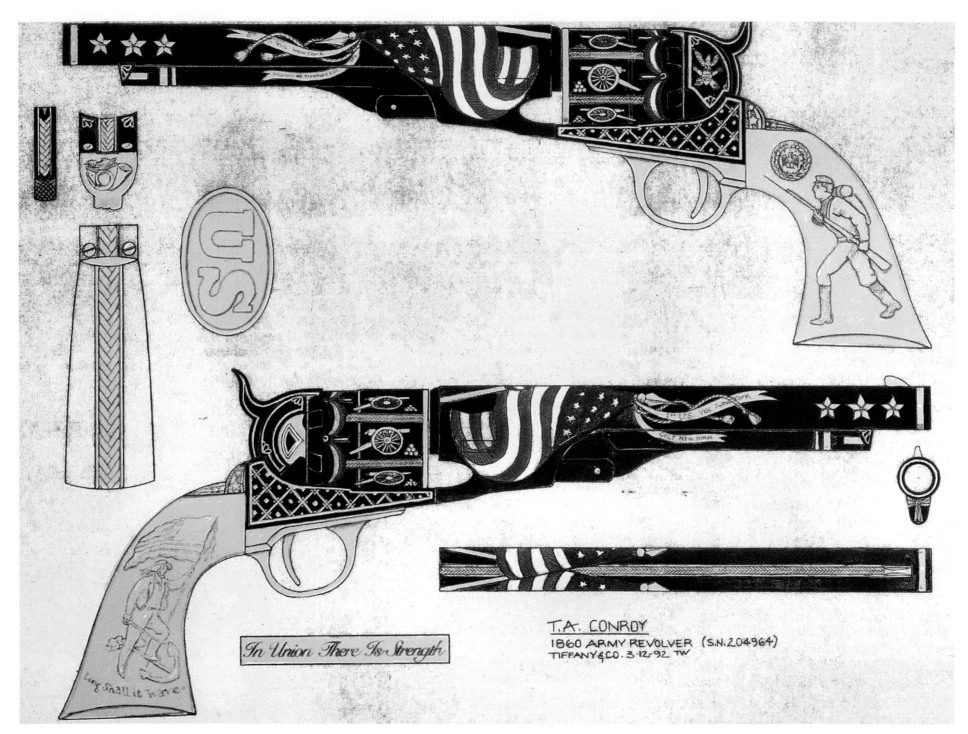

In Union There Is Strength

T.A. CONROY
1860 ARMY REVOLVER (S.N. 204964)
TIFFANY & CO. 3-12-92 TW

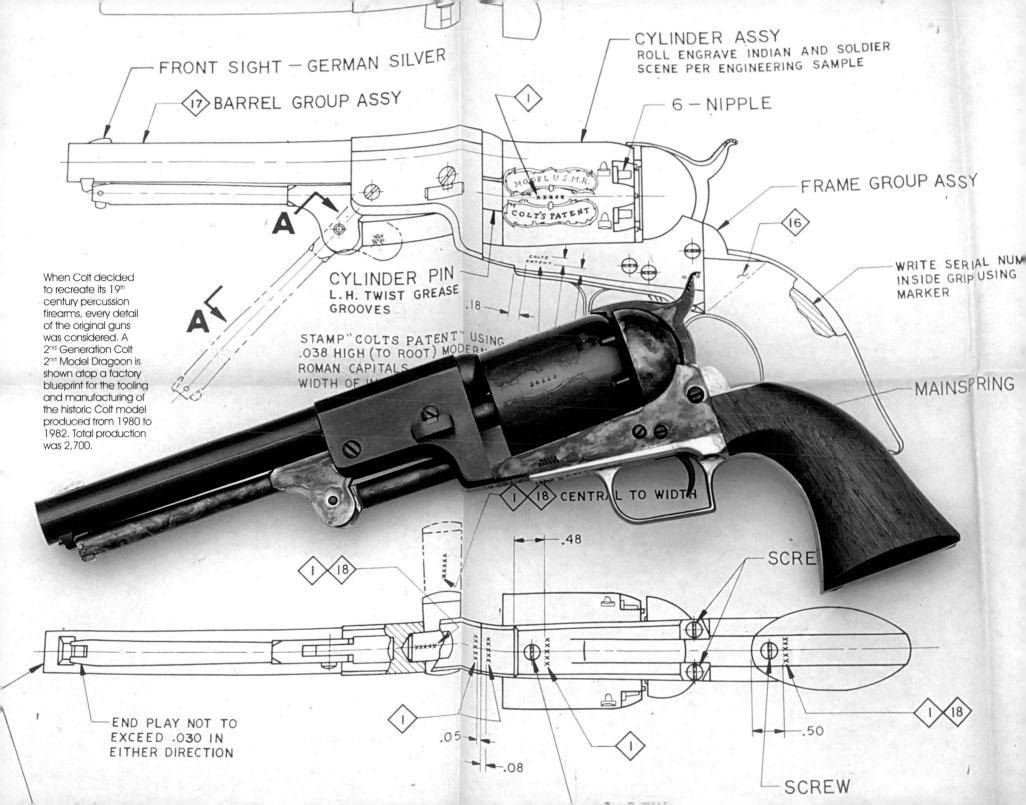

FRONT SIGHT — GERMAN SILVER

17 BARREL GROUP ASSY

CYLINDER ASSY
ROLL ENGRAVE INDIAN AND SOLDIER
SCENE PER ENGINEERING SAMPLE

6 — NIPPLE

FRAME GROUP ASSY

MODEL U.S.M.R.
XXXXX
COLT'S PATENT

WRITE SERIAL NUM
INSIDE GRIP USING
MARKER

CYLINDER PIN
L.H. TWIST GREASE
GROOVES

.18

16

When Colt decided to recreate its 19th century percussion firearms, every detail of the original guns was considered. A 2nd Generation Colt 2nd Model Dragoon is shown atop a factory blueprint for the tooling and manufacturing of the historic Colt model produced from 1980 to 1982. Total production was 2,700.

STAMP "COLTS PATENT" USING
.038 HIGH (TO ROOT) MODERN
ROMAN CAPITALS
WIDTH OF IM

MAINSPRING

1 18 CENTRAL TO WIDTH

.48

1 18

SCRE

END PLAY NOT TO
EXCEED .030 IN
EITHER DIRECTION

1

.05

.08

1

1 18

.50

SCREW

The Tiffany style cast 24-kt.gold grips are hand carved with images of soldiers, one set for the U.S. Army and one for the Confederate Army. The draping of the Union Jack and Stars and Bars over the barrels was the most difficult part of the design. The frames are outlined in gold, the inside pattern a variation of an L. D. Nimschke design.

The master of Colt engraving and engraving as a whole for the American firearms industry in the mid to late 19th century, Louis Daniel Nimschke did much of the engraving seen on Tiffany gripped Colts sold through Schuyler, Hartley and Graham in New York.

of Samuel Colt's own era. There is an air of exclusivity to having the finest of anything, and that includes firearms, old or new. Wilson finds it fascinating that the majority of collectors today like modern firearms – those produced in the 20th century. "I think engraving is the primary reason. The work today is spectacular, not only the engraving, gold and silver inlay and sculpting, but the quality of the firearms themselves."

The Tiffany Colts and Recreations

The House of Tiffany was founded in 1837 by Charles Lewis Tiffany and John B. Young. It was known then as Tiffany & Young. When Jabez L. Ellis joined the company it became Tiffany, Young & Ellis; a boutique catering to New York and New England society. Jewelry was not Tiffany's principal line; in fact fine imported silver was their stock in trade up until 1853

when Charles Tiffany took control of the company.

The new Tiffany & Co. began manufacturing its own products in the 1850s with the help of New York Silversmith John C. Moore and his son Edward C. Moore. It was the Civil War, however, that put Tiffany & Co. into the business of producing exquisitely engraved militaria, beginning with fine presentation swords in 1861. Tiffany's

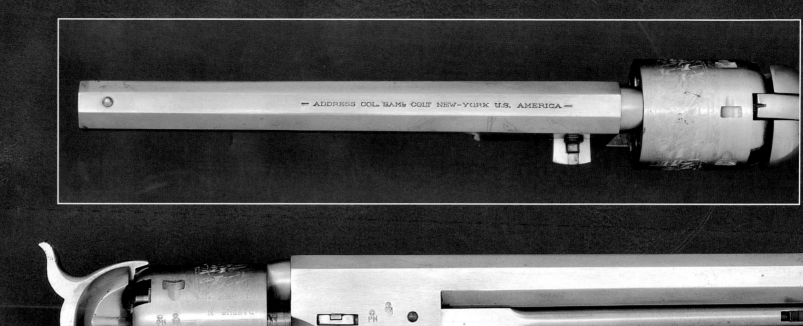

Pictured is the entire Colt 2nd Generation family of revolvers. Shown is a Walker (center) and going clockwise from top right, 1st, 2nd, and 3rd Model Dragoons, Pocket Model of Navy Caliber, Model 1848 Baby Dragoon, 1862 Police, 1861 Navy, 1860 Army fluted and rebated cylinder models, and 1851 Navy. (Author's collection)

Civil War Battle Scenes. The American and Mexican eagle were the next most popular, and the rarest was known as "The Missionary and Child." The back of the grip had a portrait of lady justice bearing a cross, with a crouching American eagle over a shield produced in high relief on the butt cap. This unique design was commissioned by the U.S. government for use on a pair of 1862 Police models presented by President Lincoln to Kibrisili Pasha, the governor of Adrianople in North West Turkey.

The Colt's custom shop often used A.A. White and American Master Engravers to produce cased engraved sets of 2nd Generation black powder revolvers like this very limited edition of 1851 Navy and 3rd Model Dragoon. The guns were done by White in an early Gustave Young vine scroll pattern. The pair was further accented with gold inlays around the barrels and the Rampant Colt emblem. Colt factory records show that the cased pair, 1851 Navy, ser. No. 24866 and Dragoon ser. No. 24575, were manufactured in 1980 and 1981, respectively, and cased as a set for Pacific International Merchandising Corporation in Sacramento, California in April 1983. (Author's collection)

clientele included Generals Ulysses S. Grant and William Tecumseh Sherman, and Admiral David G. Farragut.[1]

The War Between the States also encouraged Tiffany & Co. to venture into the field of engraved and embellished firearms for presentation, and to become the exclusive New York and New England dealer for the Henry Deringer. Colt's became a Tiffany customer during the war, as did Smith & Wesson, both of who used silver Tiffany grips on their most elaborately engraved pistols.

Tiffany gripped Colts were offered in the entire range of single action models then in production. As noted by Wilson, the elaborate, cast metal grips became "...more reminiscent of the hiltings on presentation swords of the period." Tiffany created three basic designs between 1861 and 1875, the most popular being the now famous

One hundred and twenty years after Samuel Colt introduced the 1851 Navy, the Colt Blackpowder Arms Co. produced its first reproduction. The 2nd Generation model was offered in two series, C and F and three initial versions. First was the standard 1851 model with serial numbers 4201 through 25099, produced from 1971 through 1978. A second series was introduced in May 1980 and manufactured through October 1981 with serial numbers 24900 through 28850. Finally, there was a series of limited editions beginning with the 1971 Civil War commemoratives. Pictured is one of the very early prototypes done for Colt in Italy by Aldo Uberti. Though this gun bears Italian proof marks, its purpose was to show the placement of the correct Colt barrel address. This was sample gun No. 31 c.1970. (Author's collection)

In 1971 Colt issued a pair of Civil War commemoratives, the Ulysses S. Grant and Robert E. Lee "Blue and Grey" set. The guns were sold either as two separate cased revolvers with period accessories or in a limited edition double cased set (shown).

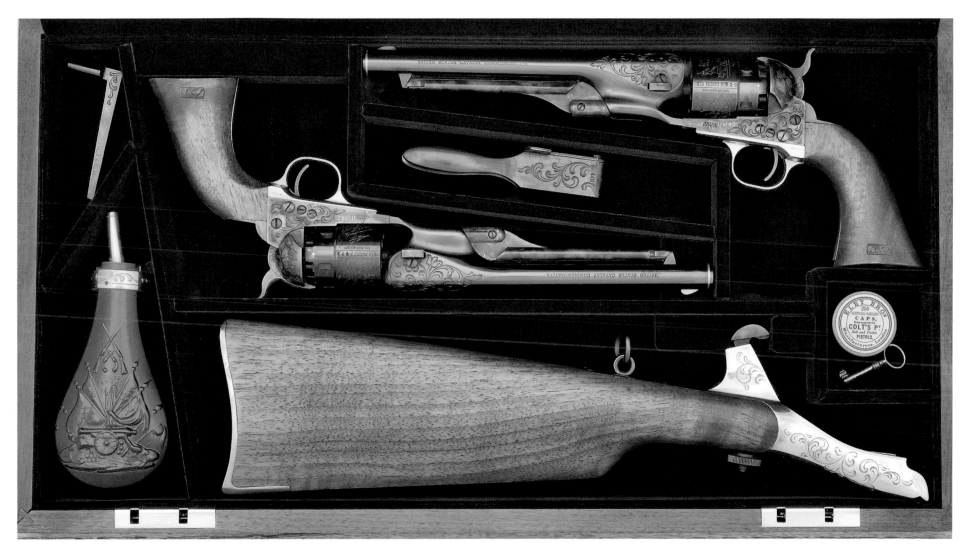

It is possible today to experience the same sense of pride in an engraved Colt revolver as it was in Samuel Colt's time. It is tribute to an art that, like the guns of the 19th century, has transcended time.

Handcrafted Civil War Era Guns

There are several ways in which commemorative Civil War era guns are manufactured today. All begin either as secondary market Colt Blackpowder Arms revolvers (produced from 1971 to 2002 in the Colt 2nd and 3rd Generation series) or new Italian-made copies of Colt and other percussion revolvers of the Civil War period. Engraving is either done by hand in the traditional method using chisels and hammer, or with an electric engraving tool (GraverMeister). A more common method today is laser engraving (which looks similar to hand engraving but with less depth and clarity), which can either stand alone as a finished piece or be hand chased to add more depth. A third style incorporates laser etching, which is usually gold inlaid with artwork more so than engraving.

One of the less seldom seen commemoratives from Colt's 2nd Generation is the deluxe U.S. Cavalry 200th Anniversary double cased set with attachable shoulder stock. While the edition from Colt's custom shop was initially limited to 40 sets, only 23 sets were made. The guns were engraved and gold inlaid with stars around the cylinder shoulders. The accessories were also period engraved to match. (Serial numbers US2972 and 2972US, from the author's collection).

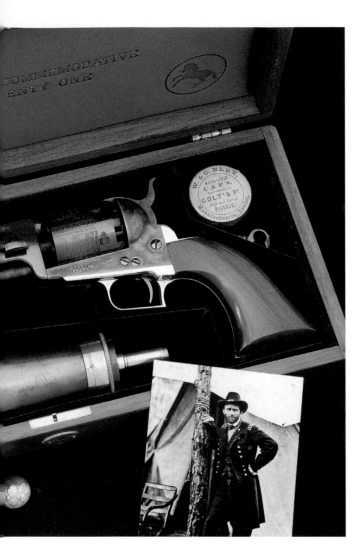

Pictured are the 1971 Ulysses S. Grant and Robert E. Lee "Blue and Grey" set. The guns were sold either as two separate cased revolvers with period accessories or in a limited edition double cased set. Shown are serial numbers 582 (Lee) and 2141 (Grant) from the author's collection. Cased pair (preceding page) from the Dennis Russell collection.

All Tiffany designs had a presentation escutcheon just below the hammer (with the exception of "The Missionary and Child") and large cast butt plates usually with an American eagle, though there were other designs. The cast Tiffany grips were either silver or gold plated and occasionally a combination of both, particularly on contemporary (20th century) examples.

The Tiffany "influence" in grip design was prolific in the 1860s and well into the post Civil War era. The design, though often called "Tiffany gripped" was not necessarily an assurance that they were cast by Tiffany & Co. In fact, most were not. Wilson is of the opinion that most of the grips were actually done by the Ames Sword Co. of Massachusetts, which also manufactured highly embellished swords for Schuyler, Hartley and Graham. In addition, John Quincy Adams Ward, the prominent American sculptor who designed the Justice and American eagle pattern Tiffany grips, was employed by the Ames Sword Co.[2]

Many of the "Tiffany gripped" Colts sold in the 1860s and 1870s were marketed through the New York retail firm of Schuyler, Hartley and Graham, which employed L. D. Nimschke and his shop as their "in-house" engraver, thus many of the finest Tiffany style Colts are Nimschke engraved. Others were done by the Nimschke shop or in the Nimschke style by other engravers hired by Schuyler, Hartley and Graham. Tiffany-style grips are also seen on Colt cartridge conversions of the 1860 Army, 1851 Navy, and Colt's Pocket Models, as well as 1873 Peacemakers and later Colt revolvers.

Today, Adams & Adams (John J. Adams, Sr. and John Adams, Jr.); Andrew Bourbon; Conrad Anderson; and dozens of contemporary artisans carry on a tradition established more than 150 years ago by Samuel Colt and his guild of engravers; Gustave Young, Louis Daniel Nimschke, Cuno A. Helfricht, their families and descendants.

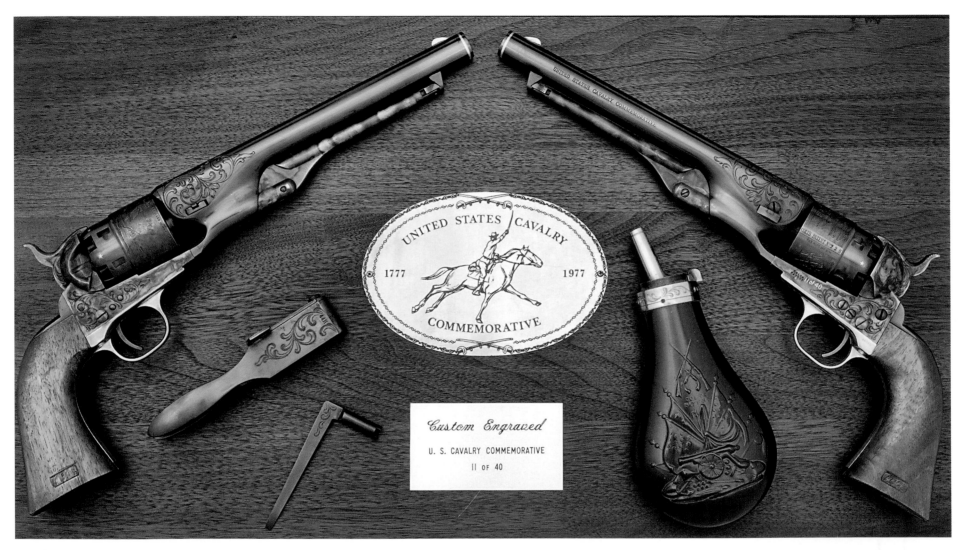

All three techniques are used today in producing Civil War commemorative arms.

Hand engraving is naturally the most expensive and examples are often limited to very small editions or even single guns. Among the finest examples in recent time is a cased pair of 2nd Generation Colt 1860 Army revolvers duplicating an original set engraved by the Cuno Helfricht shop at Colt's in the 1860s. The guns were recreated by John J. Adams Sr. for a private client and cased with authentic accessories in a period correct presentation box

handcrafted by Pennsylvania furniture maker Duncan Everhart. Adams also handcrafted the pair of 2nd Generation Colt 1851 Navy Tiffany revolvers that are pictured. The Tiffany style is very rare, even as a reproduction.

The most elaborate set of Tiffany models ever produced were a cased set designed by Tom Watts of Tiffany & Co. in 1992 and handcrafted by master engraver Andrew Bourbon. Commissioned under the Tiffany & Co. name, the intricate design incorporated the use of engraving, casting, and ceramitation, a flexible cloisonné process.

The cast grips, featuring Union and Confederate soldiers, were 24-kt.gold. As has been the case with custom built Civil War commemoratives, only one set was produced.

The one exception to this rule was the Colt Blackpowder Arms Heritage 1860 Army Tiffany-style revolver, which was manufactured from 1998 to 2002. Hand engraved in the L.D. Nimschke vine scroll style, as originally sold by Schuyler, Hartley and Graham in the 1860s, the Colt reproductions were silver plated with 24kt. gold plated cylinders, loading levers, hammer, and triggers.

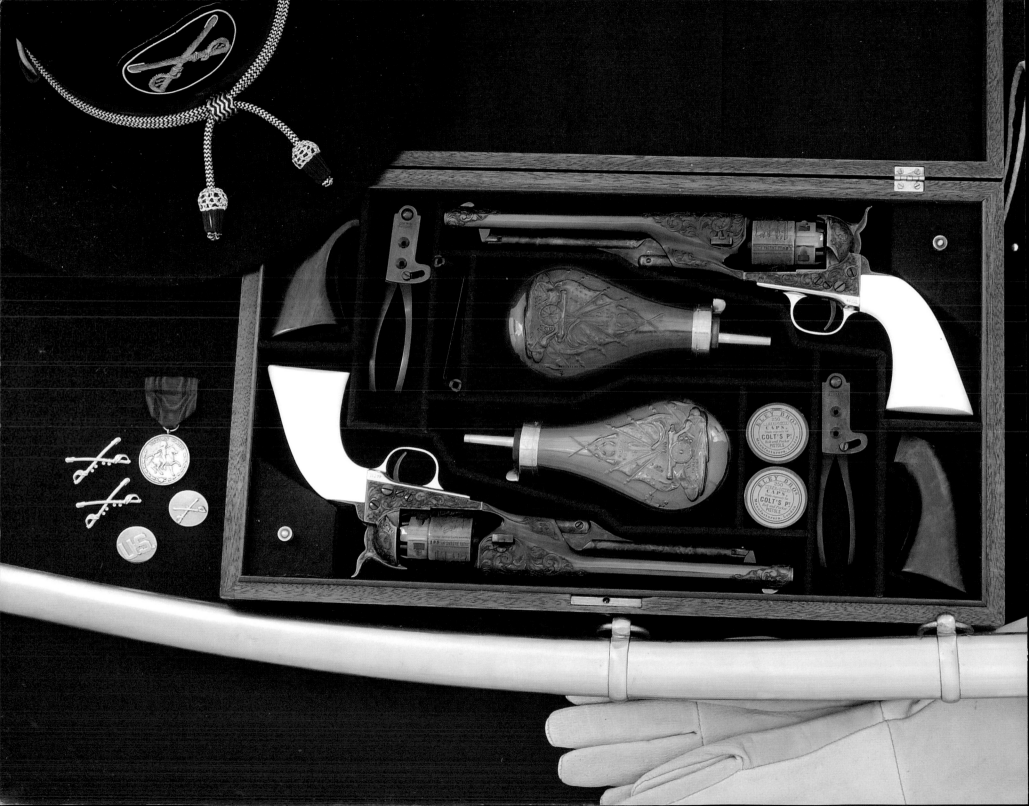

The engraving was accented by silver plated Tiffany Civil War battle scene grips. Priced at $5,000 when introduced, it is estimated that fewer than 100 were produced.

For over half a century, the Civil War has been one of the most popular themes for limited edition, custom embellished firearms. The earliest examples came from Italian armsmakers, as did the first Civil War era reproductions of Colt and Remington revolvers. Though Colt may have made the original guns, the very first reproduction Colt-style percussion models were actually created in Italy during the late 1950s for Val Forgett, Sr., the founder of Navy Arms.

Italy is where the story of most every contemporary Colt or Remington reproduction begins. Forgett had wanted to introduce a line of Colt 1851 Navy revolvers and other models in time for the Civil War Centennial in 1961. Those very first guns were crafted by Aldo Uberti and manufactured in Italy by Gregorelli & Uberti.

Forgett had established a working relationship with armsmakers Luciano Amadi,

The Deluxe engraved U.S. Cavalry set came with two 1860 Army revolvers and a single shoulder stock, just as guns were originally issued to the cavalry during the Civil War. (Author's collection)

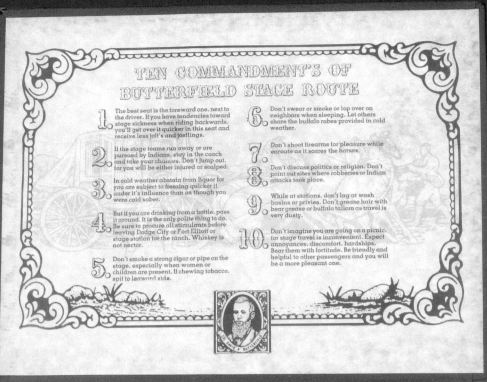

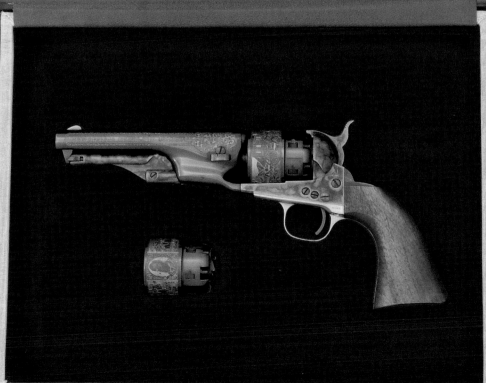

Aldo Uberti, and Gregorelli in 1957, which led to the very first prototype 1851 Navy that Uberti made by hand from an original gun Forgett had left for him to study. Those first 1851 Navy revolvers manufactured by Gregorelli and Uberti started an industry that encouraged the gun's originator, the Colt's Patent Fire-Arms Mfg. Co., to begin remaking its 19th century percussion revolvers in 1971. The rest, as they say, is history.

The original 2nd Generation Colt Blackpowder Arms (Blackpowder being the company trademark name, as opposed to the gun powder, which is two words), were manufactured through Colt Industries from 1971 to 1982; first with assistance from Forgett (1971-1973), then Lou Imperato (Iver Johnson Arms), between 1974 and 1976, with final assembly at the Colt factory in Connecticut. Colt finished its initial production from 1978 to 1982 having the guns completed at the Iver Johnson manufacturing facilities in Middlesex, New Jersey. Most of the truly noteworthy engraved contemporary Colt percussion revolvers came out of the 2nd Generation series, and all of the guns are regarded as genuine Colts. All 2nd Generation percussion models can be authenticated and lettered by the factory.

Among early Civil War Colt commemoratives were the U.S. Grant and Robert E. Lee 1851 Navy cased sets, produced in 1971. These were offered as individual cased guns and in a deluxe double cased Blue and Gray set. A total of 4,750 each of the individual cased guns were produced, and 250 double cased sets.

The second major Colt Civil War commemorate was the U.S. Cavalry cased set with two 1860 Army revolvers and a single shoulder stock, just as they were originally issued to the Cavalry from 1861 to 1865. There were several variations in this commemorative set, from plain blued guns (2,945 sets plus 40 sets with a "C" suffix) to two versions with factory engraving and gold inlays. The most elaborate set was limited to an edition of 40 but only 23 were ever made. The gold inlaid sets (no engraving) were limited to only 17 pair.

When it comes to big production numbers and Civil War commemoratives one has only to look at guns sold by America Remembers and the U.S. Historical Society.

Commissioned by the Hodgdon Powder Co., Colt produced a special run of 2nd Generation 1860 Army "Butterfield Overland Despatch" models with 5-1/2 inch barrels, an engraved cylinder picturing the Butterfield stagecoach scene, and spare cylinder engraved with a portrait of Col. David Butterfield, a Conestoga wagon and longhorn steer. The barrel was engraved Butterfield Overland Despatch. The edition was limited to 500 and came in a French fit book-style case. The example pictured with gold embellished scenes (the guns have been seen either in blue or with gold filled engraving) is serial number 201323. (Author's collection)

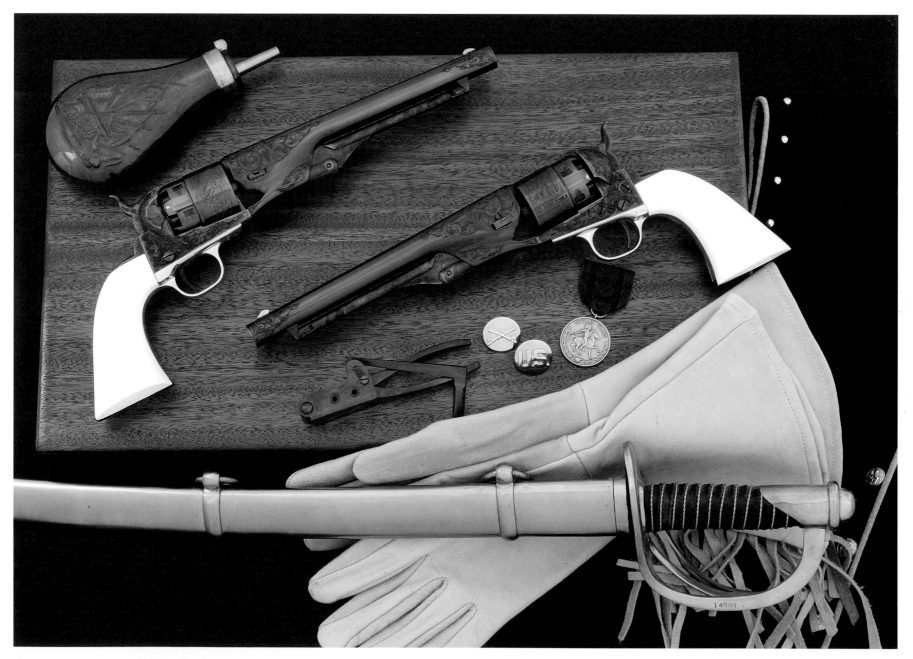

The Colt Custom Shop has been turning out extraordinary engraved guns since the 19th century and continues to do so. This cased pair of 3rd Generation Signature Series Colt 1860 Army revolvers (Ser. Nos. 223051 and 223061) was done by John J. Adams, Sr. for the Colt's custom shop in 1999. They were used as the company's display guns for the Missouri Valley Arms Collectors and NRA National Gun Collectors Show held in Kansas City, Missouri. The pair features Class "B" Expert scroll engraving and hand carved ivory grips. (Dr. Tom Covalt collection)

The Colt Blackpowder 3rd Generation Custer 1861 Navy models were among the best laser engraved guns of the period (1996). The engraving technique was a Nimschke-style period vine scroll motif. To give the engraving more depth, a punch dot background (another prominent Nimschke engraving style) was added by hand. The example shown was among the last guns built in 2002 and has a polished nickel finish. (Author's collection)

Colt Blackpowder Arms 3rd Generation 1860 Army models included the fluted and rebated cylinder variations, and among limited editions, a Cavalry model with fluted cylinder and gold etched U.S. over crossed sabers.

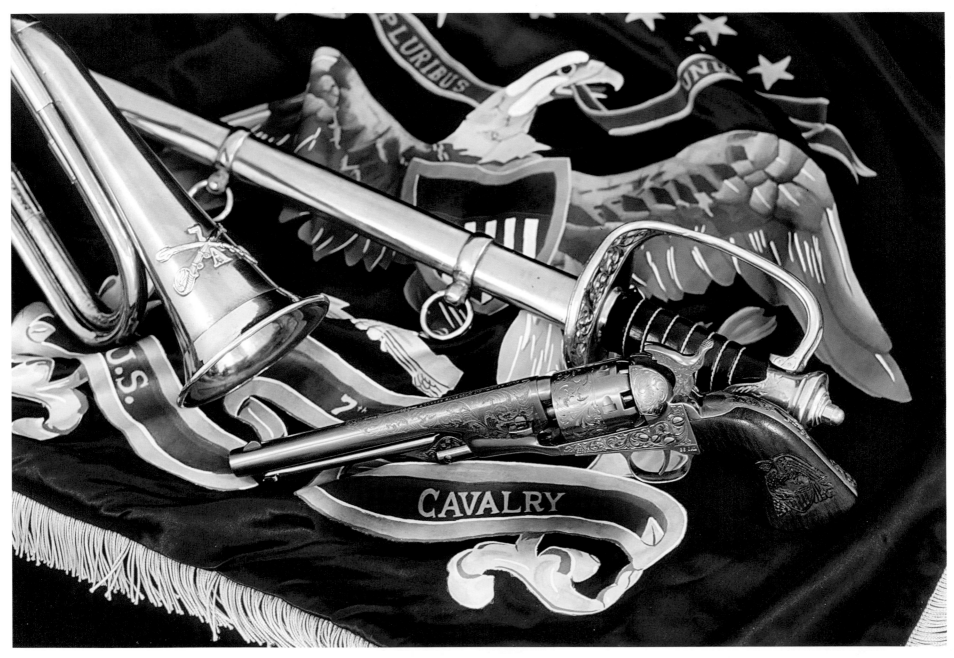

Chambered in .36 caliber percussion, the George Armstrong Custer 3rd Generation 1861 Navy had an antique silver blue finish embellished in the style of Louis Nimschke, one of the premiere engravers of Colt revolvers in the second half of the 19th century. Presentation stocks for the Custer were select rosewood, engraved with a carved American eagle over a shield on the left-hand side, with a deep checkered pattern appropriate to the era on the right. (Reproduction of Custer's 7th Cavalry flag courtesy Hugh Tracy collection)

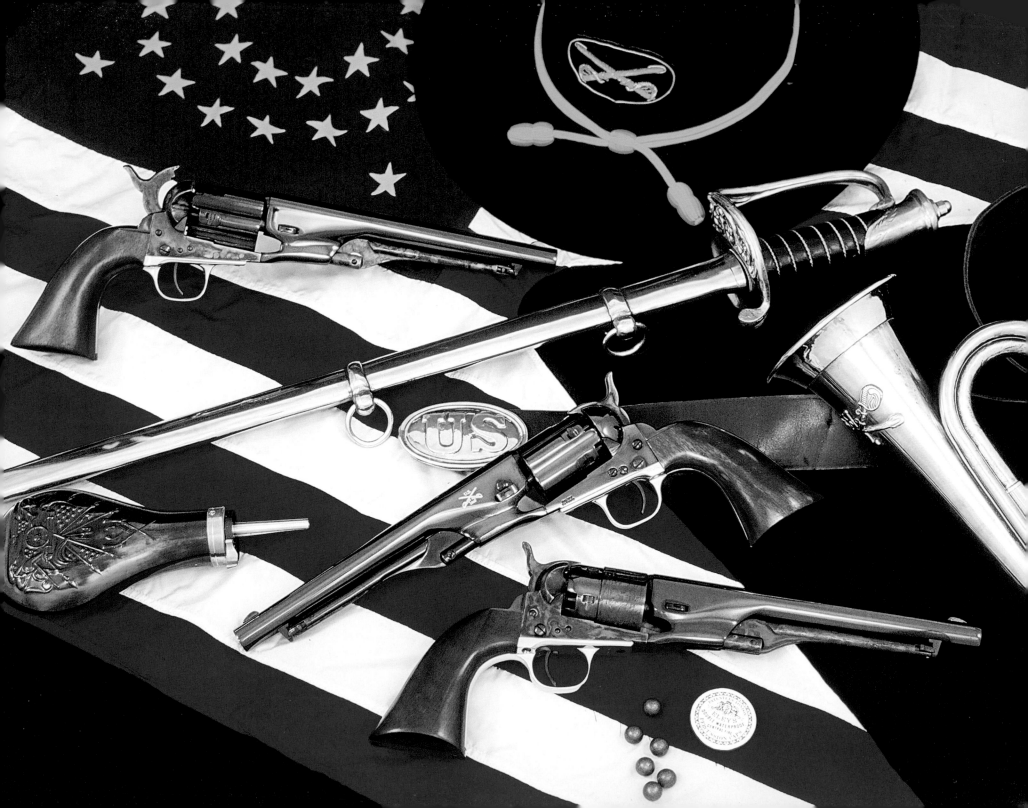

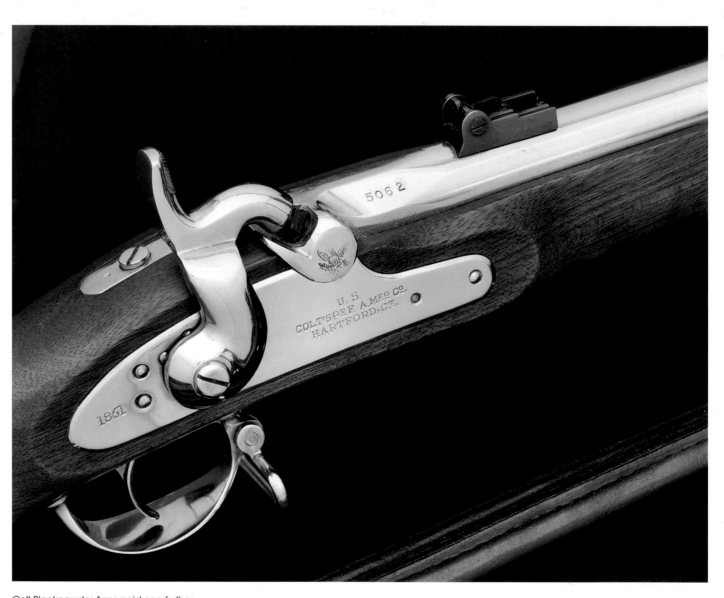

Colt Blackpowder Arms paid one further
tribute to the Civil War by reproducing the
famous Springfield Contract Model 1861
rifled musket which was produced at the
Colt factory in Hartford throughout the War
Between the States. The Colt Blackpowder
Arms Co. reproductions were also offered with
a period correct bayonet and scabbard. The
limited production longarms bore all of the
original 1861 Colt's factory markings. (Gun and
accessories courtesy J. P. Reno)

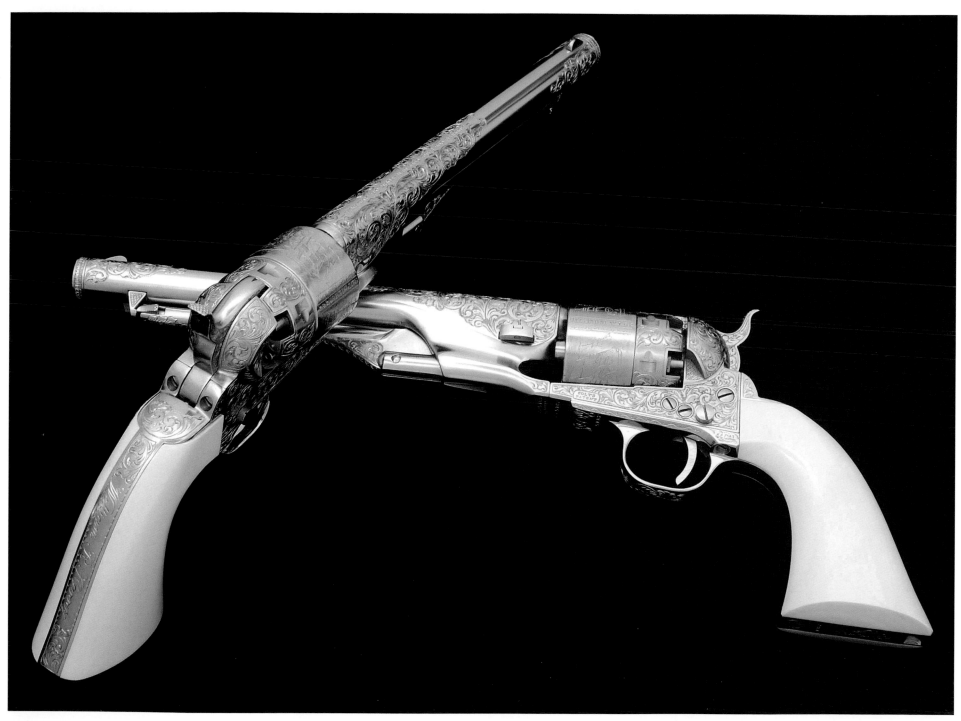

Copied from an original pair of cased and engraved Colt 1860 Army revolvers, John J. Adams, Sr. engraved this set as a private commission. The mahogany case was handcrafted from the original design by Pennsylvania furniture maker Duncan Everhart. The special accessories were done by Frank Klay.

John J. Adams, Sr. worked for Colt as an engraver during the 2nd Generation Colt Blackpowder era. Today, Adams and his son John, Jr., operate Adams & Adams Engraving in Vershire, Vermont. Adams, Sr. is shown working on one of the barrels for the 1860 Army set. While more than 140 years have past since the original Colt models were engraved by the Helfricht shop at Colt's, the techniques of hand cutting and hand engraving are the same today as they were in the 1860s. (Photos by Sarah Adams)

DEL
Fredericksburg
VA.
LONGSTREET
ROSE CRANS
GRANT
Chattanooga
23-25 Nov.
Chickamauga 19-20 Sept.
Cedar Bluff
F.S. 3 May
S. CAR.
GRIERSON'S RAID
MISS.
GRANT
McLERNAND & SHERMAN
LA.
Vicksburg
23 May - 4 July
Port Gibson
ALA.
Assault on
Ft. Wagner
18 July
Charleston
Ft. Wagner 7 Sept.
FLORIDA
New Orleans
SAM COLT

Another one-of-a-kind Civil War commemorative, this Robert E. Lee Colt 3rd Generation Model 1851 Navy was engraved in an authentic Gustave Young pattern by the legendary Ken Hurst. The 24-kt.Gold bust of General Lee was cast and inlaid by Andrew Bourbon, who also engraved a copy of Lee's signature into the backstrap, and the gold inlaid CSA on the right barrel lug. The hand carved ivory grips were done by Dan Chesiak, another Colt alumnus, who crafted hundreds of pairs of ivory grips for 2nd and 3rd Generation Colt revolvers. (Author's collection)

America Remembers Editions

America Remembers currently offers the following Civil War models:

A Tribute to the Confederacy; C.S.S. H.L. Hunley Recovery Tribute Revolver; Civil War Cavalry Leaders Tribute Rifle; Civil War Sesquicentennial Tribute Rifle; Gettysburg 1863 Revolver; Gettysburg Tribute Rifle; "God Bless Dixie" Tribute Revolver; Jefferson Davis Tribute Rifle; Mort Künstler Lee-Jackson Tribute Rifle; Museum of the Confederacy Tribute Revolver; Robert E. Lee & His Officers Tribute Rifle; Sons of Confederate Veterans Spencer Carbine; and the West Point Civil War Union and Confederate Leaders Tribute Rifles. Editions are generally limited to around 300 to 500, though there are exceptions like the 1860 Army Gettysburg 1863 Tribute Revolver which is being produced in a special run of 1,863 guns. The Civil War Sesquicentennial Tribute Henry is limited to 500.

Civil War enthusiasts were pleased with this 1860 Army commemorating the July 1863 Battle of Gettysburg. This model featured a 24-kt. gold battle scene surrounding the rebated cylinder. With each rotation of the cylinder, another piece of the Gettysburg drama unfolded. The left side of the barrel bore the legend GETTYSBURG PENNSYLVANIA JULY 1863. On the right side was an inscription from Lincoln's Gettysburg Address. "We here highly resolve that these dead shall not have died in vain." The French fitted solid walnut presentation box came with a parchment paper replica of the Gettysburg Address, and both Union and Confederate belt buckles in solid brass.

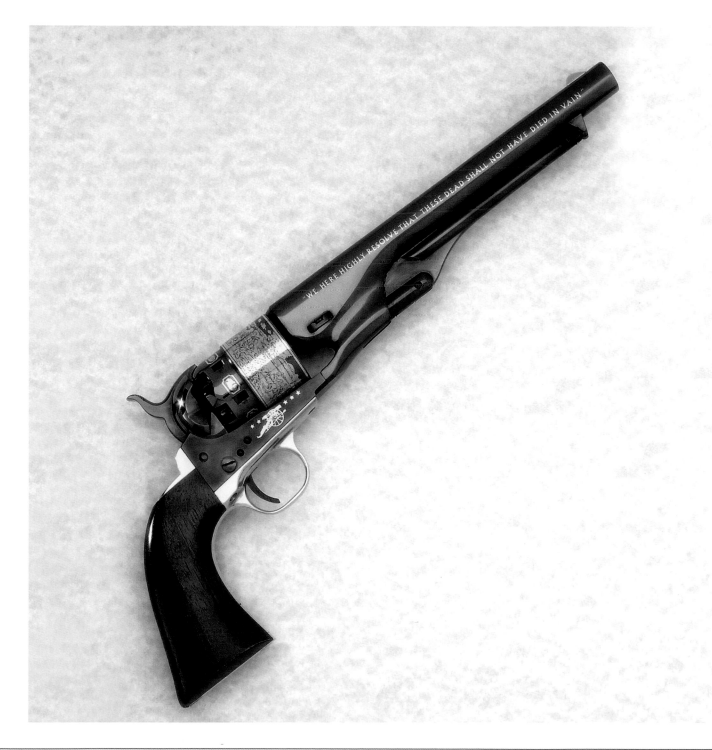

One of the finest hand engraved reproductions ever done, the Jefferson Davis 1851 Navy with shoulder stock, was produced in Italy by A. Uberti & Co. for the United States Historical Society (now America Remembers). The guns were duplicated in exacting detail from the original presented by Samuel Colt to then U.S. Senator and former Secretary of War Jefferson Davis. The original price at the time of issue in March 1990 was $2995 plus $395 for the display case. The Jefferson Davis commemorative is one of the most difficult models to find on the secondary market.

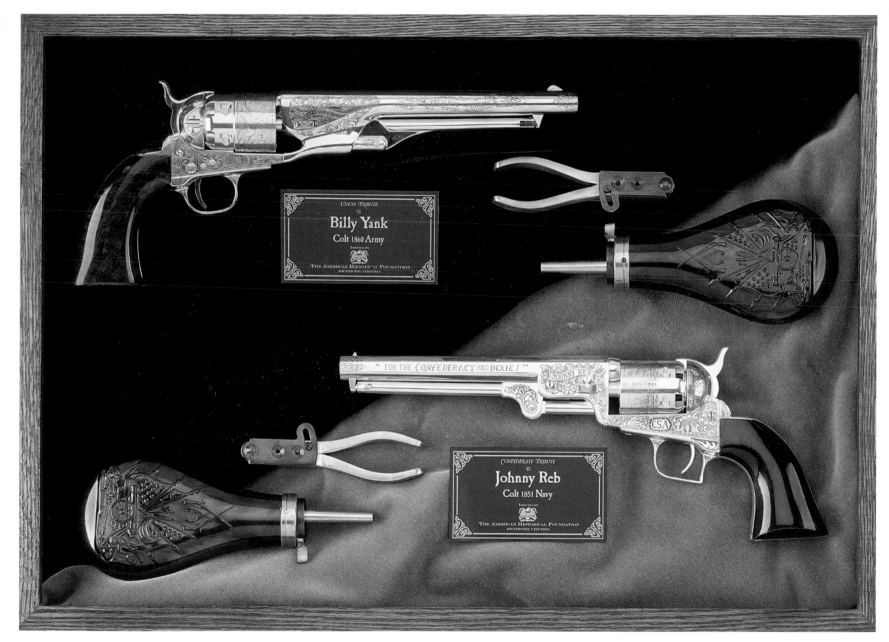

This striking pair of Union and Confederate commemoratives was issued in 1987 by The American Historical Foundation as either individual guns with flask and bullet mold, or as a cased pair with accessories. The Union Tribute to "Billy Yank" was a fully engraved 1860 Army in 24-kt.gold. The Confederate Tribute to "Johnny Reb" was an 1851 Navy hand-engraved and plated in genuine sterling silver. This series was limited to only 250 of each.

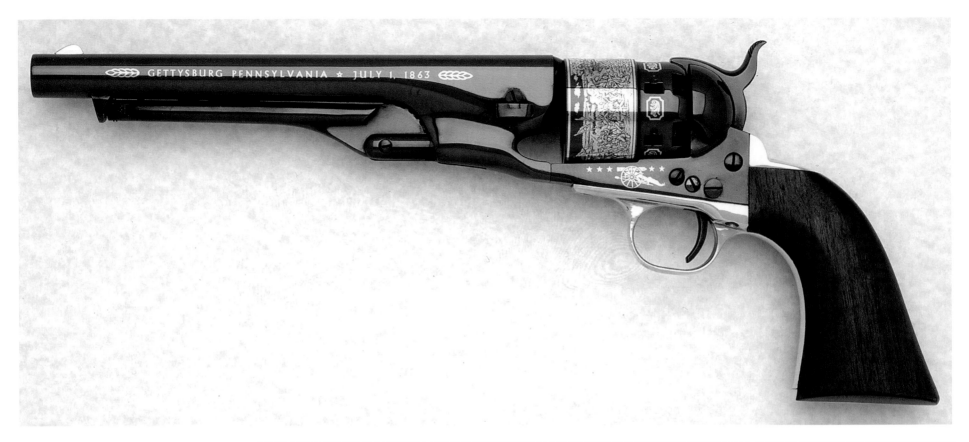

The C.S.S. H.L. Hunley Recovery Tribute Revolver, is an elegantly decorated limited edition firearm that honors a very historic event in American history, the sinking of the USS Housatonic, a Federal sloop-of-war, by the C.S.S. H.L. Hunley, on the night of February 17, 1864, off Sullivan's Island near the entrance to Charleston Harbor. The successful attack was a history-making first by a submarine against an enemy vessel in warfare. The Tribute is being issued with the cooperation of the E. Porter Alexander Camp #158 of the Sons of Confederate Veterans, the Augusta, Georgia, group that spearheaded the search that ultimately ended in the discovery of the Confederate submarine, the C.S.S. H.L. Hunley.

Another superb 1860 model from the United States Historical Society was the U.S. Cavalry Pistol, embellished with two Jack Woodson scenes around the rebated cylinder, United States Cavalry and crossed sabers along the length of the barrel, and magnificent genuine stag grips. This edition was limited to 975 examples.

There are many symbols which represent the Confederate cause, and one of the most cherished was the word "Dixie." The song *Dixie* was written and first performed in 1859, only two years before the war began. The origin of the term Dixie is not completely known. However, we do know that the song popularized the term Dixie and that it became a popular tune for Confederate forces during the war. American Remembers's "God Bless Dixie" Tribute Revolver is a handsomely gold etched revolver celebrating the soldiers, leaders, and citizens of the Confederate States and their beloved Dixie Land. A symbol of Southern pride, the Tribute is crafted from a classic 3rd Generation Colt Model 1860 Army Revolver, a favorite sidearm for both Confederate and Union forces during the war.

On the occasion of the 125th Anniversary of the American Civil War in 1986, The American Historical Foundation issued a pair of fully engraved Colt Dragoons, a 3rd Model Union in 24-kt.gold and 2nd Model Confederate Dragoon in sterling silver.

The American Historical Foundation issued the Blue & the Gray Dragoon set in 1986 in an extremely limited edition. Both guns were elaborately engraved. Authentic Colt 2nd Generation guns were used for this special Union and Confederate pair. The guns were sold separately and not as a set.

America Remembers first-ever issue of a LeMat. The Museum of the Confederacy Tribute Revolver combines the classic design of the fabled LeMat revolver with striking 24-karat gold and nickel artwork honoring the legacy of the Confederate soldiers and their leaders who valiantly fought for the cause of the Confederacy. Issued with the approval and authorization of The Museum of the Confederacy, the gun features portraits of Robert E. Lee, J.E.B. Stuart, and Jefferson Davis. The edition is limited to 500.

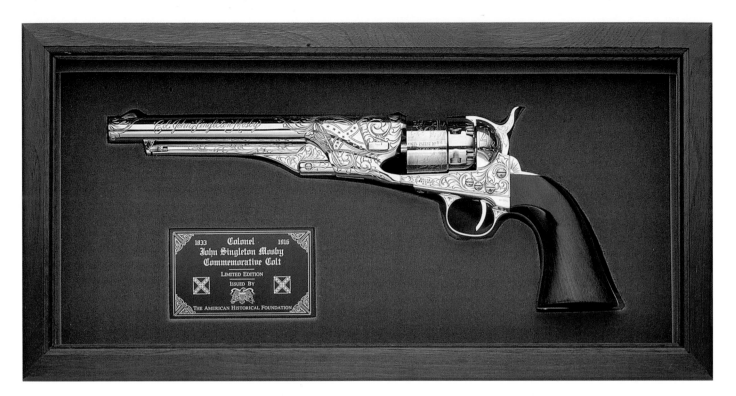

Confederate Col. John Singleton Mosby (center with feather in hat) was one of Robert E. Lee's most effective commanders. Mosby's 43rd Virginia Rangers were the scourge of the Union Army. To commemorate Mosby in 1989, The American Historical Foundation issued an edition of 150 Colt 1860 Army revolvers in sterling silver with 24-kt. gold plated cylinder. The guns were fully hand-engraved in period style and accented with the 43rd. engraved on the left side of the recoil shield, the Confederate flag along the barrel lug, and Colonel John Singleton Mosby in script style along the length of the barrel in 24-kt. gold. This was one of the Foundation's most historic offerings due to Mosby's fame among Civil War reenactors and history buffs.

The United States Historical Society produced its own commemorative Robert E. Lee 1851 Navy in 1988. Unlike the Colt version done in 1971, the USHS model featured Florentine engraving in 24-kt.gold. The Navy revolver also featured a special engraved cylinder with five important symbols in the life of Robert E. Lee, including Lee's home in Arlington and the Lee family crest. A cast medallion of Lee was set into the left hand grip and a minted solid silver medallion with a bust of Lee on the obverse side and Lee atop his horse Traveler on the reverse, was included in a French Fitted presentation case.

In the past, the U.S. Historical Society produced one of the most significant Civil War commemoratives, a limited edition copy of the shoulder stocked and factory engraved 1851 Navy that was presented to Jefferson Davis by Samuel Colt, when Davis was U.S. Secretary of War. That edition was handcrafted in Italy and limited to 1,000 guns produced in 1990. Another 250 were produced for The American Historical Foundation (acquired by America Remembers in 2005).

The American Historical Foundation was responsible for the greatest majority of engraved and custom embellished Civil War commemoratives done in the 1990s, including the Billy Yank Union Model 1860 Army; Johnny Reb Confederate 1851 Navy; The Blue and the Gray Dragoons; Col. John Singleton Mosby 1860 Army; Gen. J.E.B. Stuart LeMat; Gen. Robert E. Lee 1851 Navy; Gen. Thomas J. "Stonewall" Jackson LeMat; and the Jefferson Davis shoulder stocked 1851 Navy. Editions varied in number

The most famous owner of a Colt 1851 Navy was Union scout James Butler Hickok. The renowned "Wild Bill" was known to carry a brace of 1851 Navy revolvers both during and after the Civil War. There have been two issues of the Hickok 1851 Navy revolvers, the first in 1989 by The American Historical Foundation. Hand-engraved and plated in sterling silver, the ivory-gripped revolvers were offered as a matched pair, as Hickok carried them, or as a single gun. The backstrap was imprinted J.B. Hickok, as on the "Prince of Pistoleers" engraved 1851 Navy revolvers. The issue was limited to 500 examples. The most recent edition from America Remembers (pictured) offers the same features with high relief antiqued American eagle and Liberty faux ivory grips and a glass top presentation box. (Hickok Holsters by Jim Barnard/TrailRider Products)

The American Historical Foundation produced 500 J.E.B. Stuart commemorative LeMat Cavalry revolvers. Done with a black finish and 24-kt. gold plating, the choice of black was symbolic of mourning, a reminder that General Stuart died in the War Between the States. This was the first Limited Edition LeMat ever produced.

In creating the Mort Künstler Lee-Jackson Tribute Rifle, both America Remembers and Mort Künstler knew one rifle was the perfect firearm for this issue – the Henry rifle. The Tribute is a detailed recreation of the Henry Rifle, each produced by the incomparable artisans of A. Uberti, chambered caliber .44-40 with a blued, 24-1/4 inch half-octagonal barrel with a tubular magazine. Each of the six images on the Henry was hand-drawn by Künstler especially for the design of the rifle's receiver. Craftsmen commissioned specifically for this Tribute by America Remembers, have captured Künstler's artwork in minute detail, with a nickel decorated background serving as the canvas for the artwork. A special blackened patina highlights the artwork for maximum detail. Completing the Tribute's decorations are the polished and 24-karat gold decorated lever, buttplate and hammer. Finally, there is Künstler's own stylish signature laser-carved into the rifle's walnut stock.

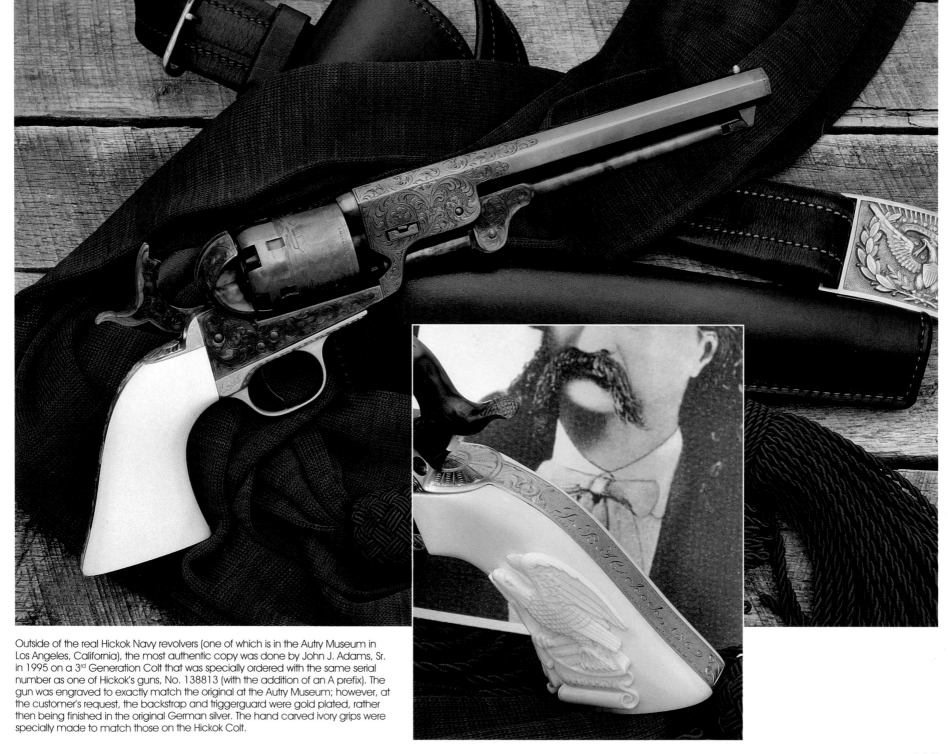

Outside of the real Hickok Navy revolvers (one of which is in the Autry Museum in Los Angeles, California), the most authentic copy was done by John J. Adams, Sr. in 1995 on a 3rd Generation Colt that was specially ordered with the same serial number as one of Hickok's guns, No. 138813 (with the addition of an A prefix). The gun was engraved to exactly match the original at the Autry Museum; however, at the customer's request, the backstrap and triggerguard were gold plated, rather then being finished in the original German silver. The hand carved ivory grips were specially made to match those on the Hickok Colt.

The America Remembers Civil War Tribute Henry features battle scenes and portraits of three famed Confederate leaders on the left side; General James Ewell Brown "JEB" Stuart, General Nathan Bedford Forrest, and Colonel John Mosby. In the center, the "Cavaliers in Gray" are featured charging into battle with the Confederate flag held high. Elegant scrollwork in 24-karat gold surrounds the images on both sides of the receiver. The right side features portraits of three famed Union leaders; General Philip Sheridan, General George Armstrong Custer, and General John Buford. The "Cavaliers in Blue" are also featured in full gallop racing into combat with the Union flag leading the way. This edition is limited to 300.

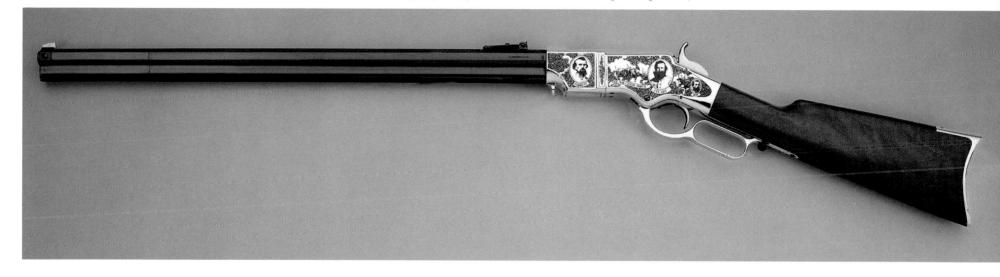

The Jefferson Davis Tribute is a recreation of the 1862 Richmond rifled musket chambered in .58 caliber percussion. The right side of the stock features an illustration of two crossed Confederate flags (the familiar Confederate battle flag and the Third National flag) laser-etched into the walnut. Both flags are hand-painted in brilliant red, white and blue. The left side of the stock features a laser-etched quote from Jefferson Davis: "The principle for which we contend is bound to reassert itself, though it may be at another time and in another form." A series of commemorative phrases are written along the blued barrel: "President Jefferson Finis Davis," "1861 – 150th Anniversary of the War for Southern Independence – 1865," and "Deo Vindice," the motto of the Confederacy, meaning "God Will Vindicate." The blued lock plate features a portrait of Jefferson Davis from the well-known photo by Mathew Brady and is decorated by elegant, ornamental scrollwork. Stamped into the plate to the left of the hammer is "1862," to the right of the hammer is the legend: "C.S. Richmond, VA."

To honor the legacy of Confederate soldiers and leaders, America Remembers introduced "A Tribute to the Confederacy" Spencer Carbine. Officially authorized by the Sons of Confederate Veterans – VA Division, the Spencer is issued in a strictly limited edition of 300 from the United States Society of Arms and Armour, the Antique Arms Division of America Remembers. Each Tribute is a detailed working recreation of the Spencer carbine produced by the old-world craftsmen of Armi Sport di Chiappa in Italy. Chambered in .56-50 caliber, each Tribute is elegantly decorated with two milestone events from the Civil War – Pickett's Charge at Gettysburg, and the Last Meeting of Generals Lee and Jackson, captured in a combination of gleaming 24-karat gold and nickel decoration with special blackened patina highlights. Each gun is individually numbered from 001-300.

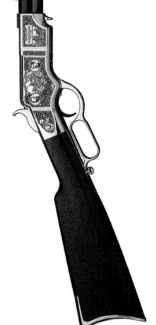

America Remembers' Gettysburg Tribute Rifle is another special Henry model by the master craftsmen of A. Uberti. The Henry is decorated with battle scenes from Gettysburg and busts of both Union and Confederate commanders, including Robert E. Lee, George Meade, John Buford, J.E.B. Stuart, James Longstreet, Winfield Scott Hancock, George Pickett, Joshua Lawrence Chamberlain, and Lewis A. Armistead. This edition is limited to 500.

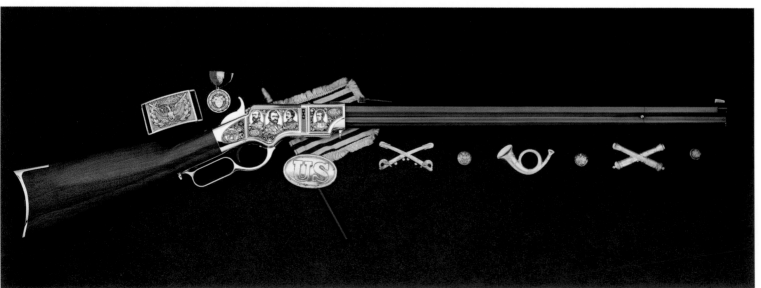

In honor of the many graduates of West Point who served so valiantly, and the famed and revered leaders on both sides of the conflict, the United States Society of Arms & Armour, the Antique Arms Affiliate of America Remembers, offers a matched pair of magnificently decorated Henry rifles honoring this epic time in American history. Officially authorized by the Association of Graduates of the United States Military Academy, the West Point Civil War Union Leaders Tribute and the West Point Civil War Confederate Leaders Tribute Rifles are issued in strictly limited editions of only 500 of each Tribute, exclusively from America Remembers.

from only 150 for Mosby 1860 Army revolvers to 500 for the majority of Civil War commemoratives.

The variety of percussion revolvers and cartridge firing rifles used during the Civil War have given modern day armsmakers a wealth of guns to recreate and with the arrival of another significant anniversary from 2011 to 2015, no doubt many more will be produced to celebrate the Sesquicentennial of the War Between the States.

Choosing a quality Civil War Reproduction

There is no easy way to recreate a 19th century revolver. What is easier is the manufacturing of the individual components that go into a gun. The final assembly, fitting and finish, however, are still a job best done by hand, and that is what separates reproduction revolvers by price.

The feel and sound of an action is an immediate clue to the quality of a firearm. If the hammer draws back smoothly and the progression of clicks as it locks back sound crisp, you probably have a well made pistol. If the action drags and the hammer seems to just stick in place when fully cocked, you have one that could use a visit to the local gunsmith for fine tuning, which may be as simple as de-burring and polishing a few internal parts.

The ease with which the cylinder rotates is another crucial point. It should be firm but not stiff, and move in perfect unison with the draw of the hammer. It's a syncopated movement that should sound and feel smooth and crisp.

The latest offering from America Remembers is the 2011 Sesquicentennial Tribute Henry rifle. Each is decorated in 24-kt. gold and nickel with a blackened patina background. The Henry is illustrated with scenes honoring major battles, pivotal moments, soldiers and iconic symbols of the war. The right side prominently features Union and Confederate soldiers engaged in combat during the Battle of Antietam. To the right is an iconic portrait of a Confederate soldier above the designation "CS." Also featured is a scene depicting the April 9, 1865 meeting of General Robert E. Lee and General Ulysses S. Grant at Appomattox Courthouse. The left side features the legendary "Attack On Fort Sumter," with Confederate troops firing cannons and mortars onto the fort. Both sides of the receiver feature a pair of crossed flags decorated in brushed nickel. On the left is Old Glory, the famous "Stars and Bars" flag hoisted into battle by the Union. On the right is the Confederate battle flag, sometimes known as "Beauregard's flag" or "the Virginia battle flag." This new edition is limited to 500.

Is it real or a reproduction? Well, experts will note subtle differences but to the general public an aged Civil War era gun looks pretty authentic. The example pictured is an A. Uberti 1851 Navy that has been artificially aged with the company's proprietary antiquing process for Cimarron F.A. Co. in Fredericksburg, Texas. Antique finishes are available on Colt 1851 Navy, 1860 Army and 1858 Remington models from both A. Uberti and F.lli Pietta. Cimarron also has matching aged presentation boxes and accessories made, so everything looks old. While most folks want a brand new gun, some more discerning reenactors and Civil War enthusiasts prefer a little "patina."

The most elegant firearm of the 1860s, the LeMat revolver was used by the Confederacy. The .42 caliber models fired 9-rounds plus a grapeshot barrel. These striking reproductions are manufactured in Italy by Fratelli Pietta, and are hand engraved by Italian artisans in Brescia. Like the very few original presentation LeMats, this pair by Pietta demonstrates the apex of arms embellishment in its own time.

The Confederate States of America were short on guns at the start of the Civil War and called upon Southern manufacturers to produce weapons. Among those answering the call were J. H. Dance and Brothers, who developed a simplified version of the Colt 1851 Navy. Like the original .36 and .44 caliber 1862 Dance models built in Texas, the Pietta reproductions are conspicuously absent of a recoil shield, thus creating a flat sided frame, which was the revolver's most distinguishing characteristic. The Dance became one of the more notable Southern made revolvers. Note the fine case colored frame on the Pietta reproduction. (Confederate holster and belt recreated by Alan Soellner of Chisholm's Trail Leather)

F.lli Pietta offers several version of the Civil War era Colt Model 1860 Army. Both of the examples shown are special models, shoulder stocked Army with fluted cylinder, and a deluxe hand engraved Army with deluxe walnut grips and lanyard ring.

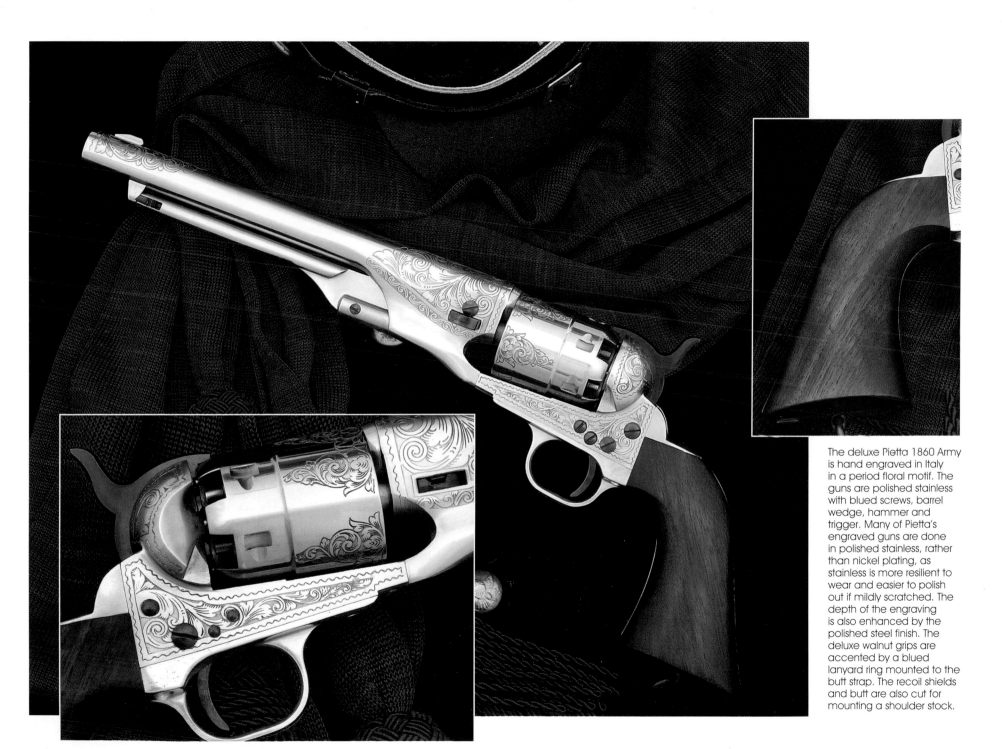

The deluxe Pietta 1860 Army is hand engraved in Italy in a period floral motif. The guns are polished stainless with blued screws, barrel wedge, hammer and trigger. Many of Pietta's engraved guns are done in polished stainless, rather than nickel plating, as stainless is more resilient to wear and easier to polish out if mildly scratched. The depth of the engraving is also enhanced by the polished steel finish. The deluxe walnut grips are accented by a blued lanyard ring mounted to the butt strap. The recoil shields and butt are also cut for mounting a shoulder stock.

The early 1860 Army models with shoulder stocks issued to the U.S. Cavalry at the start of the Civil War were all fitted with fluted cylinders. These proved to be problematic if overloaded (bursting of the cylinders around the bolt stops), and the Ordnance Department had Sam Colt go back to the drawing board. He came up with an improved cylinder design and eventually changed all 1860 Army models to the rebated cylinder style. Pietta is the only maker today that offers a shoulder stocked 1860 Army with a proper fluted cylinder. The guns come with a rebated cylinder, but the Pietta fluted cylinders are available as a special order from VTI Replica Gun Parts in Lakeville, Connecticut.

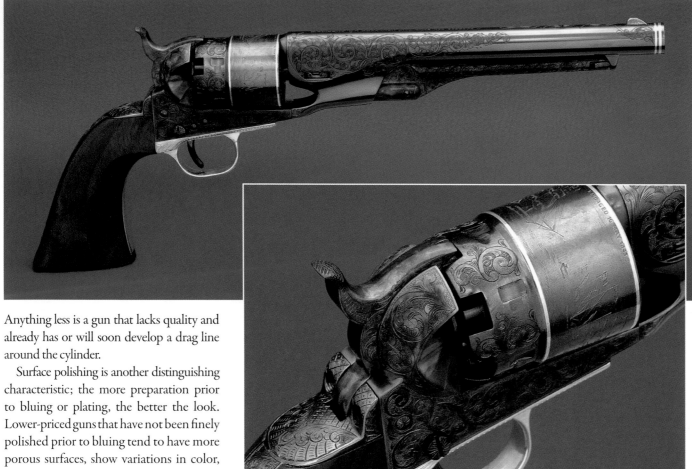

Italian Reproductions

The wheels that Val Forgett, Sr. put into motion more than half a century ago have never stopped turning. Between A. Uberti, F.lli Pietta, Euroarms Italia, Armi Sport di Chiappa, and Davide Pedersoli, there are enough accurate reproductions of Civil War guns today to have armed the North and South in the 1860s. From the most established of Civil War era revolvers and rifled muskets, to some of the most obscure handguns and rifles of the period, these long established Italian armsmakers have researched and recreated, in exacting detail, the greatest America and Europe arms produced during the 19th century.

All of the great Civil War era models produced by E. Remington & Sons, J. H. Dance, Spiller and Burr, Starr, Griswold and Gunnison, Rogers and Spencer, and LeMat, have been faithfully reproduced in Italy by F.lli Pietta, with the exception of the Rogers and Spencer revolver, which is manufactured by Euroarms Italia.

Euroarms Italia (formerly Armi San Paolo, founded by Luciano Amadi) in Concesio, is another of Italy's oldest

Anything less is a gun that lacks quality and already has or will soon develop a drag line around the cylinder.

Surface polishing is another distinguishing characteristic; the more preparation prior to bluing or plating, the better the look. Lower-priced guns that have not been finely polished prior to bluing tend to have more porous surfaces, show variations in color, and occasionally have fine underlying scratches in the finish, although on models with aged or antiqued finishes none of this means anything!

Bluing is perhaps *the* most important feature. Typical Italian bluing has an almost translucent charcoal blue hue, very attractive but lacking the depth of original Colt bluing. (Deeper high-gloss bluing is also done in Italy, but only on premium models, presentation sets, and on engraved pistols). Colt 2nd and 3rd Generation models when found on the secondary market generally have more authentic bluing and case colors as Colt Blackpowder Arms used all of the proprietary Colt processes in color casing and bluing their guns.

Case hardening is the last, but by no means least important thing to look for in a quality reproduction. Traditionally, case hardening done in Italy uses a cyanide process which renders a dusky, grey, blue, brown mottling on the surface of the parts treated, whereas true color casehardened parts are done using the centuries old method of heating and cooling the metal, producing brilliant colors such as those seen on 2nd and 3rd Generation Colts and custom finished, limited edition models sold by companies like America Remembers, Adams & Adams, and Turnbull Restorations.

historically discerning Civil War aficionado, Pedersoli makes a reproduction of the 1862 Confederate Sharps carbine (produced during the Civil War by S. C. Robinson Arms Manufactury in Richmond, Virginia, from 1862 to 1863) with a 22-inch barrel. This is a distinctively different looking model from the other Sharp's designs and does not have a patch box in the stock.

Flintlock side-by-side shotguns were developed in the 18th century (a pretty rare gun to find today), because that second shot meant a lot to frontier hunters. With the advent of the percussion lock, double guns evolved, and not just for hunting small game and birds, but with the appropriate load, bringing down an armed assailant. They were commonly used during the Civil War and even more so during the early Western Expansion in the late 1860s and early 1870s. Percussion lock doubles in gauges ranging from 10 ga. to 20 ga. are manufactured today by Davide Pedersoli, and rival the originals of the Civil War era for quality, fit, and finish.

The great diversity of manufacturers, models, and prices available today, offer collectors and shooters the finest and most extensive series of historic 19th century firearms, since the 19th century.

~~~~~~~~~

[1] *Steel Canvas – The Art of American Arms* by R. L. Wilson.

[2] Ames swords were carried by enlisted men and officers alike from obscure frontier Indian skirmishes to every famous battle fought by American military and Naval forces from the swamps of Florida and the plains of Texas in the early 1800's to the great battle fields of Europe in the twentieth century. The first presentation swords ever commissioned by Congress to honor heroes of the Mexican War were contracted to The Ames Sword Company. Excerpt from the *Ames Sword Company 1829 – 1935* by John D. Hamilton. The Ames Sword Co. is still in business, headquartered in New London, Ohio.

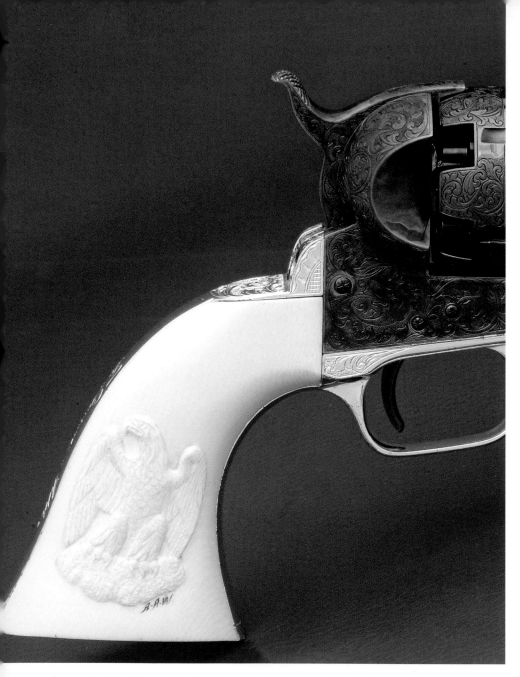

The last Colt 2nd Generation black powder pistol engraved by the late Alvin A. White was done in the Gustave Young style for the author in 1997. The master engraved Colt which was engraved by both White and Andrew Bourbon, features fine scrollwork, animal heads, and hand carved Mexican Eagle and Snake ivory grips signed by A.A. White. The fine 3rd Model Dragoon also has a silver inlaid cartouche in the left grip panel. Many original engraved Colt Dragoons from the 1870s and 1850s were carried by men during the Civil War. (Author's collection)

replica arms makers, and like Pietta has built a reputation for manufacturing rare and unusual revolvers from the Civil War era. Their most famous is the Rogers & Spencer revolver which shares some of its appearance and history with the solid frame Whitney Second Model 3rd. Type revolver originally built in Connecticut during the early 1860s. The Rogers & Spencer was produced in Willowvale, N.Y. between 1863 and 1865, however, the majority of the guns manufactured under Union contract were not delivered until after The War Between the States was over. Most became Army surplus guns in the 1870s where they saw considerable use on the frontier. The Euroarms model is an exacting, quality replica. In the past, Armi San Paolo also produced copies of the Griswold & Gunnison Navy model as well as Colt and Remington revolvers of the Civil War era.

The finest quality copy of the Rogers & Spencer is actually made in Oberndorf, Germany, by the legendary Feinwerkbau armory established in the 1950s. The Rogers & Spencer is the only percussion revolver produced by Feinwerkbau and is marketed by Davide Pedersoli.

Armi Sport di Chiappa is known for their fine reproductions of historic French dueling pistols, Civil War muskets, Sharps rifles, and the Spencer carbine and musket. Armi Sport di Chiappa, which has been in business for over 50 years, also manufactures a wide variety of Civil War era percussion lock rifles, such as the 1842 Rifled Musket in .69 caliber percussion, 1842 U.S. Percussion Musket, 1842 U.S. Short Rifled Musket, .58 caliber 1861 U.S. Springfield Musket

and the C. S. Richmond Musket used by Confederate soldiers. Chiappa also makes both versions of the 1855 Springfield Percussion Rifle, the 1863 Zouave Rifle and Muskatoon, and the 1853 and 1858 Enfield Rifle in .58 caliber.

Pedersoli has an even more historic and refined eye for the War Between the States, producing reproductions of the rare 1816 Harpers Ferry Colt Conversion Musket built between 1855 and 1858 and used during the opening years of the conflict. The company also makes what is arguably the finest reproduction of the 1861 U. S. Springfield Musket.

Both Italian firms manufacture reproductions of the Sharps percussion rifles and carbines used during the Civil War by North and South alike. Chiappa makes four; one is a modified version that uses their own patented breech design to minimize powder residue, improve ignition, and allow for more shots between cleanings; two are 1859 models in .54 caliber, an Infantry Rifle with three-band 30-inch round barrel and patch box, and a Cavalry Rifle with 22-inch single band round barrel and patch box. Chiappa also makes the later 1863 Sporting Rifle in .54 caliber with a 32-inch octagonal barrel and Schnabel forend.

Davide Pedersoli manufactures five .54 caliber black powder paper cartridge versions; 1863 Sporting Model with 32-inch rust brown finish barrel (also offered in .45 caliber), Infantry Model with 30-inch round barrel, the Sharps Berdan variation with double set trigger, and Sharps Cavalry Model with 22-inch barrel. Both the Infantry and Cavalry versions have patch boxes. For the more

The Starr was an almost forgotten gun of the Civil War until Clint Eastwood used one in his award winning western *Unforgiven*. The film's popularity led to F.lli Pietta creating an authentic reproduction of the gun, which has since become one of the armsmaker's most popular models among Civil War arms enthusiasts.

The battle between North and South was also fought in the Confederate armories that were hastily set up in the early years of the Civil War. At left, F.lli Pietta reproduces three of the most famous Southern revolvers, the .36 caliber Spiller & Burr; .44 caliber LeMat; and the .44 caliber J.H. Dance. At right, Pietta also reproduces the rare Civil War Starr .44 caliber double action revolver, the third most issued sidearm of the Union. (Holsters by Alan Soellner/Chisholm's Trail Old West Leather)

317

A. Uberti and F.lli Pietta offer their percussions models with antiqued finishes for those who prefer a gun that looks very old but still works. Pictured are (top to bottom) Uberti Paterson c.1842, Uberti Walker with aged faux ivory grips, Uberti 1860 Army with fluted cylinder, and Pietta New Model Remington with aged faux ivory grips. (Grips by Buffalo Bros.)

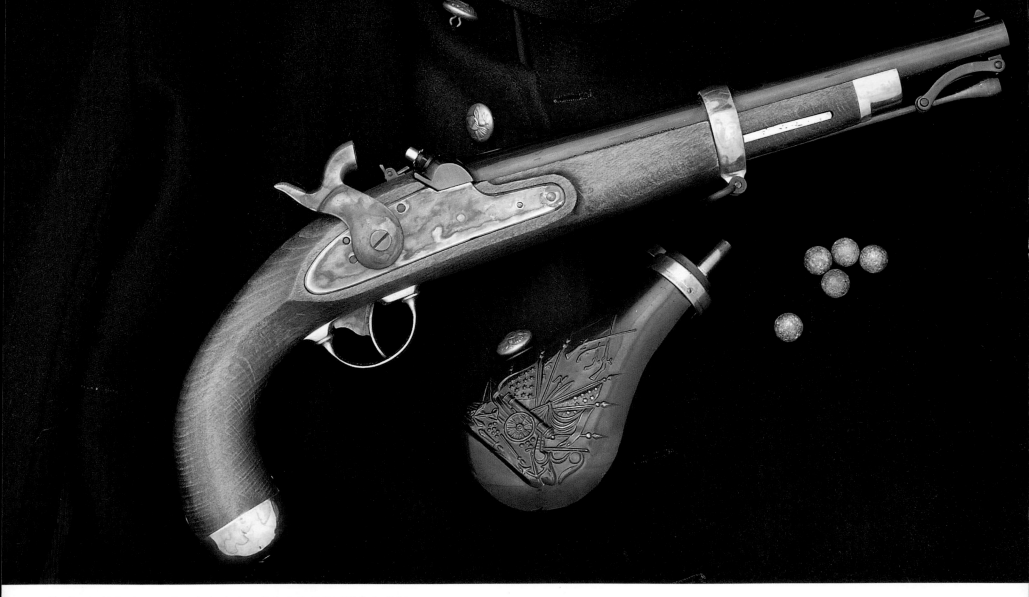

The horse pistol or large caliber single shot caplock, such as the U.S. Springfield Model 1855 with an attachable shoulder stock, was still in use by the U.S. cavalry at the start of the Civil War. The hefty .58 caliber single shot, also known as the U.S. Dragoon Pistol, used a swiveling loading lever. The reproductions, which were made by Palmetto in Italy, are nearly as hard to find as originals but far more affordable and useable for reenactments. The only source today for the reproductions is Dixie Gun Works in Union City, Tennessee. The guns feature a walnut stock and shoulder stock with brass buttplate, brass triggerguard and butt cap, brass barrel band and nose cap, color casehardened lock, and swivels for a sling. (Photos by Dennis Adler)

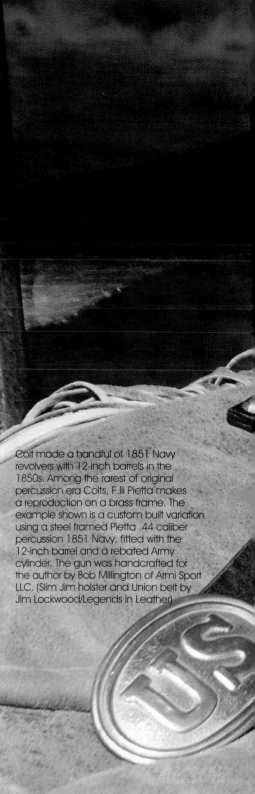

Colt made a handful of 1851 Navy revolvers with 12-inch barrels in the 1850s. Among the rarest of original percussion era Colts, F.lli Pietta makes a reproduction on a brass frame. The example shown is a custom built variation using a steel framed Pietta .44 caliber percussion 1851 Navy, fitted with the 12-inch barrel and a rebated Army cylinder. The gun was handcrafted for the author by Bob Millington of Armi Sport LLC. (Slim Jim holster and Union belt by Jim Lockwood/Legends in Leather)

F.lli Pietta makes a variety of New Model Remington Army .44 caliber reproductions. Pictured are a New Model with antique finish, Deluxe Remington New Model with color cased frame, checkered walnut grips and lanyard ring, and a standard blued New Model.

Two famous Confederate models were the J.H. Dance (top) which was styled after the Colt's Navy and Dragoons revolvers; and the Spiller & Burr, also known as the "Whitney" model because of their similarity to the 2nd Model revolvers made by Eli Whitney, Jr. at the Whitneyville armory in Connecticut. Both Pietta reproductions are very close to the original designs.

Armi Sport di Chiappa, which has been building reproduction rifles and pistols for over 50 years, manufactures this reproduction of the 1853 Enfield 3-band Musket. The original Enfields saw service by both Northern and Southern forces during the Civil War. This reproduction bears all of the original Enfield features including barrel bands, polished brass buttplate, triggerguard, nose cap and one-piece American walnut stock.

The U.S. Model 1841 Mississippi rifle, available in .54 and .58 caliber versions, features A 33-inch rifled barrel, walnut stock, brown finished barrel, buttplate, patch box, triggerguard, nose cap and band in brass, case hardened lock plate, dovetail fixed rear sight, brass front sight and polished steel ramrod with brass tip. Another Confederate rifle reproduced in exacting detail by Euroarms is the C.S. Richmond 1863 Rifle Musket. The 40-inch rifled barrel long arm has three barrel bands, is chambered in .58 caliber and comes with a walnut stock, white finished barrel, triggerguard, bands, and lock plate, brass buttplate and nose cap, 2 leaf rear sight, blade front sight and polished steel ramrod. (Photos courtesy Euroarms. Background courtesy Rock Island Auction Co.)

The U.S. government was the single largest purchaser of Sharps breech loading rifles during the Civil War. Pictured are examples of the 1863 Sharps cavalry (22-inch barrel) and 1859 Infantry (30-inch barrel) models produced by Armi Sport di Chiappa (on uniform) and four versions manufactured by Davide Pedesoli, the 1862 "Confederate" in .54 caliber with a short 22-inch barrel; Model 1859-1863 Sharps Cavalry in .54 caliber with a 22-inch barrel; 1863 Sporting Model with 32-inch barrel in .45 caliber; and the Sharps Infantry in .54 caliber with a 30-inch barrel. (Armi Sport Chiappa photo by Dennis Adler, all others courtesy Davide Pedersoli & Cie.)

Bibliography

Adler, Dennis, *Colt Single Action – From Patersons to Peacemakers*, Chartwell Books, 2007

Adler, Dennis, *Winchester Shotguns*, Chartwell Books, 2006

Adler, Dennis, *Colt Blackpowder*, Blue Book Publications, 1998

Adler, Dennis, *Black Powder Revolvers – Reproductions & Replicas*, Blue Book Publications, 2008

Adler, Dennis, *Metallic Cartridge Conversions*, Krause Publications, 2002

Allen, John B., *Fifth Edition Blue Book of Modern Black Powder Values*, 2007 Blue Book Publications, Inc.

Belden, Frank A., Haven, Charles, T., *A History of The Colt Revolver*, Bonanza Books, 1940

Boorman, Dean K., *The History of Smith & Wesson Firearms*, Salamander Books, The Lyons Press, 2002

Bowman, John S. (General Editor), *The Civil War,* 2006 World Publications Group

Breslin, John D., Pirie, William Q., Price, David E., *Variations of Colt's New Model Police and Pocket Breech Loading Pistols*, Andrew Mowbray Publishers, 2002

Carter, Robert A., *Buffalo Bill Cody – The Man Behind the Legend*, copyright 2000, Castle Books, 2005

Edwards, William B., *Civil War Guns*, 1962, The Stackpole Co.

Ezell, Edward C., *Handguns of the World*, Stackpole Books, 1981

Fjestad, S. P. Blue Book of Gun Values, 31th Edition, Blue Book Publications, Inc. 2010

Flaydermann, Norm, *Flaydermann's Guide to Antique American Firearms and Their Values*, 8th Edition, Krause Publications

Forgett, Valmore J., Serpette, Alain F and Marie-Antoinette, *LeMat – The Man, The Gun*, 1996, Navy Arms Co.

Frost, Lawrence A., *The Custer Album*, Superior Publishing Co. 1964, University of Oklahoma Press, 1990

Fuller, Claud E, Struart, Richard D., *Firearms of the Confederacy*, 1996, Odysseus Editions, Inc. for the National Rifle Association.

Houze, Herbert C., *Samuel Colt Arms, Art, and Invention*, Yale University Press, 2007

Lanier, Robert S. (Managing Editor), *The Photographic History of the Civil War,* Volumes One through Ten, 1911, Patriot Publishing Co.

McAuley, John D., *Carbines of the Civil War 1861-1865,* 1981, Pioneer Press

McAuley, John D., *Civil War Breech Loading Rifles*, 1987, Andrew Mowbray Inc.

McAuley, John D., *Civil War Pistols of the Union*, 1992, Andrew Mowbray Inc.

Metz, Leon Claire, *The Shooters*, Mangan Books, 1976, Berkley Publishing Group, 1996

Nahas, Richard, Supica, Jim, Standard Catalog of Smith & Wesson, 3rd Edition, Gun Digest Books, 2006

Paludan, Phillip Shaw, *The Civil War*, World Publications Group, 2006

Rattenbury, Richard C., *Packing Iron – Gunleather of the Frontier West*, Zon Internatinal Publishing Co., 1993

Rosa, Josepha G., *They Called Him Wild Bill – The Life and Adventures of James Butler Hickok*, University of Oklahoma Press, 1964

Rose, Alexander, *American Rifle*, Bantam Dell (A Division of Random House) 2008

Schmucker, Samuel M., L.L.D., *The History of the Civil War*, 1865, Bradley & Co.

Wilson, R. L., *The Book of Colt Firearms*, 3rd Edition, Blue Book Publications, Inc. 2008

Wilson, R. L., *The Peacemakers Arms and Adventure in the American West*, Random House, 1992, Chartwell Books, 2004

Wilson, R. L., *Fine Colts – The Dr. Joseph A. Murphy Collection*, Republic Publishing Co., 2000

Wilson, R. L., *Steel Canvas The Art of American Arms*, Random House, 1995

Wilson, R. L., *Winchester An American Legend*, Random House, 1991

Winik, Jay, *April 1865 – The Month That Saved America*, 2001 HarperCollins Publishers

The caplock side-by-side shotgun dates back to early 19th century, and like double barreled flintlock fowlers of the 1700s, changes were simply in the lock mechanisms. By the early 19th century shotguns had evolved into both long and short-barreled doubles. Pictured are Davide Pedersoli's c.1850 side-by-sides, which reproduces the look of an original English 12ga. model with walnut stock, blued 28-9/16 inch barrels, and color casehardened locks and side plates. (Photos courtesy Divide Pedersoli & Cie.)

E. Remington & Sons also played a significant role in arming the Union during the Civil War with its Model 1863 Zouave rifle, one of the most accurate and elite rifles of the conflict. Entire Zouave units were used by the Army and dressed in distinctive uniforms. The examples pictured here with a Zouave infantry shell jacket, are manufactured by Armi Sport di Chiappa. Both feature blued barrel and color casehardened lock marked U.S. with the eagle stamping. The triggerguard, barrel bands and patch box are finished in polished brass.

331

Index